Memoir of the Late James Hope ...

Hope

MEMOIR OF DR. HOPE.

JAMES HOPE ESQ.R M.D. F.R.S. &c.!

MEMOIR

OF THE LATE

JAMES HOPE, M.D.,

PHYSICIAN TO ST. GEORGE'S HOSPITAL, &c. &c.

By Mrs. HOPE

TO WHICH ARE ADDED

ESSAYS ON CLASSICAL EDUCATION,
ON THE HOPE

AND

POPULAR SCIENCE AND A JUNIOR LIFE

THE CORRECTION OF

A LATE GRANT MEDICAL &c. &c.

Third Edition.

LONDON:
HATCHARD AND SON, PICCADILLY
JOHN CHURCHILL, PRINCES STREET, SOHO
MDCCCXLIV.

MEMOIR

OF THE LATE

JAMES HOPE, M.D.,

PHYSICIAN TO ST. GEORGE'S HOSPITAL, &c. &c.

BY MRS. HOPE.

TO WHICH ARE ADDED

REMARKS ON CLASSICAL EDUCATION,
BY DR. HOPE;

AND

LETTERS FROM A SENIOR TO A JUNIOR PHYSICIAN,
BY DR. BURDER.

THE WHOLE EDITED BY

KLEIN GRANT, M.D., &c. &c.

AT SPES INFRACTA.

Third Edition.

LONDON:

J. HATCHARD AND SON, 187, PICCADILLY;

JOHN CHURCHILL, PRINCES STREET, SOHO.

MDCCCXLIV.

LONDON:
PRINTED BY G. J PALMER, SAVOY STREET, STRAND.

THIS VOLUME

IS INSCRIBED TO

CHARLES JOHN, BARON TEIGNMOUTH,

AS A TRIFLING MEMORIAL

OF THOSE FEELINGS OF SINCERE GRATITUDE FOR

MANY VALUABLE SERVICES,

AND HIGH RESPECT FOR HIS LORDSHIP'S CONSISTENT

CHRISTIAN CHARACTER,

WHICH WERE ENTERTAINED BY

DR. HOPE.

PREFACE TO THE FIRST EDITION.

A BIOGRAPHY which is not mixed up with the history of an age, seldom abounds in striking incidents, and this is especially true with respect to the details of a life devoted to a learned profession. The career of a distinguished professional man is, however, blended with the history of at least one branch of human knowledge, and is interesting to those of his own profession by presenting scenes with which they are familiar; objects which they have themselves pursued; difficulties with which they have themselves had to contend; and prospects like those which are expanding to their own view, or have already been realized or disappointed to their hopes: to those of other callings, also, the record of such a life is not devoid of interest, since it develops new phases of human existence, and new modes of operation of those

powers and principles which are common to mankind.
The latter of these remarks applies particularly to the
profession of medicine. The insulated character of
that profession removes it almost entirely from the
sphere of public observation; the statesman, the
barrister, the artist, the natural philosopher, are continually placed in prominent positions, and the steps
by which they attain to eminence are more or less
visible to the world: but the ministrations of the
physician are confined to particular occasions, and
sought for only in the hour of sickness; his professional course is unseen, and his means of success, and
his sources of embarrassment are alike unknown. A
medical biography, therefore, if faithful, and well
detailed, opens up a new scene to the mind of the
general reader, and commends itself to his reason by
the extensive materials it affords for thinking, while it
gratifies his curiosity by its freshness.

There are several circumstances which give peculiar
interest to the memoir now offered to the public. The
subject of it attained great eminence, and large practice, at an age when most physicians are only beginning to be heard of. His success was not owing to
the patronage of any great man, nor to any of those

fortunate accidents which have occasionally brought physicians suddenly into notice. He was indebted simply to his own talents, his active humanity, the weight of moral character, and the force of industry, for his rapid elevation. These circumstances render the details of his life an encouraging example to the young physician, for unhappily the qualifications above mentioned are not the invariable—perhaps truth will oblige us to confess, not the most frequent avenues to success in practice; and every unequivocal instance in which they have proved so, is a strong incentive to professional virtue, and a safeguard against the many temptations to deviate from it.

In one respect the present memoir possesses a more than usual degree of utility, namely, that the circumstances under which it has been written, enable us to trace, almost from infancy, the development of those powers and proclivities, the exercise of which has led to such fine results. It is the want of similar information that often renders the biography of individuals, however distinguished in literature, science, or art, whose life has been unconnected with great public events, meagre and unprofitable; their works are already known, and speak for themselves; their lives present no incidents different from those of ordinary mortals; and it is only by showing how the intellectual machine has been framed, and how it has worked in the production of the results we admire, that such memoirs can possess either interest or utility.

But there is a more important feature in the life of Dr. Hope than any yet mentioned; one which must commend it to the attention of all reflecting persons, and the illustration of which is a principal object in the publication of the present work. We here see an ingenuous, talented, and ambitious young man attaining great eminence at an unusually early age; yet, ere such eminence was attained, the grounds on which it had been sought had become entirely changed, and ambition had given place to a far different principle of action. Religion had become the mainspring of all his exertions, and the resting place of all his hopes, and the instance shows forcibly how poor are the motives of action which this world can afford, when generous aspirations so early satisfied, worldly hopes so early realised, are acknowledged to be insufficient sources of happiness, unstable guides to conduct, and all voluntarily and deliberately placed in subordination to the dictates of Christianity.

Considered in a religious point of view, the character of Dr. Hope is one which may be most advantageously contemplated, as it presents a striking instance of fervent piety without the slightest tinge of fanaticism, and that careful conformity of life to a professed belief, which alone can prove either the efficacy or the sincerity of religious conviction.

Thinking this memoir well calculated to do good as a stimulus to honourable exertion—an example of professional conduct—and an evidence of the all-pervading power of Christian principle, the Editor has willingly undertaken the task of giving it to the world; and in so doing, he sincerely hopes that the work may answer the desired ends, and prove extensively useful.

It has been thought that the " Letters from a Senior to a Junior Physician," from their consonance with the general tenor of this memoir, would add to its utility, and they have, therefore, been appended to it, with the permission of their respected author.

37, St. James's Street,
2nd June, 1842.

CONTENTS.

PERIOD IV.

FAILURE OF HEALTH—RETIREMENT FROM PRACTICE—DEATH.

CHAPTER I.

CHAPTER II.

CHAPTER III.

CHAPTER IV.

MEMOIR OF DR. HOPE.

PERIOD I.

CHILDHOOD—YOUTH—GENERAL EDUCATION.

THE family of the Hopes claim to be descended from three brothers, One of the brothers settled in Scotland, and was the ancestor of the Earl of Hopetown: another went to Holland, and from him are descended the Hopes of Amsterdam, and the late Thomas Hope, Esq., of London, the distinguished author of Anastasius, and other well known works: the descendants of the third brother, for he himself was lost at sea, settled in Lancashire. The subject of this memoir did not belong to the Lancashire family, though born in the neighbouring county of Cheshire; he was descended from the Scotch branch, some members of which had come to England, and settled in Manchester as bankers and merchants. There is extant a genealogical tree, which traces the family through many vicissitudes; but

B

its details possess neither sufficient accuracy nor public interest to justify its insertion in this place.

Suffice it to say, that James Hope was the descendant, in the seventh generation, of a highly respectable Scotch family; and that many of his ancestors are mentioned by Miss Hope, of Liverpool, (who has taken much pains in tracing the history of the Hope family,) as having been distinguished for piety, and having evinced great ability as architects. Dr. Hope's *great great* grandfather, and great grandfather, each attained the age of eighty-four. His grandfather, Henry Hope, died in 1765, aged forty-four. He married a daughter of James Wilde, Esq., of Manchester, who died in 1819, at the age of 89. She had five children, of whom Hannah attained the age of sixty-eight; Thomas, the father of Dr. Hope, that of eighty-five; and Mary is still living and in the enjoyment of perfect health at the age of eighty-eight. Dr. Hope's father married Miss Ann Jackson, of Middlewich, Cheshire; he was extensively engaged in business as a merchant and manufacturer at Stockport, and having realized a handsome fortune, he retired from business at the early age of forty-four, and settled in the country with what he considered an ample income of above £4,000 per annum. Being a man of decided literary taste, and of great mental and corporeal activity, he divided his time between his library and his garden, in which he did not disdain to work with his own hand. He continued to enjoy excellent health for more than forty years, and was able to walk eighteen or twenty miles in a day until a short time before his death, which took place in 1838, at the advanced age of eighty-five.

Thus it is evident that, on his father's side, Dr. Hope was descended from a family remarkable for longevity. On the side of his mother, he could not make an equal boast; but, as that lady attained the age of sixty-seven, and as no direct hereditary tendency to disease could be traced in her family, it might naturally have been expected that the joint descendants of herself and Mr. Thomas Hope would have attained, at least, an average age.

Dr. Hope was the tenth child of a family of twelve, and was born at Stockport on the 23rd February, 1801. Of this family of twelve, only four survive.

Thomas, Rector of Hatton, Warwickshire, who, in the unobtrusive duties of a parish priest, is actively and zealously engaged in the service of religion, and of his fellow creatures.

Marianne, married to the Rev. Lancelot Dixon, formerly of Wilmslow, Cheshire, but who has long resided in France, on account of his wife's health.

Eliza, married to the late Samuel Unwin, Esq., a gentleman possessed of landed property at Disley, in Cheshire, and Preston, in Lancashire, and much respected as a solicitor, in Manchester.

Emma, married to the late Rev. William Thomas Marychurch, Rector of Sudbourne cum Orford, Suffolk.

Eleven of Mr. Hope's children arrived at years of

maturity, and from their earliest childhood were so remarkable for their healthy appearance, that their lives were constantly chosen for insertion in leases. This early promise, however, proved delusive. Five died under the age of twenty-five; two others, including Dr. Hope, died at forty; and the four surviving members of the family are of a remarkably delicate constitution. In after years, when Dr. Hope's medical experience had made him competent to judge what might be the causes of so great a degeneracy in the descendants of so long-lived a family, he was decidedly of opinion that it could be ascribed, in a great measure, to the very injudicious mode of clothing and feeding children, which was then too prevalent, and which was adopted by his mother, under the directions of a surgeon of great eminence in the town of Manchester. Dr. Hope believed that exposure to cold and inadequate nutrition in childhood, sowed the seeds of the disease which was developed in later years. This opinion was the result of his own medical experience and of physiological observations on animals, in which tubercular disease may be produced by a similar mode of treatment; and as five, out of Mr. Hope's eight children who have been prematurely cut off, died of tubercular disease, the instance of this family strikingly verifies the analogy between the causes of such disease in man and the inferior animals. Of the three children who had not tubercular disease, one died in infancy, and the two others suffered from the undue exposure to which they had been subjected, since, before the age of twenty, they fell victims to acute rheumatism, terminating, in one, in inflammation of the heart.

Very soon after the birth of his son James, Mr. Thomas Hope took up his residence at Prestbury Hall, in Cheshire, a venerable mansion, which was the fondly cherished scene of Dr. Hope's earliest associations and boyish recollections. Here, amid the active sports and hazardous adventures which boys can enjoy only in the country, his character received that best of educations which nature has prepared both for the philosopher and the man of the world, and acquired the healthy force and activity which fitted him for the arduous situations in which he afterwards shone.

At the age of six or seven, James Hope was placed as a day-scholar with the Rev. Mr. Monkhouse, Curate of Prestbury, who conducted a school of some celebrity in the neighbourhood. Dr. Hope, however, had no recollection of having acquired more, under his tuition, than the art of penmanship and of drawing maps, which he executed with singular beauty and correctness. There is still extant a chart of the history of England, above a yard square, done at the age of nine, and so admirably written, as well as coloured, as not to be distinguishable from an engraving.

The school at Prestbury appears to have afforded very inadequate training to young Hope's intelligent mind ; yet such was his avidity for reading and general information, that he was constantly drawing from his father's library, and drinking in knowledge from every quarter. Nor was his reading confined to books adapted to his age, or, as it was supposed, to his capacity. When only eight years old, for example, his father found him intently perusing Milton's Paradise Lost; and having chid him sharply for poring over what he could not understand, took the book from him. The boy could not comprehend the reason of this reproof, as he felt himself much interested in the story; and at length, after many efforts, prevailed upon his father to allow him to proceed with it.

About the same time, accidentally meeting with the Arabian Nights' Entertainments, he read them by stealth under the table, and was punished for the transgression. But his eagerness for knowledge at nearly the same period, was more strikingly shown in the delight he experienced in reading Parkes' Chemical Catechism, which also happened to fall in his way, He was actually fascinated with the science, and soon began to perform many of the experiments described in the book; but was sadly mortified to find himself unable to form sulphuric acid or the gases, and more especially to be baffled in his attempts to make gunpowder for his sporting brothers. Notwithstanding, however, these failures, and the opprobrious epithet of " James's messes" applied to his enterprising experiments, he prosecuted his favourite science with no little assiduity.

Thus early did James Hope discover the intelligence and the powers of observation and steady perseverance which marked, with progressive development, every future stage of his successful career.

Parents too often forget that children are peculiarly susceptible of all impressions, and that every lesson, whether moral or intellectual, which is taught at this tender age, has an influence on the formation of the character, and produces its fruit, be it good or be it evil, even when the lesson itself may have faded from the memory. Thus we may trace to Dr. Hope's father some of the qualities which so strongly marked the character of the son. Mr. Hope was a very proud and ambitious man. He was proud of his family and his name; but his was not merely that lower kind of family pride which regards antiquity of descent alone. On the contrary, he prided himself on belonging to a family, many of whose members had distinguished themselves either in the service of their country or in the walks of science and literature. His ambition was of the same tone, and he rather desired that his sons should do credit to the family from which they sprung, than that they should attain great riches or worldly distinctions. He seems early to have discovered the rare talents of his son James, and to have centered in him a large share of his hopes. He was in the habit of stimulating him to the greatest exertions by constantly inculcating on him what high degree of excellence, according to his own enthusiastic views, was expected from any one bearing the name of Hope; while, by frequent encomiums and perpetual encou-

ragement, he fired his youthful ambition, and power-
fully urged him forward. Though the natural humility of Dr. Hope's character, aided as it was at a later
period by religious principle, obviated the most perni-
cious tendencies which might have resulted from
these lessons of family pride, yet to them may be ascribed the enthusiastic ardour which he evinced in the
pursuit of excellence, the high standard at which he
aimed, and the noble desire to be great, rather than to
appear so.

Nor did the flattering marks of approbation which
he received render him proud or conceited even at the
time when they were bestowed. He was rather a
taciturn, as well as modest and timid boy, and of a
peculiarly mild and gentle temper. While these
amiable qualities endeared him much to his relatives,
they disqualified him for fighting his way and maintaining his rights as one of a large family. Every
one who has had nine or ten brothers and sisters, must
feel that such a family is a sort of little world, where
the more lively or more noisy gain an undue share of
indulgence, while the more quiet and retiring are
pushed aside and pass unobserved. The latter seems
to have been the predicament of James Hope. While
many privileges were granted to his elder brothers, he
was always classed with " the children;" an epithet
which, he said, continued to be applied to him long
after he felt it to be unjust and opprobrious. At the
same time " the children," that is, a younger brother

and sister, excluded him from their pastimes, because
he was unable to perceive any thing amusing in some
of their games; and thus, unheeded by the elder
branches of the family as being too young, and shunned
by the younger, as being too old, he was generally condemned to solitude. Though his situation was very
depressing, and one which made him look back to his
childhood with feelings of pain, it can scarcely be
doubted but that it had a salutary influence in favouring his natural modesty and humble opinion of himself, and in checking the pride and conceit which might
have arisen from the affectionate and flattering notice
of his father.

Generally, the effect of so much commendation in
early life is peculiarly baneful. Thus, one child of a
family, more highly gifted than the rest, receives an
undue measure of praise, while the others, perhaps
equally amiable, and even more pains-taking, are
chilled with discouragement; although the more
talented may not have given half the labour to his
task, nor may require half the encouragement to proceed in it. But the injury resulting from dispropor-
tionate praise is often most deeply felt by the innocent
subject of it. He is early satisfied with his acquirements and with himself. A precocious love of distinction is generated. Superficial and showy attainments
are preferred: and, instead of a fixed and persevering
endeavour to acquire substantial knowledge and moral
worth, for their own sake, the youth is led to sacrifice

his more permanent good for those accomplishments, and that ready kind of information, which may most administer to a factitious love of applause.

When about ten years of age, James Hope was removed to the grammar school at Knutsford, then under the charge of the Rev. Mr. Vannett, where he learned the rudiments of the classics, made great progress in arithmetic, and acquired the elements of geometry. One circumstance, in reference to this school, he always alluded to in after-life with great approbation, namely, that the proceedings of the day commenced with reading two or three chapters of the Bible, each boy being expected to read at any moment his name was called, thus necessarily keeping up the attention of all. Thus, he considered, the foundation was laid for that knowledge of the Holy Scriptures, which diffused its silent influence over the rest of his life.

Having passed about two years at that school, he was placed under the care of the Rev. G. S. Weidemann, who received a few elder boys, in order to qualify them for College. That gentleman, a German by birth, was, at the time referred to, only twenty-one years of age, yet he had already evinced extraordinary talents, and had taken the first honours at the University of Strasburg.

Mr. Weidemann led his disciple over a wide range of classics, including many of the higher ones. He did not restrict himself to classical instruction, as was

too commonly the case at that period, but, besides a
due attention to mathematics, his plan embraced the
elements of a philosophic and elegant education. By
a well-managed system of catechizing, this able pre-
ceptor familiarized his pupils with the first principles
of natural philosophy and chemistry, as well as with
the outlines of ancient and modern history and belles-
lettres. For the latter purpose, Blair's Lectures on
Belles Lettres was chiefly employed as a text-book.
Mr. Weidemann was accustomed to alternate English
essays with Latin themes; and, by a critical analysis
of the former, according to the principles previously
inculcated, he imbued the minds of his pupils with a
knowledge of the general principles of style and taste;
thus enabling them to read with advantage many
standard authors, which would otherwise have been beyond their years and capacity. Under this system,
James acquired the art of elegant English composition,
became familiar with English classics, and imbibed the
sentiments of the authors selected. Nor was the last-
mentioned the least of the advantages which he derived
from so happy a method of instruction. One of the
subjects thus chosen was No. 108 of the Rambler, the
title of which is, " Life sufficient to all purposes, if
well employed." To this paper he ascribed the value
which he placed on " fragments of time ;" and he used
to say, that in the employment of these lay the secret
of his having done so much as he had crowded into his
short life. To one who knew him intimately, it is

most interesting to read this paper, and to notice how literally he acted up to his precepts; and how, after the lapse of nearly thirty years, he was in the habit of addressing to his young friends, admonitions exactly corresponding with those of the Rambler. Indeed, to this work, which was one of his early favourites, may be traced many of the sentiments which he was frequently heard to express, and many of the maxims on which he based his conduct.

To the two years spent under Mr. Weidemann's roof, Dr. Hope was accustomed to look back with the highest satisfaction, as to a period in which he gained much general and diversified knowledge, and that expansion of intellect which rendered all his subsequent labours comparatively easy. On afterwards going to a public school, where boys, for the most part, learn little or nothing beyond classics, he was called " a walking dictionary," or still more familiarly, " an odd fellow, that knew every thing."

At the age of fourteen, he was placed at the Macclesfield grammar-school, which was eligible not merely on account of its vicinity to his home, but also from the high celebrity of Dr. Davies, who, during a period of more than twenty years, had been accustomed to send an unusual number of high class-men to Oxford and Cambridge. This " prince of pedagogues," as his pupil liked to call him, was an admirable critical classic, and a most successful disciplinarian. Beyond the range of high classical acquirements, however, his knowledge and accomplishments were inconsiderable.

At first, James was placed in the third class from the head, which was lower than he had anticipated. This was occasioned by his knowledge of Greek being inferior to that of Latin. Feeling mortified at such a position, he soon proposed to a boy in the class above, to get up at four o'clock in the morning, and read through Herodotus with him. This plan, including also a portion of Thucydides, was continued for a year and a half. Before the expiration of that time, however, he was promoted to the second class, and soon rose nearly to its head. The original first class having been sent to college, the second class now became the first.

Our young scholar's memory was remarkably quick and retentive. No boy in the school could surpass, and few could rival him, in the rapidity with which he committed any task to memory; while his fluency in repeating what he had thus acquired, was almost unbroken. On one occasion only was he ever turned back from his class. The same quickness and accuracy were manifested in learning lessons of translation, &c.

Yet young Hope had not the appearance of a brilliant boy. He was too deeply thoughtful to display the showy character of a superficial mind. His natural temperament was calm and quiet. His intellectual habits were of a close and reflecting kind, not permitting him to be satisfied with an insufficient reason, or to hazard a guess instead of an accurate solution.

It may not be irrelevant to advert to the powerful
influence of physical temperament and mere animal
spirits, in producing, or at least favouring, the kind
of facility which some individuals possess of dressing-
up, and showing off their scanty knowledge to great
advantage.   Such are often designated as brilliant and
highly talented, although, perhaps, in depth and force
of thought, in general compass of mind, and in solid
attainments, they may be immeasurably inferior to
many who, with a more calm and equable temperament pursue the even tenor of their way, attracting
little observation, until, having laid a deep and firm
foundation, they gradually build up a substantial
superstructure, and their works speak for them, commanding what they never took the pains to solicit, a
high and a permanent reputation.

It would, however, be an error to suppose that the
subject of this memoir was a tame and apathetic
youth.   On the contrary, he was in as high repute
among his fellows on the play-ground, as in the school,
and was no less ambitious of excelling in the one than
in the other.   He was remarkable for the abrupt tran-
sitions which he could make without the least distraction of mind from intense study to play, and from the
most active game to intense study again.   He possessed great muscular strength and activity.   In the
exercises of running, leaping, boxing, and swimming,
as well as in the use of the sword and lance, he was
not easily beaten.   Yet was he as far removed as pos-

sible from the disposition or bearing of a bully. He was too brave and generous to lord it over any, especially if younger or less powerful than himself. In fact, he was the protector of the younger boys, and consequently a high favourite among them. They often applied to him in their difficulties, and seldom in vain, for his cool courage cowed even his seniors.

Hope had a natural intolerance of coarse language, and would never continue to talk with any party who indulged in it. If any boy in his own study employed it, he immediately requested him either to desist, or to leave the room.

Once a fortnight, he was permitted by his master to spend Saturday afternoon, and Sunday, at home. When the season, and the day were favourable, he delighted to follow an excellent trout-stream, and so fish his way home, in order that, in addition to gratifying his own love for the sport, he might present his father with a dish of his favourite fish.

The mechanical ingenuity which he evinced on many occasions, was called forth in aid of this favourite recreation. He not only made his own flies, but even his lines and rods, the latter being almost as neat and true as any that could be purchased. Like several other eminent men, he preserved his attachment to trout-fishing through life, and was an adept of the first order.

At Dr. Davies' school, James Hope continued until he was between seventeen and eighteen years of age, having read through nearly all the highest classics; Juvenal and Perseus, most of the Greek plays, Thucydides, Pindar, &c.

At this time, his mind was fixed on the bar as his future profession. He indulged the hope of going from school to the University, his father having always promised that he should follow his own inclination. Unfortunately, however, Mr. Hope had cherished a secret wish that his son should be a merchant; consequently, he had taken no measures to bespeak rooms in any of the Colleges. Nothing could exceed the mortification of our ardent scholar, at receiving this communication. He strongly objected to the plan, reminding his father of his uniform promise that his sons should select their own professions. Mr. Hope, notwithstanding, continued obstinate, until he perceived that his son's spirits had sunk into a settled gloom. This injudicious proceeding, however, sacrificed, in some respects at least, a valuable year, and prevented young Hope from securing rooms, and entering himself at College.

He was, however, of too active a mind to allow this year to be lost, although prevented from occupying it as he might have desired. He not only maintained his knowledge of the classics, for he was bent on taking a first class, but he seized the opportunity of reading through nearly the whole of those British classics and poets which he had not yet read; a task to which he came not ill prepared, as the attention which he had paid to Blair's Lectures on Belles Lettres, under his early tutor, the Rev. G. S. Weidemann, had stored his mind with the principles of taste and criticism. Even when he went out shooting, a constant amusement during the season, he always carried a book, and read as he walked during the intervals of the sport.

It was just anterior to this time that the Manchester riots, called the battle of Peterloo, had occurred; and as the country was still turbulent, new bodies of yeomanry and militia were formed. The ninth Lancers having been quartered at Macclesfield, and some of the officers having at a dinner party spoken of the impossibility of training civilians to the difficult exercises of Lancers, Mr. Cross, of Adlington Hall, undertook to form a corps of yeomanry Lancers, and enlisted under his banner many of the neighbouring gentry, including young Hope. The Prince Regent having heard of Mr. Cross's undertaking, was so much pleased as to allow the corps to be named after him, and the attempt proved most successful. In this new capacity Hope evinced the versatility of talent by which he was so remarkably characterised, and which caused him to succeed alike in whatever he attempted. He soon became so expert in the use of the lance and broadsword, that he was appointed fugleman to the corps, and on leaving his military calling, he was presented with a broad-sword, to which he always attached much value, and which is now in the possession of his family.

In after-life, it was amusing to observe the eager pleasure with which he spoke of " the time when he was a
soldier," saying, with a laugh, that he thought he might
have made a great general.

After he had spent a year at home, his father proposed to him to become a physician. To the medical
profession, he had always felt the strongest dislike,
and this proposition was received with corresponding
dissatisfaction. An eminent physician from Manchester happening shortly after to be in attendance
on a member of the family, he was requested to remove, if possible, the prejudices of the youth; and he
succeeded so well, that, on one distinct condition, the
latter consented to make trial of it, namely, that he
should be allowed to practise in London—a wish which
seems to have been prompted by a secret consciousness
of his own talents, and by that proud ambition which
made him scorn success in every field except that where
he should have to compete with the highest order of
talent.

As it was still desirable that he should graduate at
one of the Universities, he was sent to Oxford, where
his elder brother was a member of University College.
The instability of his father's intentions, however, rendered his plans abortive; and after residing for a year
and a half, without being enabled to enter, he was recalled home.

This period in Oxford was, however, profitably employed in improving himself in classics and general

knowledge. He read much with his brother, who was preparing for his degree ; and during one long vacation, he was resident in college, through the indulgence of the Dean. In this way, he derived much of the solid advantage of being connected with the University, without enjoying the éclat of being a member of it. He still, however, hoped to accomplish this by alternate residences in Edinburgh and Oxford.

PERIOD II.

PROFESSIONAL EDUCATION.

In October, 1820, Dr. Hope went to Edinburgh in order to commence his medical studies. In conformity to established usage, his first year was principally devoted to anatomy, and was to him one of disgust and unhappiness, from the extreme repugnance he felt to the pursuit.

In selecting a profession for a son, one often hears parents speak of the importance of discovering the tastes of the youth, and making the selection accordingly, under the impression that a compliance with these will promote his future success. Although there is some appearance of wisdom in such a course, it is questionable whether it be really judicious, and it can scarcely be doubted but that the open avowal of such a principle must have an injurious effect on the immature mind. How can a youth of sixteen or eighteen balance the advantages of the army, the bar, the medical profession, or the counting-house, and form a valid judgment among them ? He is sure to be influenced by some high-wrought fancy or prejudice, imbibed from a personal predilection or aversion entertained towards some individual of one or other profession. When in later life he awakes from his dream, and finds that the duties of a soldier involve more than wearing a splendid uniform and marching to the sound of gay music; that the merchant does not always reckon golden stores in his coffers; that honour and distinction are not constant attendants on him who follows a learned profession; when, in short, he discovers that in every station man is born to labour, and has only brief moments of success to cheer him on an arduous road, will he not repent of his choice, and, perhaps, in obedience to the early instilled principle of following inclination, either abandon his profession, or, pursuing it with languor, ascribe his consequent want of success to the unhappy position in which he is placed, rather than to his own want of energy and self-government?

Instead of looking to the tastes of their children, parents would do well to instil into their minds those principles of self-denial and self-control, that steady resolution to overcome all obstacles and do their best in every station, which will qualify them to fill, with usefulness and distinction, any post which the judgment of their parents, family interest, or any other guiding circumstance may assign to them.

Though Mr. Hope had always told his sons that they were to choose their own profession—a choice which he did not afterwards concede—he had not neglected to impress upon their minds the foregoing principles, which took deep root in that of his son James, and did him good service at this trying period of his life. His aversion to his profession, and especially to anatomy, was so great that many would have called it insuperable. Such a word entered not into the vocabulary of young Hope. He never had been conquered, and it was his intention never to be so. He had no idea of foregoing all hopes of future distinction because his preliminary studies were distasteful. Instead, therefore, of inquiring within himself what was agreeable or disagreeable, he calmly regarded the medical profession as that to which his future destiny was linked, as the sphere in which all his bright and ambitious dreams were to be realised. He knew that habit is one of the most powerful agents on the mind of man, and he relied on it for overcoming his feelings of disgust. He compelled himself to the diligent and persevering study of anatomy, but he dissected in gloves and with forceps, so as never to touch the body; and so strongly rooted were his feelings, that it took two years to overcome them in any great degree, and they continued to affect him slightly even six or seven years after.

Dr. Baillie was then at the head of his profession in London, and he was the model which young Hope proposed for his own imitation. He soon discovered that this eminent physician owed much of his justly-acquired celebrity to the knowledge which he derived from the study of morbid anatomy; and his own judgment enabled him to perceive that no man can hope to make important discoveries in medicine, unless he is intimately acquainted with the structure and functions of the human body. The expression which he used many years after in regard to this subject was, " that a physician, in looking at his patient, ought, in imagination, to turn him inside out." Regardless of his own antipathy, he at once determined to concentrate all his powers on the most essential though least agreeable part of his studies, and he already planned the production of a work on the morbid anatomy of the whole body, illustrated by drawings, as at that time there was no such work in existence. It is a rare thing to see a man not merely giving an ordinary share of attention to that which inspires him with disgust, but voluntarily selecting it as the subject of his peculiar study. In so doing, Hope gave a striking proof of the strength of his moral character, and the result is an encouraging illustration of the fact, that a vigorous cultivation of the intellectual and moral powers, followed by a determined concentration of those powers on one object or class of objects, is almost invariably crowned with ultimate success.

Some observations which occur in a letter written during his residence at Paris, in 1826, show that, in studying pathological anatomy, he did not fall into the error commonly imputed to the French, of following it as " mere morbid anatomy—the science of the dis-secting-room." He studied post-mortem appearances in reference to the previous symptoms; and in this, as in all his other studies, he cultivated science merely as a foundation of practical knowledge, and in subserviency to it.

At the commencement of his second session, he was introduced to Dr. James Bardesley of Manchester, who had been one of the Presidents of the Royal Medical Society of Edinburgh, the previous year. Dr. Bardesley induced him to become a member of this Society, (the only one in Edinburgh which he ever entered,) and encouraged him to aspire to be its President, by taking a regular part in the debates. To this two apparently insurmountable obstacles presented themselves. The first was his diffidence, which was such, that he thought it impossible for him ever to speak before a considerable number of persons. The second was, that the debates were confined to medical subjects, and he had never opened a book on the practice of physic!

His friends, however, encouraged him, and it was agreed that he should open the session with the first speech, which, at least, secured him an uninterrupted expression of his ideas. The subjects for discussion were papers read to the society by the members in rotation; but these papers were allowed to be circulated for a fortnight beforehand, amongst those who wished to take part in the debates. Hope examined the paper which was to form the subject of the evening's debate, and collected his materials from books. He was advised to commit his two or three first sentences to memory; and this stood him in good stead: for, on being pushed up when the dreaded moment arrived, the vertiginous state of the room and candles must, otherwise, have made him speechless. He gradually recovered breath and command of himself; and then turned out to possess unexpected facilities as an orator. He spoke for five-and-twenty minutes, during which the silence was such, that the falling of a pin might have been heard; and he afterwards commanded the same degree of attention. It is not surprising that the rich stores of a mind so highly cultivated, should make an impression on medical students, who, for the most part, are indifferently educated, and deficient both in classical and general knowledge.

Quickness and brilliancy are so seldom found united to more solid endowments, that they are generally thought to be incompatible; and the deep, reflecting man is supposed to be slow, while the superficial chatterer consoles himself for his shallowness, by the idea of his superior quickness. A closer inquiry proves that this idea is erroneous, and that, in many cases, the superficial and unreflecting are beaten, even on their own ground, by their more solid competitors. Dr. Hope's facility in acquiring knowledge at school, and his subsequent connexion with the Medical Society of Edinburgh, remove every doubt that he had all the

C

qualifications necessary for making him a brilliant man ; and that, had he had no higher ambition than that of shining in society, he might have excelled in that sphere, as much as in the one he chose. He possessed, in a remarkable degree, the power of " getting up" a subject ; and his mode of study seems to have consisted in " getting up," successively, the various subjects to which he applied his mind. While aiming at the acquisition of extensive information, he was far from despising accuracy. This is evident from the very copious and careful notes which he took of all the lectures that he attended during his medical education, and which, covering many quires of paper, are still in possession of his family. He also made an analysis of every medical book which he deemed of sufficient importance to be seriously studied ; and he used to say, that he never left such a book until he had completely " got up" its contents. Many of these analyses are still extant. Another very useful plan which he adopted, was to have the ordinary and standard medical and surgical works, those which he made his text-books, bound up with alternate blank leaves ; and on these he inserted, each in its appropriate place, the scraps of valuable information which he picked up in visiting the infirmary, in conversation with his teachers, or from the perusal of works which, though containing some useful matter, were not worth the trouble of being entirely committed to memory. He always attached much importance to the arrangement of his ideas, and to the art of selecting from the enormous mass of knowledge presented to an inquiring mind, those portions which would prove of ultimate benefit, and this method of interleaving his books assisted him in the accomplishment of both these objects.

Dr. Hope's connexion with the Medical Society occasioned an incident which first turned his thoughts to the selection of diseases of the heart, as the subject of his chief investigation. Each member of this society is required to write a paper, which is made the subject of an evening's debate. Dr. Hope wrote one on diseases of the heart; it was highly applauded, and a wish was expressed that it might at a future day be expanded into a book. He used to say, that this first led him to give the subject particular attention, though his decision was formed on more substantial grounds, as will hereafter be stated.

Towards the close of the year 1823, Dr. Hope was elected one of the four Presidents of the Society. We shall give some extracts from a letter written on this occasion to his friend Dr. George Julius, of Richmond, who seems to have enjoyed a larger portion of his intimate confidence than any other of his acquaintances. It will here be seen, that while he could scarcely brook any honour except the first, he was far from being actuated by that spirit which inclines a man to seek his own elevation, by depreciating the merits of others, and to deem himself unjustly treated when others have been preferred.

" You have heard that I have come in only a second. I do not murmur.   Hannay is a worthy and deserving fellow, and has hitherto acquitted himself to admiration.   I am satisfied, too, with the Society; they elected me in the most handsome manner. But to you, my dear George, I feel ashamed to acknowledge that I am second.   Like that unreasonable fellow, Cæsar, I would rather be first in a village, than second in the world.   Pray let me not sink in your estimation.   Try if you can exculpate me, on the count of an unfortunate combination of circumstances: that as you were all absent, I was friendless in the Society; that the other candidates were of thrice my standing in the profession; that the destruction of votes was unfortunate; and, what actually cast me, that I had to encounter the envious malignity of certain of my antagonists.   But, ohe! satis!   *   *   *"

Dr. Hannay, who, on this occasion, gained the first place in the Presidency of the Medical Society, was one of Dr. Hope's earliest companions in the study of auscultation, and to him he, therefore, dedicated the third edition of his work on Diseases of the Heart. He is now one of the first physicians in Glasgow.

Dr. Hope had never relinquished the expectation of returning to take his degree at one of the English Universities, and, at the expiration of his third session, he proposed graduating at Edinburgh, and then returning to Oxford. He went up to Edinburgh in October 1823, to prepare for his examination. Soon after, in February 1824, he was elected to the office of House-Physician to the Royal Edinburgh Infirmary, an appointment which was too valuable to be declined. As he perceived that the present was the only time previous to his settling in practice, which he could spare for the English University, he found himself forced to select between the substantial advantages of increased medical knowledge and experience which the Edinburgh Infirmary offered, and the greater éclat of an English degree—for so extended and so finished had been his classical education, that it was only éclat which he could gain by the latter. He decided in favour of the Infirmary. Though he never had reason to regret the choice, yet, as it is not always fair to judge of the wisdom of a step by its results, he used to say that it was not a wise one, and that, had he been aware of the strong feeling then operating in the profession in favour of Fellows of the College of Physicians—a rank which, under ordinary circumstances, was attainable only by graduates of the English Universities, or of Trinity College, Dublin—he would not have ventured thus to place himself at a disadvantage.

In November 1824, the office of House Surgeon to the Infirmary was offered to Dr. Hope, and he accepted this also; one reason being, that he had often, as a student, heard the surgeons remark upon and ridicule the ignorance of physicians in surgery. He, therefore, determined to study the two equally up to the time when he should commence practice, and even to obtain a diploma in surgery, which he accordingly did in London in the year 1826. He used to say in after-life, though he restricted himself rigidly to medicine, that his knowledge of surgery was of the greatest use to him, and gave him a confidence which he could never otherwise have enjoyed. In his lectures, he always recommended a similar course to young men designing to be physicians.

He had often been heard to observe that the two years spent in the Edinburgh Infirmary, were the most valuable of his life, as he literally lived at the bed-side of his patients, where the sphere for observation was unlimited.

It was a rule of that institution, that the person holding the office of House Physician should have graduated; but the managers made an exception in Dr. Hope's favour, permitting him to postpone taking his degree till the following year. In August 1825, it was duly performed. The subject of his inaugural thesis was Aneurism of the Aorta, which had been declared by Laennec to be impossible to make out. In the Edinburgh Infirmary, Dr. Hope had paid particular attention to these cases, and, as if in anticipation of his future discoveries, had already succeeded in doing that which had baffled Laennec. His thesis was noticed for its pure Latinity and classical idiom, and possessed, what we believe to be a rare excellence, that of having been written by him whose name it bore. Its motto was a quotation from his favourite Rambler, and we cannot refrain from inserting it, because it indicates his intention that this essay should not be a solitary result of his successful investigations; but should form the first step in a series of researches, which, when brought to a happy close, might immortalize himself no less than benefit mankind:—" All the performances of human art, at which we look with praise or wonder, are instances of the resistless force of perseverance. It is by this that the quarry becomes a pyramid, and that distant countries are united with canals. If a man was to compare the effect of a single stroke of the pick-axe, or of one impression of the spade, with the general design and last result, he would be overwhelmed by the sense of their disproportion; yet those petty operations, incessantly continued, in time surmount the greatest difficulties, and mountains are levelled, and oceans bounded, by the slender force of human beings."—(*Rambler*, No. 43.)

It may here be mentioned, that on the occasion of Sir James M'Grigor's visiting Edinburgh, immediately after the examination, and being entertained by the professors with a public dinner, Dr. Hope and his friend, Dr. George Julius, of Richmond, were invited, and their health was drunk, as having passed the two best examinations of the year.

Although during the five years he spent in Edinburgh he was thus gaining the first honours in medicine ; yet he, notwithstanding, found time for various collateral studies, especially that of the fine arts. The sleepy hour between dinner and tea, he devoted to learning the flute, though without any other preceptors than operas, concerts, &c., of which he was a frequent attendant. He so far overcame the difficulties of the instrument, as to begin to be invited out as an acquisition to musical parties. He had the finest taste and most accurate ear, and was at that time remarkable for the richness, sweetness, and variety of his tone. Here, however, he stopped short, finding that music was too seductive. After leaving Edinburgh, he seldom touched his flute, and, on commencing practice in London, he threw it aside entirely. It may be remarked, however, that his accurate ear was one reason of his excelling in auscultation ; as this gave him a fine perception of the distinction of allied sounds. It is a striking fact, that a number of the best auscultators, including Laennec, who excelled on the violoncello, have been musical amateurs ; whereas, persons who cannot distinguish one tune from another, are almost incompetent as auscultators.

Of painting, he was a still more devoted and successful follower.

From his earliest childhood, he had showed an unusual facility in the use of his pencil and brush. He used to say, that he never had any instruction except that which he received from his elder sister,

Martha, who was herself a very fine artist, and who taught him to do Sepia drawings. A recent reference to the family Bible shows that this lady died when her brother was only seven years of age, a circumstance which proves how early his talent for drawing was manifested. On going to Edinburgh he lost no opportunity of seeing and studying good pictures, and eliciting from eminent artists and connoisseurs all that he could of the principles of the art. He likewise practised oil painting (merely, however, as a copyist) with a degree of success not commonly attained by amateurs. A copy of a small Vanderveld was thought worthy of a place in the collection of the Hon. Charles Hope, Lord President of Scotland; and a copy of Stirling Castle, by Simpson, about 3 feet by $2\frac{1}{2}$, is in the possession of Professor Monro; both of whom are able connoisseurs in the art.

It was principally, however, to subjects of morbid anatomy that he devoted his pencil, notwithstanding the great violence it did to his tastes and inclinations. When elected House Physician to the Edinburgh Infirmary, he began to carry into execution his idea of a work on morbid anatomy embellished with plates. He employed an artist for some months, but at length discovered that it took more time to superintend and correct him, than to execute the drawings for himself. He, therefore, adopted the latter plan, and tried every expeditious mode that he could devise for curtailing the process. His general rule was, to finish each drawing at a single sitting, or, at the utmost, two, in order to avoid changes of colour in the specimens from too long exposure to the air. To show how readily he succeeded at the first attempt, we may instance a drawing of ulceration of the fauces and adjacent parts, the first drawing from nature that he ever made, and which was afterwards published in his work on morbid anatomy, Fig. 46. It is a bold and effective sketch, full of truth to nature, and in no way inferior, as a sketch, to any of his subsequent productions. His collection slowly accumulated, in the space of ten years, to the number of three or four hundred, and comprised examples of almost every important change of structure. The specimens that he selected were, for the most part, small, both for the convenience of rapid execution and of subsequent cheap publication; and they have a double value from being drawn by one who, as a thorough morbid anatomist, understood what he was representing, and could give it a degree of accuracy and expression unattainable by the ordinary artist.

He left Edinburgh in December 1825, after having spent five continuous years at that University.

Dr. Hope's whole career in Edinburgh was one calculated to flatter the vanity of a young man. His acknowledged superiority in general and professional attainments, his amiable disposition, his gentlemanly manners, and, above all, that unpretending modesty and delicacy of feeling, which prevented his seeking to

8

display his own superiority at the expense of others, made him a general favourite among those of his own standing; while his high principle, uncompromising rectitude, and strictly moral conduct, gave him a high degree of influence in his own immediate circle. At the same time, his connexion with the Medical Society, and his conspicuous position in the Infirmary, caused him to be extensively known throughout the Profession as a young man of eminent talents and excellent promise. He was, in consequence, distinguished from his fellow students, and admitted to the best society which Edinburgh affords. Among his companions he retained his former character acquired at school, of excelling in every thing which he attempted; and Dr. Beilby, in introducing him to Dr. Burder, speaks of him as leaving Edinburgh " to the great regret of all who knew him." The letters which he wrote at this period are remarkable for the buoyancy of spirit which they breathe, and show what keen and exquisite enjoyment he derived from every amusement and occupation. " Age quod agis," was one of his favourite maxims, and whether in the play-ground, the school-room, the hospital, the midnight study, or in society, he acted up to its spirit, seeming for the time to have no object beyond that in which he was engaged. In after years, these feelings of enjoyment were very much subdued by the labours and anxieties of his profession, but they continued to influence him so far as to give great cheerfulness to his mind, and that happy disposition to be easily pleased—happy no less to its possessor than to those with whom he is connected.

In January 1826, Dr. Hope went to London, for the purpose of studying surgery, in which department the London school was more distinguished than that of Edinburgh. He entered at St. Bartholomew's Hospital, because the names of Abernethy, Lawrence, Vincent, Earle, and others, together with its magnitude, gave it a first-rate character; but still more, because two of his personal friends, Dr. Charles, of Putney, and Dr. George Julius, of Richmond, were already attached to that institution. He took a dressership under Mr. Vincent. After having learned the peculiarities of the London manipulations, he was permitted by that gentleman to transfer the lighter dressing department to some junior friends, while he devoted himself to more scientific researches and observations, not only on his own cases, but also on those of the other surgeons.

In the spring of 1826, he passed his examination before the College of Surgeons, being determined to have this last proof of his competency in surgery. He was examined by Mr. Cline alone, partly on anatomy, but principally on practical points, who dismissed him in seventeen minutes, with the remark, " You know your profession, Sir; we need not detain you."*

---

* By a rule of the London College of Physicians, no physician,

Immediately after this examination, Dr. Hope went to Paris, intending to devote two years to visiting France, Italy, and Germany. He had imbibed the popular error, common to his countrymen, that there was nothing to be learned in medicine, out of England. It was, therefore, his object to acquire general knowledge, rather than to devote any special attention to his profession. But, on arriving in Paris, he met Dr. Lombard, of Geneva, who had received his medical education in Edinburgh, and for whom he entertained a warm friendship. This intelligent young foreigner took him the round of every thing professional in Paris, and soon convinced him of the French superiority in many departments of medical science. His objects now were completely changed; he determined to spend a full year in Paris, and it proved to be one of the most laborious in his life. A grand difficulty confronted him in the very outset. He had already picked up, in fragments of time, which would otherwise have been wasted, a good knowledge of French and Italian, so far as mere reading went, and he imagined, like many others, that a little practice on the road would enable him to speak the language sufficiently to carry him through his tour; but it was a very different thing to hear the lessons of professors,

practising in London, is permitted to be a member of the College of Surgeons. Previously to commencing practice, Dr. Hope was, therefore, obliged to pay a fee to the College of Surgeons for the privilege of erasing his name from their books.

or to converse with the natives of the country. Of
this he found a very humiliating proof. He went to
engage apartments at a private hotel, but after a pan-
tomimic performance of some twenty minutes between
himself and the landlady, it was found that neither
could, in the slightest degree, understand the other ;
and, after laughter and reciprocal bows, he retired in
despair. Having settled at another hotel, he now
determined to devote twelve hours a day to the mere
practice of speaking French. His first step was to
engage a French master for twelve lessons, and to
make him go through the drudgery of reading three
words at a time, while he mimicked them as closely as
he could. This was singularly disagreeable to the
master, but it was all that Dr. Hope wanted, and he continued inflexible : he thus secured himself against any
gross error in pronunciation. He happened to possess a Wanostrocht's Grammar, with a Key to it—a
grammar which is remarkable for the great number
of simple exercises which illustrate each rule. He now
translated these exercises, vivâ voce, from English to
French, correcting himself by constant reference to the
Key. In this way, he went two or three times through
the grammar in the space of a month, gaining flexi-
bility of tongue, and losing the fear of hearing his
own voice. He, at the same time, adopted another
device, suggested by his friend Dr. Lombard ; namely,
he went to dine daily at a small and crowded restau-
rant, frequented by the garde-du-corps, where the

company was so closely packed, that he could not avoid overhearing the conversation of two or three contiguous tables. In this way his ear got familiarized with all the sounds of the French language, whether quick or slow, correct or provincial. At the end of a month he ventured to sally forth, and having a fancy for the rooms of the private hotel, to which he had originally gone, he again waited on the landlady. On entering, he addressed her in fluent French, explained his wishes, &c. The landlady, meanwhile, with upraised arms, and an air of utter amazement, exclaimed, " Voilà, un miracle ! You cannot be the same gentleman that called here a month ago, and could not speak a single word of French !" " The same, notwithstanding." After some explanation, and much congratulation on her part, the rooms were duly taken, and he resided in them during the remainder of his stay in Paris. They were in the Faubourg St. Germain, and were selected for the convenience of attending the hospitals.

He now began his attendance on the hospitals at the early hour of five in the morning—such being the custom of French students and professors. He visited most of the important hospitals for two or three weeks or more, especially the Hôpital des Enfans; but he settled at La Charité, where M. Chomel was Professor of Clinical Medicine to the University; where also Andral, Lerminier, Louis, Roux, Boyer, and other distinguished men, were either students or pro-

fessors. Chomel soon singled out the diligent Englishman, and, complimenting him on his perseverance,
proposed to him to undertake a series of measurements
of the chest in empyema. Dr. Hope thanked him,
but explained that he had come to Paris to study
medicine universally, and not to restrict himself to any
one point. M. Chomel now showed him much kind
attention, and shortly after proposed to make him one
of his clinical clerks—an offer which was gladly accepted. These clinical clerks were six or eight in
number, and consisted of gentlemen who took charge
of six, eight, or ten cases each. Their duty was to
take most accurate notes of the cases, to offer their
opinion of the treatment, which M. Chomel corrected,
keeping it virtually in his own hands, and to write
out the post-mortem examinations. After the round
of the patients, M. Chomel and the class adjourned
to the lecture-room, where he gave a clinical lecture on
the cases just visited, and, finally, exhibited to the
class any specimens of diseased structure which might
have resulted from the post-mortem examinations of the
preceding day. If any of these proved to be good
subjects for the pencil, Dr. Hope was immediately
called for by M. Chomel, who was aware of his
anxiety to obtain the best materials for a series of
drawings on pathological anatomy, and the specimen
was delivered over to him, with a request that it might
be returned, along with the drawing, for exhibition
the next morning. Finally, if a case terminated

fatally, the clinical clerk read its whole history aloud to the class, together with the details of the post-mortem examination. This was the most formidable part of the duties of the young and diffident Englishman, and he was often glad to get a friend to read for him.

From specimens of morbid anatomy procured in this way, and from various other sources, he compelled himself to make three or four drawings per week, during the remainder of his stay in Paris; each drawing taking him from two to eight hours, according to its size, and to the attention devoted to it. He has often been heard to say, that this proved the most irksome task that he ever performed. His repugnance to anatomy, though greatly subdued, was not totally eradicated, and' this occupation was consequently so alien to his taste, that it was only by the strongest mental effort that he could compel himself to proceed. It was far, he used to say, from being a mere mechanical employment like copying; for, in making original drawings, one paints with the head, not with the hand alone: every touch, every shade of colour is a thought, and thus the intellectual process is a severe one. Notwithstanding, he thus occupied himself five hours daily, and he satiated himself so thoroughly with it, that he never afterwards could settle to drawing of any kind, except from pure necessity; his taste for the art continuing however unimpaired.

Towards one or two o'clock, the medical labours of the morning terminated, except when the drawing was large. He then sallied forth for the double purpose of exercise, and of examining all that was curious in Paris and its environs. On these occasions, he was often accompanied by his friend Dr. Lombard. He avoided the society of all Englishmen, except two or three particular friends, including Dr. Charles, of Putney, and the late Dr. James Gregory, of Edinburgh.

He entered in only a limited degree even into French society; going so much only to the soirées of a few select families, as to give him an insight into the manners, habits, and general character of the French, without trenching seriously on his time. He never went with the view of making patients by making connexions, for he had judgment enough to know, contrary to the prevailing opinion, that a man is less esteemed by his friends than by strangers; and that the very last persons to employ a physician are his acquaintances. He considered, that " the only true, legitimate, and unfailing key to professional success, is superior knowledge and experience;" and to these, in conjunction with the simple and unsophisticated, though not neglected manners, which nature and cultivation had bestowed upon him, he trusted for success.

On the 6th July, 1827, Dr. Hope left Paris, weary after a year of toil, and joyful at the idea of visiting the wild beauties of Switzerland. A friend challenged him to pedestrianise through it for two months, at the rate of twenty miles per day, and Dr. Hope who, during some similar tours in the Highlands of Scotland, had with ease walked thirty miles in a day, willingly accepted the challenge. The journal which he wrote during this tour, teems with information of every sort, and breathes the eager interest which he took in all that was presented to his mind or eye. Botany, mineralogy, traits of national character, popular customs, historical anecdotes, classical reminiscences, all take their turn, and are intermingled with the most vivid and poetical descriptions of scenery. One is equally struck with the intellectual activity of the traveller, with the numerous quotations which evince his familiar acquaintance with ancient and modern authors, with the brilliant imagination linked alike with poetry and painting which renders him so exquisitely alive to the beauties of nature, and with the exuberant spirits of youth which find pleasure in difficulty and hardship, and discover something to amuse, if not to instruct, in every incident and vicissitude of the journey. The tour was evidently performed in the spirit of exploring an unknown country, and it is only to be regretted that the scene of his researches was not some region, as new to the world at large, as Switzerland was to the intelligent young traveller. As it is, we refrain from making quotations from this journal, because we feel that the subject itself is worn so threadbare, that the most valuable journal can possess no interest, except to the personal friends of the writer.

After crossing the Simplon, and visiting the northern lakes and towns, the friends parted company at Milan, as had been agreed upon.

Having had a lesson in France on the inconvenience of being unable to speak the language of a country in which one is travelling and studying, Dr. Hope guarded against a similar inconvenience in Italy. Before leaving Paris, he improved his pronunciation of Italian, by taking twelve lessons in the same manner as he had formerly done in French, and he provided himself with a brief, practical Italian grammar, with exercises referring to the rules, and a key to them. During the tour in Switzerland, it was agreed that he should walk in advance of his friend for one hour, daily, in order to give him an opportunity of practising these exercises vivâ voce. This plan answered perfectly. At the end of the time he spoke Italian fluently; though he was occasionally rallied for using too classical words, such as are found in the old poets only; a circumstance which resulted from his giving the Italian termination to the first suitable Latin word that crossed his mind. During the early part of his residence in Italy, as in France, he avoided the company of his countrymen, and travelled with Italians exclusively.

In company with some Italians of rank and distinction, he visited the northern towns of Italy, Rome, and Naples, dividing his time among the medical schools and hospitals, the galleries of the arts, and the public buildings. At Naples he began to feel the extreme pressure of solitude; the solitude of having been so long alone, even in a merry crowd, in a foreign land, far from home, and far from any friend. He hurried back to Rome, which was to be his winter quarters, intending, at length, to associate with his countrymen; for he had now accomplished his object of becoming familiar with the language, and with the exterior manners and customs of the nation.

His residence at Rome was rendered peculiarly delightful, by an unexpected rencontre with a valued friend, whom, in a letter to Dr. George Julius, he justly denominates " the father, rather than the friend of all in whom he interests himself." This gentleman was Mr. Eneas Mackintosh, of Montagu Square, London, brother of the present proprietor of Raigmore, Inverness-shire. As we shall hereafter have occasion to mention him, we cannot introduce him better than by quoting from some letters which Dr. Hope wrote at this time to Dr. George Julius.

" Imagine my delight at meeting Mr. Mackintosh in the street. It seemed to me incredible, after the joking that had passed between him and your father. You will easily conceive how much his company has enhanced the pleasure of my sojourn in Rome. In fact, I know not whether I should not ascribe to this cause, principally, the profound attachment which I have formed for the ' eterna città,' as its charms are tenfold more charming when viewed in the state of mind created by the company of such a man as Mr. Mackintosh." Again, he says, " I can scarcely describe to you how happy I am in the company of Mr. Mackintosh. He has a most ample share of feeling and imagination ; and though there is many a scene which I should enjoy differently with my dear friend of Loch Katrine, yet I never saw a man of his age, who could reduce himself more happily to the tone of his juniors. But what a model of a character ! I consider myself fortunate in having such a one to study in circumstances which enable me to examine it thoroughly. It is impossible to behold his benevolence, his liberality, his piety, his manly principles, and his universal philanthropy, without feeling better, and consequently happier, for the lesson. The singular acuteness and clearness of his judgment, has not only excited my astonishment, but has rendered me important service."

In the society of one who inspired him with such enthusiastic feelings of admiration and attachment, Dr. Hope visited all that gives such varied attraction to Rome, and which his taste for the fine arts and his classical attainments fitted him peculiarly to enjoy. He regularly attended the hospitals, and was received with much kindness and flattering attention by the distinguished Roman professor, Tagliabo, who used to say, with characteristic warmth, " Siamo quasi fratelli insieme."

In February 1828, Dr. Hope left Rome in the company of Mr. Mackintosh, and selected the beautiful road through Spoletto and Perugia to Florence. Here a tempting offer was made to him. Dr. Thomas, who had, for a series of years, been physician to Lord Burghersh, and enjoyed the principal practice among the English in Florence, was recalled to active duty in the navy. He offered Dr. Hope a gratuitous introduction to Lord Burghersh and his practice. His books showed receipts to the average amount of £1000 or £1100 per annum, and there was no opposition worth considering. This income in Florence was equal to two or three times the amount in London. Dr. Hope, however, was not to be diverted by any thing from the mark on which he had kept his eye steadily fixed, namely, London; and he had sagacity enough to see that, viewing Florence as a mere stepping-stone to London, a few scattered connexions made there, could not be of the least service to him. Not one twentieth of these would ever reappear in London, and, as for the rest, on the same principle that they employed him as the first physician in Florence, they would employ some of the first physicians of London on arriving there; self-interest, not friendship, being almost invariably the principle on which patients select a physician. This is human nature. He, therefore, declined Dr. Thomas's kind offer.

Journeying onwards through Ravenna, Bologna, Modena, Ferrara, Mantua, Verona, and Padua, they arrived at Venice, where they spent three weeks. Here they were in constant and intimate communication with the late estimable British Consul, Mr. Money and his family, who were universally esteemed and respected by their numerous visitors, not only for their frank hospitality, but for the consistent religious conduct which prevailed throughout their cheerful household. In a letter in which Mr. Money's family is mentioned, we may perceive the impression made on Dr. Hope's mind by his intercourse with them, and trace the first indication of that change of opinion and feeling which soon became evident in his actions, and altered the complexion of his after-life.

" The extreme kindness of this amiable and estimable family has almost domesticated us with them. Mr. Money was formerly in India, and subsequently a Member of Parliament, and East India Director. The prominent feature in the character of the family is an ardent and sincere piety, and it is a most impressive lesson to see how happy they are under the influence of such feelings. Whatever the world may say, my dear George, it is a clear case to me that the saints have the laugh on their side. If wishing would add me to their number, I would get enrolled tomorrow. * * * * *"

On leaving Venice, they crossed the Tyrol into Bavaria. It had been their intention to have visited

Vienna, and made the tour of Germany, but as both had urgent calls to return home, it was resolved to take the shorter route homewards by the Rhine, and the principal towns in the Netherlands. Finally, arriving at Calais, they crossed to Dover the 2nd June 1828, with those feelings of joy, which all Englishmen must experience on visiting their native shore after an absence of nearly two years.

Preparatory to settling in his profession, Dr. Hope spent some months in visiting his family and friends in England and Scotland.

While staying at his father's an incident occurred which he took much pleasure in repeating. We have already noticed how warm was the affection which Mr. Hope felt for his son. A change, however, had come over the character of the former, since the days when he used to stimulate the school-boy by the prospect of worldly honours and family distinction. The loss of three daughters; the more recent death of his eldest son, whose fine character and brilliant talents had filled a father's breast with pride and ambitious hopes; the still more recent separation from her who had been the companion of nearly half a century; severe pecuniary losses—all had bowed the old man's spirit, and sending him to his Bible for consolation, had taught him to lay up his treasure where there is no death, and where sorrow is unknown. Thus it is, that messengers of mercy often come disguised as instruments of wrath and chastisement. Mr. Hope

D

felt a natural anxiety on placing his son in the world, and, with the characteristic formality of the old school, to which he belonged, he thought it incumbent on him to give him a little advice for his future guidance. His intention being notified, was received by Dr. Hope with suitable thanks ; for he was tenderly attached to his father, and loved to humour him in all the eccentricities of age. He often reminded his father of his promise, but the fulfilment of it was always deferred to some season of becoming gravity.

It ought to be premised, that Mr. Hope had a supreme contempt for the medical profession. Having attained the age of nearly eighty, without having, to his remembrance, taken a dose of medicine, he ascribed his good health and great activity mainly to having " kept out of the doctor's hands." He therefore concluded that all medical practitioners must necessarily be either fools or knaves. Still, being both fond and proud of his son, he hoped that, by dint of good advice, he might form a bright exception to the rule. To this end, he did not fail to recommend to his especial notice a book of no ordinary quack receipts which he possessed, and which, according to his belief, comprised the whole of medical art and science—a recommendation which Dr. Hope never failed to receive with suitable respect.

At length, the day before Dr. Hope was to leave his father's house, Mr. Hope invited him to take a walk in the adjoining park of a nobleman. The invitation

10

was accepted. For some time they talked on indifferent subjects. Suddenly Mr. Hope stopped, drew himself erect wiih an air of great dignity, and, as if preparing for an important speech, said, " Now, James, I shall give you the advice that I promised, and if you follow it, you will be sure to succeed in your profession.

" *First*,—Never keep a patient ill longer than you can possibly help.

" *Secondly*,—Never take a fee to which you do not feel yourself to be justly entitled. And,

" *Thirdly*,—Always *pray* for your patients."

A short time before his death, Dr. Hope said that these maxims had been the rule of his conduct, and that he could testify to their success.

PERIOD III.

PROFESSIONAL PRACTICE—AUTHORSHIP—LECTURING.

CHAPTER I.

Plans and views on settling in London—Two modes of getting practice
—Opinions on various points of professional tactics.

WE have brought the subject of this Memoir to
the termination of his preliminary studies. We have
pointed out the influence of trivial incidents in calling
out the natural tastes and qualities of mind; the importance of early habits and systematic training in mo-
delling the future man; and, what is more rare, we have
shown how the strongest antipathy may be overcome
by a powerful mind, and all the previous cultivation
of the intellectual faculties be concentrated and made to
bear on that which, however distasteful, is to form the
sphere of future usefulness, and the criterion of future
renown or insignificance. We are arrived at the point
which is to try the efficacy of the previous educational
training, to realize or destroy for ever the ambitious
hopes of the young aspirant to fame, no less than the
fond prophecies of admiring relatives and friends,
who had already, in imagination, placed Dr. Hope

at the head of his profession. How many a clever, brilliant youth has deservedly won the applause of provincial societies, and yet, like Crabbe's country squire, has dwindled into comparative nothingness when placed beside the brighter luminaries of the metropolis! Family connexions, superficial qualities, a higher species of charlatanism, may gain a reputation in the country where comparatively few are qualified judges; but in London, every action is exposed to jealous and able scrutiny; and in order to come out of the large crowd of men who really are possessed of very good average abilities and education, a man must be truly superior. In London every man finds his level, be it mediocrity, or a grade higher or lower.

Fully aware of what was required to be at the head of the profession in London, Dr. Hope shrunk not from the ordeal through which he had to pass, in order to attain what he esteemed the sole object worthy his ambition. He had already refused the most flattering prospects at Florence; he was now urged to settle in Edinburgh, in Manchester, in York, in various other places where he had connexions, or where his former fellow-students were already beginning to taste the sweets of success. He turned a deaf ear to such solicitations, determining either to be nothing, or to be the first physician in the first metropolis of the world. His past success in *every* situation in which he had been placed, justified him in believing that his natural abilities were not inferior to those of others, and he had taken care that none should gain an advantage over him by more assiduous application, or by superior opportunities for study. His cool judgment, therefore, formed the rational conclusion that where his equals or inferiors had succeeded, he could only fail through his own fault. The knowledge of the dangers and difficulties which awaited him, served to awaken his prudence and animate his zeal; but his predominant feeling was that of impatience to enter the field. This sentiment is expressed in the following letter to Dr. George Julius, written from Cheshire :—

"*August* 28th, 1828.

"You could not easily have devised a stronger temptation than the York Festival in such company; but, alas! the obstacles are insuperable. I am pledged to appear before the College of Physicians at the end of September: three or four weeks' preparation will be necessary, and I shall be previously occupied in house-hunting. - - - - - After all, I think I should be a damper on your merriment at York, and, accordingly, should not enjoy the amusements: for I am so weary of idleness, and so impatient to expose myself to the onus which you, from repletion, reprobate, that every other object has lost its charms for me."

Dr. Hope came to town a few days after this letter was written, passed the College as a licentiate, and, on the 8th December, 1828, took possession of his house in Lower Seymour-street, the same which he continued to occupy till he retired from practice. In the choice of this situation, he afterwards found reason to believe that he had been mistaken. He said, at the close of his career, that it was the only error in professional tactics into which he had ever fallen. Having never been in London, except during the few months when he was a student at St. Bartholomew's Hospital, and when his studious habits made him avoid all society, and choose a residence in the immediate neighbourhood of that hospital, he was ignorant of the strong line of demarcation which Oxford-street forms. He naturally supposed that a few yards north or south of that barrier of fashion could not make much difference; especially while he was surrounded by so many families of rank and wealth in the adjoining squares and streets. He had also a further inducement from the promises of Mr. Mackintosh to introduce him into an Indian connexion, with whom he had much influence, and who, for the most part, reside in this quarter. In a few years he was sensible of his mistake in this respect, and he would willingly have corrected it; but many difficulties lie in the way of a physician's change of abode. Setting aside the inconvenience to patients from the country, a physician ought never to move from one house to another of equal size and appearance: every step must seem to be in advance. If it be not so, there are many too

ready to look upon the removal as an indication of
want of success.   Such, at least, was Dr. Hope's
opinion, and this made him defer, from year to year,
a step of which he daily felt the increasing necessity.

Before commencing a narration of the events which
marked Dr. Hope's professional career, we shall give
a brief sketch of what were the advantages and disadvantages with which he commenced it ; what were
the special objects of his ambition, and what were
the means which he adopted to attain them.   This example may be peculiarly useful to those desirous of
following in his track, because chance, as it is commonly
called, had nothing to do with his subsequent success.
Every step of his after life was arranged from the first ;
and having once traced out a path for himself, he
followed it perseveringly, undaunted by opposition and
unseduced by temptation, until he had arrived at the
summit of his wishes.   How few, at the close of life,
can look back and say, as Dr. Hope might have done,
that, so far as this world is concerned, they have accomplished all that they had planned, and attained all
that they had desired !

The sole advantage which Dr. Hope possessed on
settling in London, lay in his natural powers of mind,
his superior education, and a robust constitution.
We mention this last, because, though often over-
looked, he considered it an indispensable requisite to
professional success.   His reasons were founded on
the opinion that natural abilities can do little without

application ; that native talent is more equally distributed than might be supposed from the various success of after life ; and that he who, by dint of unbroken physical powers, can superadd the largest portion of study to its natural gifts, is certain to bear off the prize. It is unquestionable that without a very robust constitution, Dr. Hope could not have accomplished all that he did, especially in so short a time.

As for his education, it had not been hurried over, as is too frequently the case, with the greatest possible economy of time and money : nor had he come prematurely to settle at the place of his future destination. On the contrary, his medical education had been extended over nearly ten years, and had been conducted in the first schools in Europe, and under the most eminent men in Edinburgh, in London, in Paris, and in Italy. Instead of coming to town immediately after graduating, and loitering away in idleness those years when his extreme youth would necessarily have excluded him from practice, he had spent this time in making observations on foreign practice, and in collecting the materials for his future works. He had resided for two years as house physician and surgeon in one of the best regulated institutions in the United Kingdom ; and he could make, we believe, the singular boast of being no less able as a surgeon and a chemist than as a physician. Testimonials of merit are so easily obtained, that they are of small value, unless they enter much into detail, and use no ordi-

nary terms of commendation. The numerous testimonials which Dr. Hope had obtained from the first
men, both at home and abroad, decidedly possess this
characteristic, and it is curious to see how unanimously these individuals, of various nations, habits,
and characters, point him out as the one who must
occupy the first position in his profession. M. Andral
writes,

" Je me plais à reconnoître en lui un medicin déjà
très distingué et qui est appellé à occuper le premier
rang dans votre profession. Je pense que ce sera
toujours un grand profit pour la science qu'on lui
confiera une place soit dans l'enseignement, soit dans
les hôpitaux." And such is the unvarying tone of
the others.

To counterbalance these great advantages of education, Dr. Hope lay under disadvantages of so serious
a character that they would have been sufficient to
deter any one of less determined courage and energy,
or who did not possess such a consciousness of his
own powers. It may safely be affirmed, that no one
who has arrived at such early and such great eminence
in his profession, started with so few adventitious
circumstances in his favour. In the first place, not
having taken his degree at an English University, he
was not a fellow of the College of Physicians. At
that period, when reform had not begun its innova-
tions, this seemed an insuperable barrier to the attainment of any public appointment. The esprit de

corps was so strong, that if opposed to an election
by a fellow, he would have had to contend against
the whole college. Of this he had an opportunity of
judging when canvassing for the Marylebone Infirmary. On soliciting the assistance of a leading physician, who on all other occasions, maintained a very
friendly conduct towards him, he was told, with many
expressions of friendship and of regret, that, as one
of Dr. Hope's opponents was a fellow, it was impossible for another fellow to take an active part in Dr.
Hope's favour; adding, however, that Dr. Hope need
not feel any uneasiness on the occasion, as it was
utterly impossible that he should be defeated by so
incompetent a candidate!

The second disadvantage was so great, that it is
strange how he could have had the hardihood to fix on
London as his sphere of practice. He often said, that
he had but *one* private acquaintance, his quondam
travelling friend, Mr. Mackintosh, who himself was
not then resident in town; and we believe that his
medical acquaintance did not extend beyond his
teachers at St. Bartholomew's Hospital, and Dr.
Henry Holland, whose father had long attended Dr.
Hope's family in Cheshire. A physician now in extensive practice in London, is said to confess how much
he owes to the kind offices of an eminent surgeon who,
from friendly motives, scarcely allowed a day to pass
without sending him a patient. Others can doubtless
testify to similar, though not such powerful aid ren-

dered by friendship. But Dr. Hope was not so favoured. He had formed but few friendships, and
by a strange chance, if chance it can been called, the
more eminent of his youthful friends had settled at
a distance from London.* He stood alone, and to
his professional merits only, under Providence, could
he look for success.

There are two ways by which a physician may
obtain practice in London. The one, which is the
more commonly adopted, is that of private connexion.
While this is the easier mode, for one who has a good
family connexion, or private introduction, it is the
less certain, nor does it lead to the highest eminence,
and the largest practice. A man selecting this method
may be clever, or he may be an ignoramus: how can
it be known? He is necessarily excluded from the
more easy and lucrative walk of consultation practice,
and must not expect to gain more than a meagre com-
petence.

The second way of getting into practice is through
the medium of professional reputation; and when a
man possesses the average share of abilities, united to

---

* It is singular that the two friends with whom he was most allied
by amity and by talent, have, like himself, sunk early martyrs to their
profession, and preceded him to the tomb. We refer to Dr. James
Gregory, of Edinburgh, for whom Dr. Hope felt the warmest affection; and to Dr. Becker, of Berlin, who translated Dr. Hope's work
on Diseases of the Heart. They were both young men of the highest
promise, and must have attained the first professional honours, had it
pleased the Almighty to have spared their lives.

great diligence and common prudence, this is the more certain mode, as well as that which leads to the greatest honour and wealth. To follow this course, he must seek to make himself known by his writings, by his lectures, but especially by attaching himself to an hospital, with the hope of being its physician at some future day. As a senior pupil, he follows the physicians in their visits to the wards, takes notes, becomes known both to the officers of the institution and to the junior pupils, and while he is adding to his stores of information, has an opportunity of gaining a character for general diligence and talent. But at the same time, he is exposed to the jealous scrutiny of many who are his competitors in the race of fame; and, therefore, he must be careful that the character he gains, be a good one. When he takes a higher stand, as a lecturer, or a physician to the hospital, he has a field for the display of the practical and scientific knowledge which he has been storing for many years; and a fair reputation gained in the wards of an hospital, is sure to lead to private consultation practice among the numerous medical men of all classes who frequent the hospital, originally as students, and afterwards as practitioners. But those whom he has outstripped, or whom he is likely soon to outstrip in the race of professional eminence, continue to maintain a strict watch over all that he teaches or prescribes. Students, too, like school-boys, are always prone to detect faults in a teacher. Such a practice cheats a man into the pleasing belief of his own superiority. And when it is remembered that in these students are to be found the practitioners who, in a few years, will be scattered over the whole kingdom, their favourable or unfavourable opinion is by no means unimportant to the physician, as it is to the pedagogue.

To pass successfully through this ordeal in London, is indeed a test of talent, and it may be said, that no man gains reputation in this way, and retains it, without deserving it.

Dr. Hope had long ago resolved that he should adopt the latter mode of securing private practice, because he considered it the only certain and legitimate means for securing his end. His was not a vulgar ambition, which sought wealth and honours simply for themselves. We have before said, that he was ambitious *to be* good and great, rather than to be thought so; and while seeking his own aggrandizement, he never lost sight of the hope of being useful to mankind at large. He never sought to employ the public for his own interest, but he desired that it should be their interest to consult him. He had, therefore, spent his time in acquiring knowledge rather than connexions; and thus, on settling in London, while he was peculiarly destitute of the means of succeeding in the former of the courses which we have delineated, he was eminently qualified for the latter. He may be considered a good specimen of the working class of the profession, and his career strikingly shows what may be done in the brief space of twelve years by reputation alone, unaided by private connexions.

One of the means which Dr. Hope selected for bringing himself before the public and the profession, was the publication of the results of his previous studies. As, however, he had marked out for himself a high game, he did not think it prudent to waste his strength in writing pamphlets, papers for journals, or any of those minor works which bring a man into notice, simply by having his name seen in print. While he sought to be known, he avoided making himself conspicuous; and desired to wait until he could write that which would really do him credit, and procure him fame rather than notoriety. With this view he assigned to himself the execution of the two works which he had long planned; viz. A treatise on Diseases of the Heart, and a complete work on Morbid Anatomy, illustrated by plates: and for the completion of these works he allotted seven years. The materials for the work on Morbid Anatomy were nearly complete, and the only difficulty which he had to encounter in its publication was the enormous expense— an expense which he had already reduced, and hoped still further to reduce, by being his own artist. The treatise on Diseases of the Heart was a work, the execution of which was not so easy, nor so certain. This subject was then very little understood, and though Dr. Hope had already unravelled some of its intricacies, yet so much still remained uncertain and inexplicable, that he often doubted whether he should succeed in his object. At all events, he was determined not to publish until he should be fully competent to do so. To this end it was essential that he should continue his studies at some large hospital, and he selected St. George's, as being the one to which he hoped one day to be physician.

As the governors of St. George's Hospital include in their number the first nobility, and wealthy gentry residing in its neighbourhood, and as its wards are visited by the principal apothecaries whose practice lies in that quarter, Dr. Hope preferred attaching himself to it, as he perceived that a reputation gained within its precincts, must be an introduction to the first practice in the metropolis. To be one of its physicians was then an ultimate object of Dr. Hope's ambition; but as there were already several candidates in the field, who he feared might reasonably hope to precede him in the course of election, and many years must, therefore, elapse before the attainment of his end, he desired in the interval to be physician to the Marylebone Infirmary. This post was then held by Dr. Hooper, whose advanced age and declining health, made it probable that a vacancy would soon occur. Besides offering a field of observation which Dr. Hope always held to be unequalled, a salary of about 500*l.* per annum was then attached to this office, and this made it no undesirable situation for a junior physician.

.The same motives which had influenced Dr. Hope

in not publishing until he could do something which would be really creditable, prompted him not to seek a petty distinction, by being elected physician to any dispensary or minor public institution. Being desirous, at the same time, of possessing some field for the acquisition of practical knowledge, he established a private dispensary in 1829, in connexion with the Portman-square and Harley-street District Visiting Societies. His professional skill, no less than his humane and gentle manners, soon made him very popular among the poor of the neighbourhood. The number of his patients increased rapidly, and he calculated that he must have seen a thousand patients annually. He held this dispensary until he was appointed physician to the Marylebone Infirmary in November 1831.

Though Dr. Hope had hitherto acted on the principle of not seeking to form connexions as an introduction to practice, he judged that the time was now come when he might, in some degree, depart from his prescribed rule and conform himself to the custom of most other members of his profession. In yielding so far to the experience of others, he was not sanguine of success, and, therefore, he did not give himself much trouble about the cultivation of general acquaintance, except as a means of recreation ; nor did he sacrifice to this object much of that precious time which he felt certain was better and more wisely spent in the furtherance of strictly professional objects. In Mr.

Mackintosh, Dr. Hope had an attached and influential friend. This gentleman introduced him to several families of his acquaintance as a physician who would soon be at the head of his profession, and in families with which he was intimately connected he did not hesitate to recommend him as the future medical attendant. By means of this zealous friend, and through the medium of a few letters of introduction, Dr. Hope was soon introduced to a tolerable numerous circle of acquaintances. This did not fail to make his residence in London more agreeable, by relieving him from the wretched feeling of loneliness in a crowd, which must weigh down the spirits of every stranger arriving in that great metropolis. Mr. Mackintosh's efforts were also in some degree successful in procuring him his first patients, but the success was by no means commensurate with the wishes and expectations of that gentleman. Though Dr. Hope always met with a friendly reception from Mr. Mackintosh's friends, and was at once admitted to the intimacy of their families, yet, in numerous instances they objected to employ him as a medical attendant. One thought him too young; another could not think of employing an unmarried man; a third was already provided with a medical adviser in whom he had the greatest confidence. Every day Dr. Hope saw more and more clearly the wisdom of not seeking to make friends with the hope of making patients. He had always been a close observer of human nature, so as to analyze the motives of action operating as general laws throughout mankind; and though the kindness of his own feelings led him to form a more favourable opinion of human nature than he was enabled to do when his judgment was matured by experience, yet he had discrimination enough to perceive that man will seldom sacrifice to considerations of friendship what he conceives to be his interest. To ask a stranger to dinner on the recommendation of a friend, and to give him a peculiarly courteous reception, is no great stretch of friendship, especially where the individual himself may fairly be considered an acquisition to a social circle. But to trust your life to the hands of the said stranger is really too much to ask from friendship. There is scarcely any subject on which the generality of the world are more ignorant than on the merits of medical men, and as to what are the data on which the opinion of those merits should be formed. They are, therefore, not only open to the impositions of fraud; but as the usual accompaniment of ignorance, they are peculiarly capricious, prejudiced, and unreasonable on the subject. There is a vulgar proverb, which makes familiarity the parent of contempt, and in the case of medical men this is strikingly verified. When a man becomes known as an agreeable man in society, as a musical performer, as an artist, as an adept in general science—in fact, as any thing but a professional man, he loses his chance of securing a patient in almost the same ratio as he gains popularity. Dr.

Hope used often to notice this; and he remarked not
only that his friends and acquaintances were the last
to discover his professional merits; but that, even
when converted into patients, he had much less influence with them than with those whom he had first
known as patients, and who were afterwards changed
into friends.   He used often to tell, with much zest, a
story illustrative of this opinion.   A gentleman, an old
friend of Mrs. Hope's family, lived for several years
within three doors of him, but never dreamt of trusting his life into the hands of a young man like Dr.
Hope.   This gentleman having been taken dangerously
ill at Glasgow, was recommended by his medical adviser (Dr. Hannay, we believe), to come to town in
order to consult Dr. Hope.   " What!" said the old
gentleman, " you do not mean the man next-door to
whom I have lived so many years?"   He came,
however, and with great naïveté related the story himself, laughing at the notion of having been obliged to
travel to Glasgow to discover the merits of his neighbour.

Dr. Hope's experience led him to form the conclusion, that in a professional point of view only one
benefit can be derived from a large circle of acquaintances.   In canvassing for public appointments, their
friendly exertions may be useful; or, at all events,
they convey an idea of the influence which a man can
command, and this very idea conduces to success.   In
the three contested elections which Dr. Hope had to

stand, he derived this great benefit from the very warm
and active exertions of many friends. At the same
time, he acknowledged that had he been dependent
solely on the aid of friends, and destitute of the
powerful co-operation of his professional brethren, he
could have made but a very feeble opposition to any
candidate who was supported by the latter, even though
otherwise friendless.

As we are speaking of the value of non-professional
connexions, it may not be inappropriate to notice the
opinions which Dr. Hope entertained with respect to
some other measures and adventitious circumstances,
which are commonly supposed to lead to private practice. These opinions were either formed from his own
experience, or strengthened by its results; and as the
wisdom of his plans was attested not only by his great
success, but by its rapid attainment, they may be interesting, and possibly not quite uninstructive to the
public.

It is very generally believed that a physician should
marry early, and that his practice will be benefited
by his assuming the character of a married man. Dr.
Hope at one time participated in this notion, but his
own experience so completely changed his opinion,
that he was in the habit of warning his young friends
against being led into a similar error. He rather advised, if they were influenced by considerations of
policy alone, to defer forming this connexion until an
increased practice might enable them to do it with

more advantage. He confessed that before his marriage he had believed the professions of some who,
while regretting that they could not employ him as
an unmarried man, had given him to understand that
the change of his state would make a corresponding
change in their conduct. He found that this event
made no addition to his practice, and that the hopes
held out to him were fallacious. At a later period, he
observed that the patients who came to him on professional grounds alone, neither inquired nor cared
about the matter. Some even professed surprise on
discovering accidentally that he was married, thereby
proving that he had been consulted as an unmarried
man.

There is another measure very frequently recommended to young physicians, and scarcely less frequently adopted by them—that of giving dinners to
apothecaries and other members of the profession, in
hopes of securing their professional assistance. This
was a low device, from which Dr. Hope's good taste,
no less than his pride, revolted. From the first, he
set his face against it, and he believed it to be an equal
loss of time, trouble, and money. The persons thus
invited, at once see through the motive ; they make a
favour of accepting the invitation, praise the dinner,
laugh at the host, and go away determined on following their own interest or inclination, uninfluenced by
any recollection of the interested hospitality. · Once a
medical gentleman, who had been a patient of Dr.

Hope's, told him, that he regretted he could not assist him in his canvass, because he had occasionally dined with Dr. Hope's opponent. Dr. Hope contrived to convince this gentleman that he was so sure of success, that the assistance of one individual was not of moment, and this consideration soon banished the remembrance of the dinners. Acting on the principle that he had laid down, Dr. Hope never gave a medical dinner until after his election to be physician to St. George's Hospital; he then invited, in succession, all practitioners, as well as students, who had assisted him in the canvass, with a few who had opposed him. He then found that he associated with them on much more agreeable terms when he had nothing to ask or to hope from them, and when they could only regard his hospitality as an earnest of his friendly feeling for the future, or of his gratitude for the past.

Finally, Dr. Hope often spoke of the imprudence of a man commencing his career in style, or setting up his carriage at too early a period. Of course, a certain respectability of appearance must be maintained from the first, and after some time the removal to a handsome house and the setting up of a handsome carriage may be beneficial, as giving an impression of professional success. But if these are assumed at an early period, when it must be evident to all, that they are supported from private, not professional resources, the owner loses all benefit from them at the time, and the power of resorting to them, when he is legitimately

entitled to do so.   In his own case there were special
reasons for avoiding all such advertisements of success.
He had often been warned that his unusual pros-
perous career would awaken much jealousy, and he
was advised to allay such feelings as much as possible.
He acted invariably on this principle, and we believe,
that, however fortunate he was supposed to have been,
the reality of his success exceeded the opinion generally
entertained of it.   Thus, prudence, as well as taste,
would have prevented Dr. Hope from resorting to an
expedient which, in common with all similar ones, he
despised, as being worthy alone of those who have no
other means of introducing themselves to the notice
of the public.

CHAPTER II.

Pupil at St. George's Hospital—Auscultation—Experiments on the sounds of the heart—Treatise on Diseases of the heart—Physician to the Marylebone Infirmary—Work on Morbid Anatomy.

IMMEDIATELY after settling in Seymour Street, Dr. Hope became a pupil and a governor in St. George's Hospital—the former, in order to be entitled to gain knowledge and experience, by following the physicians in their visits to the wards; and the latter, with a view to his future election by the governors to the situation of physician to the hospital. In commencing his professional career, Dr. Hope felt so strongly the necessity of concentrating all his powers, all his thoughts, to the attainment of his great end, that he sacrificed to it every other taste and gratification. He discarded his flute, restricted his pencil to professional objects alone, and even imposed on himself the restraint of not looking at a newspaper, or reading any work of general interest, until he should have completed the task of publishing his works on Diseases of the Heart and Morbid Anatomy.

As a senior pupil at St. George's, Dr. Hope soon

E

became conspicuous for his regular attendance and
unvarying application.   He was always to be seen
with his stethoscope, his book for taking notes of cases,
and a small ink-bottle attached to his button.   At
that time the physicians of St. George's had no clinical clerks, and the taking of notes was much neglected.   Dr. Hope induced Dr. Chambers to introduce
this arrangement, so productive of advantage both to the
student and the physician, and he was himself the first
medical clinical clerk in St. George's Hospital, holding
that Office to Dr. Chambers.   On the intermediate days,
when Dr. Chambers did not make the round, Dr. Hope
went to the Marylebone Infirmary, and for a year he
was a regular attendant of Dr. Hooper's in that institution.   At this time the prejudice against auscultation was very strong in England, and especially at St.
George's, in consequence, chiefly, of several persons
having brought it from Paris, and having undertaken,
without paying any attention to the *general* signs of
the various cases, to form the diagnosis by the *physical*
signs alone.   They were constantly in error, and thus
their undue pretensions brought discredit on the whole
system.   Dr. Hope determined to remove these prejudices, and he adopted a most judicious course.   He
never spoke nor argued in favour of auscultation, but
allowed facts to speak for themselves.   He was always
to be seen, stethoscope and journal in hand, at the
bedside of every chest case : he took the most minute
notes of them all, wrote the diagnosis in as great

detail as possible, and, before proceeding to a post-mortem examination, publicly placed his book on the table, in order that it might be read by all: his diagnosis was invariably correct. Attention was soon drawn to him; his diagnosis was generally asked for and read aloud; its accuracy silenced every objection, and all intelligent and candid men became convinced of the utility of the stethoscope.

The injudicious conduct of one of the opponents of auscultation served to show its superior claims to the notice of the profession. Dr ———— having observed, with some annoyance, the progress of a theory which he regarded as unsound, and being unconvinced by the proofs of the superior facilities it afforded for forming a correct diagnosis, announced that it was high time to put a stop to such proceedings, and that he would come down to St. George's and drive the auscultators out of the field. He said that he would choose half a dozen cases, write the diagnosis, and defy all the auscultating gentlemen, with their pipes, to throw more light on the cases than he had already done. Dr. Hope desired nothing more than such a public examination, and he joyfully accepted Dr. ————'s challenge. One case was chosen. Dr. ———— *said* that it was hydro-thorax, but did not *write* his diagnosis, though frequently urged to do so. Dr. Hope wrote it down as " Hypertrophy and dilatation of the heart. Hydropericardium. Little, if any, hydrothorax. Lungs gorged and emphysematous."

The patient died, and a post-mortem examination was to set at rest for ever the claims of auscultation.

On arriving at the room appointed for the purpose, Dr. ———, though not producing a written diagnosis, repeated his opinion that the case was one of hydro-thorax. Dr. Hope read out his diagnosis as above specified. The case proved not to be hydro-thorax, not an ounce of fluid being found in the cavity of the pleura; and, on the other hand, every item of Dr. Hope's diagnosis was verified. This is the case of Bryant, the first mentioned in the Treatise on Diseases of the Heart. From this time, Dr. ——— was silent on the subject of auscultation, and the half dozen cases were not again heard of.

While thus standing up as the champion of auscultation, Dr. Hope was simultaneously prosecuting his researches on diseases of the heart.

We have already shown how the commendations bestowed by the Royal Medical Society of Edinburgh, on his paper on Diseases of the Heart, and the expression of their wish that, at some future day, the paper might be expanded into a book, had first caused Dr. Hope to turn his attention to the subject. He had afterwards two more weighty reasons for the concentration of his mental powers on this point. These were, first, that, being a wide subject, researches in it were more likely to be useful, than similar care devoted to the individual branches of any more explored branch of medical science: secondly, that having been left in an unsatisfactory state by Laennec, there was the more room for investigation. In these two reasons, which were thus expressed by himself many years after, may be observed the ruling principles of Dr. Hope's natural character; great intellectual activity and the benevolent desire to serve his fellow-creatures.

In the Edinburgh Infirmary he made observations on aneurisms of the aorta; and, though Laennec had said, that it was impossible to make out these cases, Dr. Hope succeeded in doing so. He chose this as the subject of his thesis on graduation in Edinburgh. In France and Italy, he had continued his observations; but though he had overcome many difficulties, much still remained doubtful and intricate. While such was the case, he would not publish. He could not be satisfied with merely laying before the public more than was already known, or with embodying in an able work the conjectures of those who had preceded him. As he himself expressed it, " he did not feel *justified* in publishing on a subject till he fully understood it." With this impression, he continued his examination of cases of disease of the heart, but with little prospect of arriving at the desired conclusion. At length he devised his ingenious experiments on the ass, and these, by enabling him to satisfy his mind as to the cause of the first sound of the heart, suddenly dissipated the greater part of the difficulties with which he had been contending.

As the subject of the sounds of the heart, though connected with medicine, belongs also to physiology, which may be considered as possessing more general interest, we will endeavour to state the objects and results of these experiments in a manner intelligible to the non-professional reader.

The action of the heart gives rise to certain sounds, which are heard very distinctly in the cardiac region, and more obscurely over an extent of the chest, which varies in different individuals. If the ear be applied, with or without the intervention of the stethoscope, to the cardiac region of a healthy person, two successive sounds will be heard ; then a brief interval of silence ; then the repetition of the two sounds ; then another interval ; and so on in a series, which is perfectly regular, and susceptible indeed of being represented by musical notation. The two sounds heard at each pulsation of the heart differ from each other both in kind and duration. The *first* sound is grave, louder at its commencement than at its termination, and seems to be suddenly interrupted by the *second* sound, which is short and acute, and has been compared to the flap of the valve of a pair of bellows. The first sound is synchronous with the impulse of the heart against the ribs, and with the pulse in the arteries nearest the heart. The existence of these sounds in the state of health, and the important indications afforded by the changes which they undergo in various diseases of the heart, had been established by Laennec, and were al-

ready familiar to those practised in auscultation. With
respect to the causes of these sounds, Laennec had
given an opinion which for some time remained undis-
puted ; namely, that the first sound was occasioned by
the contraction of the ventricle, and the second, by
that of the auricle. Mr. Turner was the first to show
that the second sound could not depend, as supposed
by Laennec, on the contraction of the auricle, because
the contraction of this cavity in reality precedes that of
the ventricle. Dr. Hope's first experiments on the ass
were made in August 1830. The animal was stunned
by a blow on the head with a hammer, so as to render
it insensible to pain, and the action of the heart was
sustained by the maintenance of artificial respiration.
The chest and pericardium being then opened, the
central organ of the circulation was exposed to view,
pulsating, as in health ; such, at least, was the case in
the second of two experiments performed on the same
day ; for in the first, the action of the heart was found
to be considerably enfeebled. Dr. Hope's general conclusions from these experiments were, that the first
sound is connected with the *contraction* of the ventricle, and the second sound with the *dilatation* of the
ventricle ; but the immediate causes of the sounds yet
remained to be determined.

In three series of experiments made in 1835, on
asses poisoned with woorara, Dr. Hope obtained certain results, which he deemed conclusive as to the
causes of both kinds. He maintained that the *first*

sound was compound, and consisted, first, of the sound caused by the extension of the auricular valves; secondly, of the sound caused by the sudden extension of the braced muscular walls of the ventricle; and thirdly, of the prolongation, and possibly an augmentation by *bruit musculaire*, or the sound attendant on muscular contraction in general.

The cause of the second sound he determined to be simple, and to consist in the sudden expansion of the valves at the mouth of the pulmonary artery and aorta, resulting from the recoil of the columns of blood upon them.

In his explanation of the first sound, Dr. Hope admitted a greater number of influential circumstances than had previously been done; his view was less exclusive, and probably more correct than others; but it must be acknowledged that considerable obscurity still hangs over the causes of this sound.

His explanation of the *second* sound was derived from an experiment of a very exact and conclusive nature, in which the obstruction naturally caused by the valves was removed and replaced at pleasure, with a corresponding absence and restoration of the sound; and the same result having been obtained by other able inquirers, the question may be regarded as nearly decided.

These experiments, whether considered in reference to the importance of the practical points which they tend to elucidate—the ingenuity with which they were devised—or the cautious and sagacious manner in which they were conducted—deservedly rank as the most important experimental researches connected with medicine which have been instituted for many years, and have conferred, by universal consent, the very highest reputation on their author.

A large proportion of obscurities that enveloped his subject being now removed, Dr. Hope no longer hesitated about publishing. It was true, that several points still remained unexplored; but, on the other hand, he was enabled to present so much new matter, to offer so much information on the diagnosis and treatment of these maladies, that he did " feel himself justified" in presenting himself and his discoveries before the public. He accordingly set about the work, and he wrote with such diligence that he completed it in one year, though it was an octavo volume of above 600 pages. It had long been his custom to work with little intermission, from seven in the morning till twelve at night; but, when once engaged in any work of interest, he seemed not to feel fatigue, and not to know where to stop. When writing this book, he frequently sat up half through the night. When completing it, he often rose at three in the morning. On one occasion he rose at three, wrote without cessation till five the following morning, then went to bed, and at nine o'clock Mrs. Hope, for he had been married a few months before, was at his bed-side writing to his dictation, while he breakfasted.

E 5

This work met with the most favourable reception
from all the principal reviews.   It was hailed with
a high degree of satisfaction, and his analysis of the
sounds of the heart was pronounced to be the only
great accession which the science of auscultation had
received since the death of its memorable author,
Laennec.   Dr. Hope was said to have produced the
best work on the subject which had yet emanated
from the public press—an encomium, however, which
can no longer be applied to this production, because
its author subsequently eclipsed himself in his third
edition.   It was translated into German, passed rapidly
through several editions in America, and found
its way even into Italy, a country where, of late years,
the progress of medical improvement has been slow,
and the medical literature of other nations is little
cultivated.

Early in October 1831, Dr. Hooper resigned the
office of Physician to the Marylebone Infirmary.   As
the advantages of an admirable field for study, and a
considerable salary, made this post a very desirable
one, several candidates were soon in the field.   Though
all of these were considerably senior to Dr. Hope, both
in age and in professional standing, he did not shrink
from opposing them.   It was supposed that the new
physician would stand in the same position as Dr.
Hooper, with the sole exception of a reduction in the
amount of salary, the proposal of which had led to

Dr. Hooper's resignation. Shortly before the election, however, the following was passed by the Board of Guardians :—

" Resolved,—That the gratuity hitherto given to the physician be discontinued : that two physicians be appointed in the place of Dr. Hooper, and that they be allowed to have their pupils accompanying them, subject to such regulations as may be hereafter made."

Although this resolution considerably diminished the value of the appointment in a pecuniary aspect, yet, to Dr. Hope, the change seemed unimportant. Nothing was further from his intention than a gratuitous attendance at the infirmary. He conceived that the above resolution placed the infirmary on the same footing with the hospitals of the metropolis, and the instruction of pupils being very congenial to his taste, he rather rejoiced at a measure which threw the institution open to the profession. On the other hand, had he felt disposed to retire, he could not have done so without confessing himself vanquished ; for, as the candidates had been several weeks in the field, and this resolution was passed only a few days before the election, it was pretty generally known how the votes would be given. Dr. Hope was opposed by eight candidates, most, if not all, of whom were at least ten years his seniors. Dr. Hope had 11 votes, Dr. Sims 10, and the other seven candidates divided 23 among them.

The result of the election was announced to Dr. Hope by one of the guardians in a letter from the board-room, addressed to him as " the senior Physician to the St. Marylebone Infirmary"—a title which he accordingly affixed to the first edition of his work on the heart. The board afterwards directed that the two physicians should stand on an equality.

Dr. Hope always acknowledged the deepest obligations to Dr. Young, of Devonshire Place, to whose very warm and friendly exertions he considered that he owed his success. This gentleman had held high appointments in the East India Company's medical service, but had never practised in England.

Preparations were now made by the parochial guardians for the reception and accommodation of pupils. Clinical journals were furnished at the expense of the institution, prescription cards were placed at the heads of the beds, a new room was appointed for post-mortem inspections, the name of the medical portion of the institution was changed from workhouse to infirmary, and the hours of attendance, and certain other regulations, were specified. Great, therefore, was the surprise of the medical officers when, about a fortnight after the election, they were summoned before a committee at which only three guardians were present, and informed that the number of their pupils was restricted to one or two each! They objected to this restriction, as being subversive of their contract with the board; and so strongly did Dr. Young, who was one

of the three guardians, feel the injustice of their treatment, that he gave up his seat at the board.

It may now be asked, why the medical officers did
not resign their places? The result proved that this
would have been their most dignified course of action,
and would have completely exonerated them from the
imputation of letting down their profession by volun-
teering to do gratuitously, that for which an adequate
salary had hitherto been received. But as the restriction had been carried at a sub-committee, where only
three members were present, and one even of these
three strongly objected to it, they very naturally supposed that by temperate remonstrances to the individual members of the board, and an appeal to a meeting
where more persons should be present, they should
succeed in placing themselves on a footing more in
accordance with the spirit of their contract and the
honour of their profession. With this view, Dr. Hope,
during the whole period of his connexion with the
infirmary, left no means untried to recall this measure.
Not only did he urge his claim on the grounds of justice to himself and his colleagues, but he pointed out
that, by the admission of pupils, apprentices, house-
surgeons, and house-physicians, who would pay for the
advantages they enjoyed, the work which had previously been done by paid dispensers, &c., would be
accomplished more economically, in a superior manner,
and with greater regularity. His efforts, however,
were made at an unfortunate period. The new Vestry

Act was then coming into play, and the regulation of parochial concerns was thrown into the hands of a new class of men. In the Marylebone Vestry, as in many others at the same time, a few noisy, ignorant demagogues usurped the management of all affairs; and, if opposed, they did not scruple to carry by abuse and invective that which they could not support by reason. Such discussions did not suit the tastes of the gentlemen who still remained members of the board; some resigned, others absented themselves from their places, and many refused to stir in a measure which did not concern themselves personally, and which they could not have carried without exposing themselves to a stormy debate.

That the medical officers were justified in the construction which they placed on the terms of their election, and that, by accepting their offices, they did not place themselves on a different footing from the medical staff of most of the metropolitan hospitals, is evident from the fact, that about two-thirds of the persons who composed the vestry at the time of the election concurred with them in opinion. We have now lying beside us letters and certificates signed by fourteen out of twenty-two of the guardians, alleging that they " did truly mean the physicians should at all times consider their pupils as a remunerating medium in the place of the abolished gratuity :" or, in other words, that " the principle on which their salaries had been discontinued was, that they might be put on a footing

with the medical officers of other public institutions."
The following extract of a letter from Mr. Pope, another guardian, shows that he also acknowledged the
principle which the medical officers advocated, and that
he only differed from them in the time and mode of
accomplishing their object :—

" DEAR SIR,

" Reflecting, after you left me, on the remarks relative
to pupils, I fancied, that perhaps you considered that
I was rather opposed to the system of pupils. Pray
allow me to remove such an impression, if it did exist
in your mind; for I can assure you, that in suggesting
the present arrangements, it has been with the view to
rid us of the *old system* of things, and in due course
of time to bring into play the high and legitimate advantages to the honorary officers; or else, why should
I have urged that of pupils, (as now admitted,) only
on a limited scale, but with ulterior views ?"

But it was not alone his own interests and those of his
profession, which Dr. Hope so warmly advocated while
he held the office of physician to the Marylebone Infirmary. The welfare of his patients equally engaged
his attention. An outcry had been raised against the
old vestry for squandering the parochial funds, and
their successors, the reformed vestry, were zealous in
endeavouring to prove their own superiority by carrying economy into every department. In the infirmary
and workhouse schools it was pushed to its extreme

limits, and Dr. Hope saw with pain, that the health of his patients was compromised. He remonstrated again and again ; but, generally, in vain. Experience proved to him that he was not to expect justice from bodies of men ; and he used to call them the most untractable of all creatures, doing collectively what each, singly, would be ashamed or afraid to propose.

A physician cannot be expected to enter into the private circumstances of his numerous patients at a public institution. Dr. Hope, however, was in the habit of doing so with the view of ascertaining, whether any were so friendless or so poor as not to be supplied with those comforts and trifling luxuries which were not allowed by the institution, and for such he never failed to provide. On his removal to St. George's Hospital, there was not equal room for the exercise of private charity ; but he evinced the same careful interests in his patients, for he never ordered them to wear flannel, without finding out whether they had the means of obeying him, and furnishing them if necessary.

Though Dr. Hope met with much annoyance in this post, yet the advantages it afforded him for scientific research and the acquisition of practical knowledge, fully counterbalanced the attendant evils. He had the charge of ninety beds, more than double the number that he afterwards had at St. George's Hospital ; and as the patients were of the very lowest order of society—of a class who seldom give way to illness till it has reached a formidable height—the cases were of a more severe character than is usually met with. He always considered that this circumstance, united to the large number of beds under his care, made it an unequalled field for the study of acute diseases.

Dr. Hope now turned his attention to the publication of his work on Morbid Anatomy, the drawings for which had occupied him since the commencement of his medical education in Edinburgh. On first coming to town, he had made some inquiries on the subject, and had found the expense so enormous that no bookseller would undertake it. On meeting with an obstacle, his sole idea was how to overcome it. Undismayed by the enormous undertaking, he determined to lithograph the whole of the folio plates, and actually had completed three very beautiful ones on the lungs, when the discoveries relative to the sounds of the heart induced him to suspend the morbid anatomy until the treatise on the heart should have appeared. In the course of the summer of 1832, he persuaded Messrs. Whittaker and Co. to undertake the publication of the morbid anatomy on terms which experience had taught him to consider very advantageous. These were, that he was to provide all the drawings and lithography, and they were to be at the expense of the printing and the colouring of the plates. After having paid all their own expenses, Messrs. Whittaker agreed to divide the profits with him. After a lapse of three years, Dr. Hope received between £60 and £70 for his share; a sum which would not even have remunerated him for the expense of the lithography, had he been compelled to employ a regular artist for its execution. Bad as this bargain may appear to the public at large, he considered himself very fortunate in gaining such terms. The expense of similar works is so great, and the sale so limited, that no other respectable bookseller would hear of its publication, except on the stipulation of Dr. Hope's making himself responsible for the whole expense.

He had originally proposed his work in folio, but he afterwards consented to its appearing in its present large octavo form, because he found that, in folio, it would be too expensive to be at all within the reach of the student. He, therefore, determined to sacrifice, in some degree, its value as a work of art to that consideration, which was always uppermost in his estimation—public usefulness. This work met with a reception no less favourable than that on the heart, and, in a pecuniary light, more than answered the expectations of Messrs. Whittaker.

Dr. Hope's collection of original drawings had the rare advantage of being executed by one no less excellent as a draftsman than as an anatomist, a circumstance which gave them a truth and a medical value possessed by no similar work. This advantage he managed to extend to the lithographed plates; for, although he had not time to do these himself, yet they were done under his roof, subject to his constant super_vision and explanation; and when they were brought to a certain point, he took the pencil, and, devoting a day to their completion, gave accuracy to their anatomical character. In the same way, he coloured the first plate of each as a pattern to the colourers, and when completed, all the coloured plates were inspected by him and altered if they were not true to nature. Most, if not all the copies presented to public libraries, he coloured himself. The first five numbers came out monthly. The complicated labours of writing the portion of letter-press attached to each, of superintending the colourers, and of directing and finishing the lithography, at a time too, when he had the charge of ninety beds in the Marylebone Infirmary, were, however, more than he could manage. He found it necessary to make the intervals of publication longer, and the last seven numbers were published every two months. The whole work was completed in nineteen months, the first number having appeared on the 1st January, 1833.

While making arrangements for the publication of the morbid anatomy, Dr. Hope formed the design of giving a course of lectures on diseases of the chest, and fixed upon St. George's Hospital as the place best suited to his purpose. He mentioned the subject privately to some of the medical officers of that institution, but was given to understand that permission would not be granted, as he was not *officially* connected with the hospital. He, therefore, never made a formal application. In accordance with the rule which he had laid down not to connect himself with institutions of secondary rank, he preferred lecturing at his own house to doing so at one of the minor schools. These lectures were intended not for students, but for practitioners. He accordingly, in the autumn of 1832, delivered about five and twenty lectures at his own house, and commanded a regular attendance of from thirty to forty, which, considering that they were all practitioners, was more than he could have expected. The lectures were highly esteemed by those who heard them, and tended to increase his professional reputation.

Notwithstanding these numerous avocations, and the very great labours which Dr. Hope underwent in rapid succession, his health was remarkably good. He had never had a day's illness except an attack of lumbago, which confined him to his room for no more than three days. A cough was unknown to him. He could, with ease, walk twenty miles, and, when in the country, and led on by his passion for trout-fishing, he was in the frequent habit of doing so. If, at any time, he seemed over-worked, a day or two spent in the country, in fishing, shooting, or any other strong exercise, was sufficient to recruit him. On one occasion, while working almost night and day at the morbid anatomy, urgent business required him to make a hurried journey. He travelled twenty-four hours without stopping ; and, so far from being fatigued, he was refreshed by the country air and relaxation from study.

CHAPTER III.

Domestic life—Religious opinions and feelings—Employment of time—
Marriage—Practice—Jealousy of senior practitioners.

WHILE reading of the public career of a man whose
name is ennobled by the achievements of military or
civil greatness, or by eminence in the less ostentatious,
though perhaps more useful pursuits of science, our
admiration may be called forth, and the emulation of
the young may be fired at the bright example set
before them. But when we draw aside the veil from
private life, when we enter on the details of those
social virtues and warm affections which have characterised the same individual in domestic retirement,
when we go further, and inquire what has been the
main-spring of action and the true source of feeling,
then the picture grows vivid and life-like : each observer finds that which has a responsive chord within
his own breast, and receives at once a stimulus and a
guide to imitation.

Though it is far from our intention to infringe the
sacred privacy of domestic life, we hope to be excused

for entering into its details so far as may be conducive
to the object above stated.

The following extract from a letter, written by the
Rev. John Rate, of Trevery, in Cornwall, gives a
graphic description of Dr. Hope's character and
habits of mind. As Mr. Rate was on terms of the
closest intimacy with him, often spending several
months together under his roof, no one could have had
a better opportunity of judging of him, and we may
add that Mr. Rate's own character peculiarly qualified
him to enter into that of Dr. Hope,

" I think it was in the autumn of 1828, soon after
Dr. Hope had returned from the continent, that I first
met him at Richmond. His conversation, full of interesting thought and information, and his manners,
indicative of a peculiarly amiable and gentle disposition,
did not fail at once to attract my regard. It was
about the end of this year that I first went to stay
with him. He began, I believe, about that time to
compose his work on Diseases of the Heart, and that
on Morbid Anatomy. I was struck with the remarkable power he possessed of concentrating his mind at
once on any subject to which he turned his attention.
When he sat down to write, he could so fix his thoughts
on his subject, that he was not in the least disturbed by conversation or noise in the room, however
great. When he had finished what he intended to do,
he could enter, with equal interest and power of fixed
attention, on any other subject to which he directed his

mind. It was his habit to recline in an easy chair after dinner. Often, on such occasions, I have spoken to him, and, receiving no answer, have concluded that he was asleep; when I afterwards found that he had been deeply occupied in pursuing a train of thought. When walking with him, he would at times become similarly abstracted. His mind was always in a high state of activity, and when not engaged by any immediate object, seemed to be engrossed with subjects relating to his profession. This was one great secret of his success, as it is the great secret of the success of almost all those who have attained eminence in any department of science. Sir Isaac Newton himself, when asked how he made his discoveries, answered, ' by always thinking about them;' and at another time he declared that ' if he had done any thing, it was due to nothing but industry and patient thought.' Dr. Hope was so strongly impressed with this idea, that he used often to say that natural genius will do very little for a man without hard labour; and that almost all men who have distinguished themselves in literature or science, have been men of diligent study.

"But Dr. Hope's thoughts were not so totally absorbed by his profession as to shut out other subjects. On the contrary, his tastes and acquirements were almost universal. There was no topic of importance which came in his way in which he did not interest himself, and on which he did not exercise his powers of reflecting and judging. He used to say that

he had no peculiar talent or taste for any one pursuit
more than for another, and that he found all equally
easy when he directed the energies of his mind to the
attainment of them.

" The most remarkable feature in his mind and
character was, I think, the uncommon symmetry of
both. His intellectual powers and his moral dispo-
sitions were both so finely balanced that each faculty
and each disposition seemed to hold exactly its proper
place, and its just proportion among the rest. He
had a considerable share of imagination, but it was
so kept in check by the predominating influence of a
sound judgment, that it never transgressed the rules
of a correct and refined taste. His temper was calm
and even, seldom greatly elevated or depressed. Nothing like passion or violent feeling ever showed itself during the whole period of my acquaintance with
him. Reason seemed to hold constant and undis-
puted sway over all his faculties and feelings. Though,
at that time, he was not in the habit of saying much
on the subject of personal religion, yet it was evident that his mind was very much under its influence. He used to attend very regularly at Long Acre
Chapel, which was about two miles from his house,
to hear the late Mr. Howels, to whose ministry he
was much attached. He took an interest in district
visiting, and other societies for the religious improvement of the lower classes; and the high standard
of conscientious and correct moral feeling which evi-

dently ruled his conduct and deportment, was such as seldom, if ever, exists, except when it is the result of religious principle. To one of these societies, I believe, he gave his professional services gratuitously. Afterwards, his religious character became much more evident and decided."

In the first part of this work, we have pointed out how early Dr. Hope was stimulated to exertion by motives of worldly ambition, and by the desire to add lustre to the name he bore. His father had pushed these principles to their utmost limit, and, by keeping in the shade the more sordid inducements of wealth, and that aggrandizement which is strictly selfish and personal, had inspired his son with notions which in the world would have been considered enthusiastic. This ambition had, hitherto, led him to use the greatest diligence and the most unwearying perseverance, to practise remarkable self-denial and control over his natural tastes and feelings, and to rest unsatisfied so long as there was one individual who surpassed him. It was so far removed from all vainglorious desires to enjoy the appearance alone of greatness without its reality, and so united to true elevation of character, that, in ordinary phraseology, it would have been called a laudable—a noble ambition; but, when viewed in the light of revelation, no feeling which has self for its ultimate object, or which extends only to the brief space of this life, can be denominated laudable or noble. This was a truth which had been

F

recently impressed on Dr. Hope's mind, and which, by its secret and growing influence, changed the character of his subsequent life.

Though at a later period Dr. Hope's family adopted sentiments similar to those which, in the course of this narrative, will be found to be his, yet his parents, at the time when their children were under their roof, belonged to that numerous class who deem mere morality to be religion, and who think that, by setting a good example to their families and the poor, by a regular attendance at church, and by a consistent course of honesty and integrity, they are performing that which constitutes vital Christianity. Hence Dr. Hope did not find under his parents' roof that actions were tried by motives, and motives tested by the letter and spirit of scripture.

On going to Edinburgh, he attended the fashionable English church. His life was quite unsullied by any of the dissipation of youth, but this he ascribed to the natural refinement of his feelings, and not to religious principle. He continued the observance of Sunday in the same manner as he had been taught to do at home, never studying on that day; but he did not then keep it as at a subsequent period. He used to think in later years that a blessing attended even this conscientious, though partial, observance of the sabbath; and when he kept it more strictly, he attributed to it many of the blessings which he enjoyed.

It was in Paris in 1826-7, that he was first led to hear evangelical preaching. One Sunday, Dr. Nairne happened to call on him, and inquiring whether he was going to church, Dr. Hope answered in the negative, assigning some trivial reason for not going to the Ambassador's, and adding, that there was no other place to which he could go. " Oh !" said Dr. Nairne, " I will show you where to go ;" and he accordingly took him to the chapel of Mr. Lewis Way. With his preaching, Dr. Hope was delighted, and was a regular attendant during the remainder of his stay in Paris.

His clear judgment, now first exercised on this subject, and aided by that Spirit which is promised as our guide to truth, made him perceive that if religion was anything, it must be everything. The same activity of mind which spurred him on in the pursuit of scientific truth, prompted him to bring his whole mental faculties to the investigation of that *immutable truth*, the importance of which so infinitely surpasses that of all others. During the remainder of his residence abroad, he eagerly embraced every opportunity of conversing on the subject, and of eliciting the opinions of those whose conduct bore evidence of their being under the influence of religion ; but it was not till after his arrival in London, that he found time calmly and dispassionately to investigate the subject ; and without such an investigation he could not receive any doctrine, whether relating to his

F 2

profession, to matters of general interest, or to his spiritual concerns. Dr. Hope was always slow in forming a conclusion on a new subject; not because he experienced difficulty in comprehending it, but because he considered it irrational to hold, and much more to utter, an opinion on any subject until he should have fathomed all its depth; and his comprehensive mind could see further, and discover more intricacies to unravel, than a more superficial intellect would have done. When this part of his character is borne in mind, his testimony in favour of the religion of the Bible acquires manifold weight; and the young sceptical student, or pseudo-philosopher, ought to pause before he slights this additional testimony to the truths of Christianity, furnished by one who, naturally gifted with the clearest reasoning faculties, uninfluenced by the prejudices of early education, and after calm and deliberate investigation, desired to devote all his talents to the service of the Gospel, and to bring every thought under its purifying influence.

Dr. Hope had always distinguished Sunday from the other days of the week; but now he endeavoured to " keep it holy," by devoting the entire day to religious purposes. He was induced to do so because he believed that it was required by the spirit, as well as the letter, of the divine command; and also because he practically felt the value of this portion of time redeemed from his temporal occupations for the care of his immortal soul. On Sunday he studied with the same ardour as on other days, the subject only being changed. He always attended divine service twice, and sometimes three times a day. The intervals between services were employed in study, which he conducted on the same plan that he had already found useful in attaining professional knowledge. Among his papers has been found the cover of a large book labelled " Notes on Sermons," which shows what was his custom ; though, unfortunately, the pages have been carefully cut out. There are also many loose scraps containing texts, collected under various heads, tabular views, and analyses of scripture. Also an analysis of Paley's Evidences of Christianity, made with the utmost care, and evincing the caution with which he received even the fundamental doctrines of religion. In a letter written to Dr. Burder, many years after, he alludes to this feeling, and says, " You do not know with what anxious timidity and diffident labour others are permitted to acquire a distinct view of the first elements." His reading was chiefly confined to his Bible, on which exclusively he professed to found his religious faith and practice.

In matters of practice, Dr. Hope observed the same rational caution as he did in forming his creed. Because he had embraced certain opinions he did not think himself bound rashly to join a party, and to fashion his conduct to that which others deemed necessary, and of which, at a future day, he might repent. While he paid remarkable deference to the judgment of those whom he believed to be his superiors in religious knowledge and practice, he would not openly profess that of which he was not internally convinced. The result was, that his conduct answered to the scriptural definition of the Kingdom of Heaven, in the comparison of it to leaven, which, put into one corner, worked imperceptibly until the whole was leavened. Dr. Hope was rather a practical than a professing man. He did not *say* much on the subject, for, with the humility natural to him, he feared by his unworthy conduct to do injury to the pure religion which he professed. This reserve did not arise from want of courage; for, when called on, he was ready openly to avow his sentiments. While however, he spoke but little, his friends could not do otherwise than admire the even consistency of his conduct, the unflinching courage which he evinced in acting up to what he believed, and the steadily increasing ascendency which religion gained over him. From this time it was the mainspring of his actions; and the desire to glorify God by the full use of every talent committed to him, was its chief stimulus. Believing that there was no station, in which a man could not serve his God, he did not leave the sphere in which Providence had placed him; and while he foresaw that the professional and scientific eminence which he hoped to gain, would give him much moral influence, he eagerly anticipated the day when he might,

even in his profession, the more effectually advance the
glory of God.

But let it not be supposed that Dr. Hope's religion
was a cold philosophy, affecting the intellect and the
outward conduct alone; no,—it warmed every feeling
of his heart, and these feelings were only the more
to be admired and trusted, because they were sanctioned by reason and reflection. He was gifted with
a rare combination of intellectual and moral qualities;
and it was remarkable to observe the beautiful equi-
librium and proportion maintained throughout these.
While his feelings never got the better of his reason,
his reason was not allowed to quench the warmth of
his feelings. A few days before his death, when referring to this period, he spoke of the " craving"
which he had then felt, and which never left him,
" to be permitted to be Christ's soldier militant." An
observation which he made to Mrs. Hope very soon
after his marriage, gives a clue to what was his mode
of governing his feelings. Mrs. Hope was complain-
ing of the irksomeness of evangelical religion, because
she believed that it required the feelings to be constantly worked up to love God. " Do not trouble
yourself about that matter," answered he; " do not
think whether you love Him or not, but only endeavour to keep your thoughts fixed on the individual
and collective blessings which He has bestowed on you,
and then you will not be able to do otherwise than
love Him." Many years after, he was much pleased to

find a similar course recommended in a very valuable little work, called "Think of these things," by Dr. Abercrombie.

The point in which his religion was most apparent, was his habit of referring everything, whether great or small, to a special Providence, believing that in the eye of an Almighty Being, all things are of equal magnitude. Thus, he was a man of prayer, both in the ordinary occupations of life, and in the more extraordinary positions in which all are occasionally placed. No work was commenced without asking for the Divine blessing ; no important step taken without an application for Divine guidance ; when harassed by professional vexations, he regained by prayer his wonted serenity ; and, when surrounded by difficulties and threatened with disappointment, he found in prayer a strength not his own, united with submission to the Divine will, whatever it might be.

The details of the day of a studious man are so little varied that they would scarce be worthy of a place in this memoir, were it not that they show what portion of study Dr. Hope thought it necessary to give to the object on which he had concentrated his mental energies.

At this time he was in the habit of breakfasting at seven. During this and his other meals he generally read, or followed some other intellectual pursuit. After breakfast, he continued his studies till one o'clock. From one to three o'clock, was occupied in following the physicians in their rounds of St. George's Hospital, or the Infirmary, or in seeing his own patients at the Dispensary which he had established. He then paid any private visits which might be on his list, and hurried home. This part of the day was the only portion which seemed to afford any recreation; but as his mind was busily at work, either in prescribing or in studying the practice of others, there was no intermission of mental labour. On his return home, he recommenced his studies, and with no other interruption than that of dinner, at which he not unfrequently read, he continued them till after midnight.

Thus his time was fully occupied; not one minute was wasted. And even at a later period, when his increasing practice varied his pursuits, when there was no longer necessity for such unremitting attention to study, the same custom of completely occupying his time was maintained. The visits of patients, whom he then saw at home from ten till twelve, and an increasing number of visits abroad, diminished his hours of study, without, however, affording a relaxation from mental exertion; he had so strongly imbibed the habit of never being idle, or rather, the occupation of time had become so evident a duty, that he could not be happy when disengaged. He especially deprecated the very common custom of daily spending three or four hours after dinner in gossiping; and as his temperate mode of living, and almost total abstinence from wine, rendered his intellectual faculties as vigorous after dinner as before, the evenings in his family were always devoted to some rational occupation. Nor can this habit of constant mental activity be attributed to an undue ambition for professional advancement, for his pursuits were not always professional. Many " fragments of time" were " squeezed out" for the service of his relations or friends, and at a later period, for the cultivation of the fine arts and general literature. Great, too, was his delight when he chanced to hit upon an expedient which redeemed, by a non-professional pursuit, some odd half or quarter of an hour which had hitherto been unoccupied.

On the 10th March, 1831, Dr. Hope married Anne, second daughter of John Williamson Fulton, Esq., of Upper Harley Street, an Irish gentleman, who had spent the principal part of his life in Calcutta. A remarkable similarity of tastes and suitability of disposition, rendered this union a peculiarly happy one.

Entering the married state made little difference in Dr. Hope's mode of life. It is true that he sometimes complained of the impossibility of reading during meals, and the loss of " fragments of time," which he was tempted to spend in conversation. For the last, however, he managed to gain rather an advantageous equivalent, by interesting Mrs. Hope in his occupations, and allowing her to undertake many of those minor and almost mechanical details which fritter away much of the valuable time of a professional or studious man, and require more patience than intellect. As to the meals, though irrecoverably lost to medical studies, he was satisfied to have them redeemed from idleness by frequently engaging Mrs. Hope to read works of general interest, to analyze them, and to repeat the substance at those seasons—an occupation which was no less instructive to herself than advantageous to him.

Notwithstanding the natural reluctance of most persons to employ the young stranger, Dr. Hope was so fortunate as to fall in with some who were less scrupulous. It thus happened, that he had more practice the first year after his settling in London than he had anticipated, and than generally falls to the lot of a young physician. At the close of the year, Dr. Holland kindly inquired how he was getting on. Dr. Hope answered in cheerful terms, and mentioned how much he had made. "It does not signify," answered Dr. Holland, "how much or how little you have made; but what connexions have you formed, and what hold are you gaining on your patients' confidence?" Dr. Hope saw the force of the observation, and perceived what was to be the aim of his conduct towards his patients, and the criterion of his success. A few years afterwards he practically felt its truth. The casualties which cause a London population to be always changing, removed some of the families which he attended, before his reputation was so far established as to bring him others to supply their place. His practice diminished, and the third year of his residence in London, that which preceded the publication

of the Treatise on Diseases of the Heart, he made a
smaller sum than at any other period. He then saw
more than ever what must be the uncertain nature of
every practice which rests solely on private connexions,
and he congratulated himself that he had not trusted
to such contingencies.

From the publication of the Treatise on Diseases of
the Heart, in November 1831, a work which rapidly
and widely spread Dr. Hope's reputation both at home
and abroad, we may date the commencement of his
practice, for the chance patients whom he picked up
before, scarcely afforded anything worthy of that
name. It could not be supposed that in the first year
after the publication of the book, his income would
experience any remarkable increase. But he observed, with hope and pleasure, that he was consulted
by many physicians and surgeons, and two patients
sent to him, the one from Gibraltar and the other from
Corfu, gave him high promise for the future. He remembered Dr. Holland's remark; and though the fees
of these two patients figured in his account-book but as
two single guineas, yet they were in his eyes worth as
many hundreds of his former profits. From this period his practice never fluctuated, but rapidly and
progressively increased, till he left town a few weeks
before his death.

It has sometimes been said that junior physicians
are retarded in their progress by the jealousy of senior
practitioners, who eagerly exclude them from every

family into which their merits have happened to introduce them. In an elegant modern publication, a story
is told of the young intruder being turned out by a
senior physician who, with many commendations of
the young man's talents, persuades the patient that
change of air alone can complete the cure so ably begun.
In this part of his career, Dr. Hope had not reason to
complain of any such jealous interference. One ludicrous instance, however, occurred, in which the fear of
being displaced by the young physician, prompted a
poor apothecary to play a bold but unsuccessful game.
After the death of the apothecary, Dr. Hope narrated
the fact, to the great amusement of the patient whom
it had concerned.

A young lady, whose family Dr. Hope always attended, came to town on a visit to her aunt. Her
health being delicate, she placed herself under Dr.
Hope's care. Now it happened that the aunt was one
of those who had objected to admit Dr. Hope into her
family as being too young, and who preferred confiding her health to an apothecary, who was certainly
one of the least enlightened of his class, who was more
frequently drunk than sober, but who, by dint of address, had contrived to insinuate himself into the confidence of many of his patients, and of this lady among
the rest. She was much attached to her niece, and
was, therefore, not quite satisfied in having her en-
trusted to such a juvenile practitioner as Dr. Hope.
Her alarm was not diminished by finding his opinion

at direct variance with her own. She believed her niece to be consumptive, while Dr. Hope was unable to discover any symptoms of such a disease. At length, her affectionate anxiety for her relative conquered her feelings of delicacy, and with as much politeness as was possible, she expressed a wish that Dr. Hope would not object to consult with Mr. ————. For a physician to be thus called to consult an apothecary is contrary to professional rules. Dr. Hope, therefore, explained that he could not do so; but, at the same time, feeling for the lady's alarm, he said that he should have no objection to see Mr. ————. They met, and after visiting the patient retired to an adjoining room. Mr. ———— began an eloquent harangue on the merits of the said Mr. ————, on the wonderful cures which he had performed—in fact, there was not such another practitioner in London, perhaps not in the whole world. So eager was he to convince his patient auditor, and so fruitful did the theme prove, that Mr. —— continued it during the whole time generally occupied by a consultation. At length, the aunt, anxious to know the result, ventured to enter the room, and to inquire whether they had come to a decision?

" Oh, yes !" said Mr. ————, " our opinion is—"

" Excuse me, Sir," interrupted Dr. Hope, " you forget that we have not yet formed our opinion."

The lady once more retired, and the medical men proceeded to that task for which they had not yet found leisure. Again the apothecary took the lead.

" Come," said he, " I will tell you what we shall do ;
we shall send Miss——— to Madeira ———"

Dr. Hope stared.

" And you shall go with her as her physician.
They have plenty of money, you know, and it will be
a very good thing for you."

The secret was now revealed. Dr. Hope could with
difficulty restrain a smile ; but, thanking Mr. ———
very cordially for his kind and disinterested offer, he
intimated that such a plan would not suit him, for
" plenty of money" was not what he wanted. As for
their patient, before sending her to Madeira, they must
prove that she is consumptive.

" Of course," added he, " you have some reasons for
forming that opinion. I suppose you have detected
such a symptom ?"

" No," answered the other.

" Or, perhaps, such another ?"

" No," again answered Mr. ———

" Possibly so and so ?"—and, thus going through
the whole list of consumptive symptoms, and getting
an answer in the negative to each, he forced the unwilling apothecary to the opinion that the young lady
was not consumptive—probably the only opinion which
he ever gave in opposition to that of a patient. It
may be added, that the fears of the poor apothecary
were not realised, but that he continued undisturbed
until he retired from practice some years after.

10

CHAPTER IV.

Assistant physician to St. George's Hospital — Professional anxieties
and disappointments—Submission to the Divine will.

In May 1834, Dr. Chambers had so serious an
illness that it seemed probable he would be obliged
to resign the office of physician to St. George's Hospital. At that time, there were four physicians, who
divided among them the care of the medical in-
patients and out-patients of the hospital. A statement which is inserted in a subsequent chapter, shows
that the medical out-patients amounted to about one
half of the whole number of patients, both medical
and surgical. In order to lighten the duties of the
physicians, and, more especially, to retain the valuable
services of Dr. Chambers, it was proposed to create
a new office, that of assistant physician, to whose
province it would belong to prescribe for all the
medical out-patients—a measure which would diminish
the labours of Dr. Chambers and the other physicians,
by considerably more than one half. An assistant
surgeon was already attached to the institution : but

the surgeons thought that it would be desirable to have a second. The two appointments were, therefore, proposed to the Board of Governors, by the majority of the physicians and surgeons : but as the prescribed forms of the hospital required the lapse of some time before they could be confirmed, the canvassing of the candidates was tediously protracted over nearly six months.

On ordinary occasions, it is the custom for the medical committee to assemble as soon as possible after a vacancy has been declared, to consider who is the most eligible candidate, and to give their collective support to that individual. Should there be a difference of opinion, it is the etiquette, that if the vacancy be among the physicians, the candidate who has the suffrages of the majority of the physicians shall be preferred ; while if the vacant place be that of surgeon, the choice shall fall on him who is supported by the majority of the surgeons. A candidate thus recommended to the governors is certain of success ; for, as the latter are necessarily ignorant of the professional merits of the candidates, by far the larger part are in the habit of placing their votes at the disposal of the physician or surgeon, of whom they chance to have the highest opinion.

On the present occasion, the physicians having given a pledge of neutrality to the governors until after the creation of the appointment should have been confirmed, the surgeons also declined declaring their sentiments until the wishes of the physicians should become known. Thus, the candidates were thrown on their own resources, and the contest was a very severe one. Six candidates started, independent of Dr. Williams, who, from the first, avowed his intention of giving place to the superior pretensions of Dr. Hope. After a very tedious struggle, all the candidates, except Dr. Dunlap and Dr. Hope, successively retired. The election took place in the beginning of November 1834; Dr. Hope succeeded by a majority of about two to one; having as many votes, within two or three, as Mr. Cutler, the successful assistant-surgeon, who had been openly assisted throughout by Sir B. C. Brodie, and the majority of the surgeons. Dr. Hope had been most warmly supported by many of his private friends, to whom he acknowledged the deepest obligations; and this is a solitary instance of any benefit which he derived from a long list of non-professional acquaintances. Before this election enabled Dr. Hope to see into the principle on which many governors of hospitals give their votes, he had often contemplated the possibility of being obliged to become a candidate in opposition to the medical officers. After the experience of this election, he used to rejoice that he had not been ignorantly led into a measure which could not have been successful, and which, by making him personally obnoxious to a large body of governors, might have excluded him for ever from the post which he sought. His advice, therefore, to all young candidates was, never, under any circumstances, to stand a contested election in opposition to the medical officers of the institution.

On this occasion, Dr. Hope gave a very decided proof of the strength of his religious principles. After he had been for some days engaged in the canvass with little apparent prospect of success, a party of very influential medical governors sent to offer him their support. This communication was made at ten o'clock on Saturday night, and, as persons naturally feel their own honour interested in the success of their candidate, these gentlemen stipulated that he should canvass most actively, and under their guidance. To this, Dr. Hope made no objection, and they proceeded to point out his work for the following day, Sunday. To observe the sabbath was, however, a principle from which he could not swerve. He preferred risking the offered support, to offending his God. He urged that, without the Divine blessing, his election could not prosper, and that he could not expect that blessing while acting in opposition to the Divine commands. It was in vain that his new friends argued, intreated, and even threatened to withdraw their support. Dr. Hope was inflexible : and they finally yielded the point, thinking him, no doubt, an odd fellow who could prefer religion to self-interest, and who would rather trust to the promises of God, than to his own exertions.

On being appointed assistant physician to St. George's

Hospital, Dr. Hope resigned the office of physician to the Marylebone Infirmary.

Scarcely six years had elapsed since Dr. Hope arrived in London with but one acquaintance, and since he had marked out for himself a path of high ambition and hard labour. He had allotted seven years for the accomplishment of that portion which depended on his own industry; but in five years and a half his work was completed, and his books were published. In a few months more he had attained the objects of his ambition—a remarkable success—which filled him with gratitude to the Giver of all good. It is true that he was only assistant physician; but as in case of a vacancy in the higher post of physician, it was customary to give the vacant office to the assistant-physician, unless he should have forfeited his claim by misconduct, Dr. Hope naturally felt that it also was gained.

On taking a retrospect of Dr. Hope's career, on observing that he, a friendless stranger, gained by his merits alone, under Providence, every object which he sought, and on finding that throughout his life, he never met with *one* professional disappointment, the student, or young physician about to commence practice, may be dazzled by so brilliant a prospect, and believe that the course of a successful physician is free from thorns, and offers an easy avenue to fame. Just as the inference may seem when the result alone of his labours is proclaimed, and when the lapse of years has worn away the remembrance of much that was most painful when the happy result was uncertain, it would scarcely be just to sanction the propagation of so delusive a hope. None but those who have themselves been in the profession, or who have been admitted into the most secret confidence of a professional man, can tell the anxieties which attend him. He who depends on private connexion cannot but feel his dependence on the fancies and caprices of his patients, for the most part totally disqualified to judge of his merits. The physician who places his trust on professional reputation, is free from these cares, and is rendered happily independent of each individual patient. But he exchanges these anxieties for others of much greater weight. While the former practitioner may be compared to one playing at a game of chance for paltry stakes, where the constant fluctuations of fortune keep him from being alike a great gainer or loser; the latter is like the gamester who stakes his all on each throw of the dice, and who while he may be ruined by one unlucky cast, can gain but little by a fortunate one. In every step that the latter takes, his character is pledged; and so delicate is the nature of a good name, so easily is it tarnished, that while one rash act may demolish it for ever, its brilliancy cannot be much enhanced by a judicious one. Who then can tell the prudence and foresight which must belong to every successful physician? Who can reckon the anxieties that disturb his peace?

No professional man can hope to be totally free from these cares ; but Dr. Hope's situation exposed him to an uncommon share of them. While his decided superiority, his early reputation, and unvarying success, roused much jealousy, and caused many eagerly to listen to, and industriously to circulate, any misrepresentation which was repeated to his disadvantage, he had not one professional friend whom he believed to be sincerely interested in his success, and to whom he could apply for counsel on any trying emergency, or before taking any important step. There are always plenty of ill-natured individuals, who are ready to repeat to a man, all the on-dits against him. Dr. Hope's fine sense of honour and integrity, made him peculiarly sensitive to every impeachment of his conduct, and his prudence pointed out to him that no accusation, however paltry, should be allowed to remain unrefuted with those on whose opinion rested his success. While the generality of men have little minds, no prudent man who is dependent on others, will dare to despise little things. It is really curious to know the trifles which may make a man obnoxious.

Feeling the dangers of his situation, and knowing that he was condemned by his friendless position to act, as it were, in the dark, Dr. Hope took the very wise precaution of preserving all letters which he received, and copies of all that he wrote on matters of professional business. When any little circumstance occurred which he thought capable of misconstruction,

he immediately took notes of the facts, and obtained
the signatures of witnesses. He thus supplied himself
with documentary evidence which might at any time
be produced, and after such precautions, he could with
safety banish from his thoughts all recollection of the
disagreeable transaction.

It may seem that this conduct of Dr. Hope's arose
from a morbid sensitiveness to censure, and from a
desire to perpetuate disputes. So far from the latter,
the notes being once taken, they were locked up and
never looked at till the conduct of others brought them
once more to his attention; and experience proved to
him that he had not exercised any unnecessary prudence. After the lapse of several years, he sometimes
found that the most serious charges were based on
trivial incidents; and he then rejoiced to be furnished
with documents which at once removed every shade
from his character. For some years before Dr. Hope's
death, when he had secured his objects, he perceived
that the power of others to injure him was gone, and
he, therefore, no longer paid the slightest attention to
these trifles, but conscious of his own rectitude, and
standing on the firm basis of his reputation, he acted
on those principles of independence which were most
in unison with his own feelings. In after years, Dr.
Hope used to speak with much feeling of the labour
and anxiety which must be inseparable from the career
of a physician aiming at high professional honours.
When talking of the future profession of his only son,

he invariably added, with warmth, " I could not have
the cruelty to bring him up to my own profession."

There was a disappointment which Dr. Hope felt,
arising entirely out of an erroneous estimate of facts ;
and as many others participate in this error, it may
not be amiss to mention it.   He had formed much too
favourable an estimate of his profession, and believed
that the wealth which rewarded those who attain
eminence, was both greater and more early acquired
than he afterwards found it to be.   Physicians, in
practice, attach so much importance to the appearance
of success, that there is no subject on which they
preserve such inviolable secrecy, as the amount of
their practice.   It is only when a man has got into
very large practice, that he dares to depart from this
rule, and thus the young practitioner has no means of
judging of the various steps of the ladder which he is
about to mount, nor to estimate the time which it will
require to attain each.   On arriving in London, Dr.
Hope was led into the belief that the first twenty
physicians in that metropolis, divided about £80,000
annually between them, and that a successful physician might hope to be established in good practice in
five years.   To be one of so large number as twenty
seemed no difficult task, and, therefore, he ignorantly
hoped, that, if he succeeded at all, he should be making
£4000 per annum, in about five years.   As he soon
found that his practice did not seem likely to realise
these hopes, he began to look around for the causes

of what he deemed his slow progress. First he attributed it to the small number of his acquaintances; then to his not being married; afterwards to his not having made himself known by any publication, or being attached to any public institution. Each of these obstacles gradually vanished from his speculations. He found that having many friends, and being married, made no difference; and that though there was decided proof that his reputation was increased by his publications and his being physician to a large infirmary, yet that the practice seemed to be making very tardy approaches to £4000 per annum. He often tried to discover wherein lay his fault, (for such he thought it must be,) until he was relieved by the observations of two of the first physicians in London, two of the few who could dare to speak on the delicate subject of practice. Dr. Chambers told him that it was absolutely impossible for any man who did not keep a carriage, to find time to make more than £500 per annum at the very most. Sir Henry Halford, while giving him very powerful assistance on the occasion of the St. George's election, and congratulating him on being in the number of the successful few of his profession, told him that if he made £1,000 per annum by the time he was forty, he might feel certain of attaining the first eminence that the profession could offer. Dr. Hope's career terminated at the age of forty, and he was then making four times as much as Sir Henry had led him to expect.

G

He did not, however, consider himself as a fair criterion of the probabilities of professional success, as he was universally considered to have attained very early eminence, and his own observation led him to believe that this opinion was not unfounded. He often used to smile in secret when he heard opinions, similar to those he had once held, expressed, not only by non-professional men, but by students who were luxuriating in golden dreams of the future. But he had not yet risen to that pitch of eminence in which a man is free from equals and from rivals, and, therefore, he was bound to maintain the grand professional secret, or at most, without exposing the naked truth, to strip the fair delusion of a few of its golden ornaments.

While on the subject of professional profits, we cannot refrain from remarking on the peculiarly bad fortune which attended Dr. Hope in his public appointments. His predecessors, both at the Marylebone Infirmary and St. George's Hospital, had been handsomely remunerated for their services; but he, on succeeding to those services, was in the one case deprived of that to which he thought himself entitled by contract with the board; and in the other, by the creation of a new office, he was obliged to perform, gratuitously, the most onerous duties that ever fell to his lot. It may with safety be affirmed that no physician ever did so much gratuitous work, for he calculated that during the first ten years and a half of his residence in London, he must thus have prescribed to nearly 30,000 cases.

We would not, however, number the loss of these salaries among the discouragements which Dr. Hope had to encounter. Though, as a man whose fortune was not made, he was not insensible to them, yet he esteemed the situations so highly on professional and scientific grounds, that the pecuniary emolument was quite a secondary consideration. He had also a very deep conviction that all sublunary events are under the guidance of a wise Providence. He could not, therefore, forget that, though man was the apparent instrument, the event itself was ordered by Divine wisdom, which, for some reason he could not penetrate, saw it expedient to withhold wealth from his grasp. When dying, he used often to remark on the circumstance that while all his hopes of eminence had been realised, all his professional wishes, all his ambitious plans had been crowned with success, riches alone seemed to elude his grasp. The truth of this observation was the more apparent, because at the time he made it, he was on the point of being removed from the golden prospects which his practice offered, and when he had seemed to have been on the eve of becoming rich. These frequent pecuniary disappointments, so far from raising a murmur in his heart, inspired him with the conviction that wealth would have been unsuited to the characters of himself and his family, and detrimental to their spiritual and eternal welfare.

He remembered our Saviour's declaration of the difficulty of a rich man's entering the kingdom of heaven,
and with filial submission and heartfelt gratitude, he
thanked God for having cheered him with hopes which
were only disappointed when wealth might have been
injurious, and for always giving him a sufficiency to
supply his need, while denying him a superfluity.   In
the spirit of the Eastern patriarch, he praised the Lord
equally for what was given and for what was withheld.

In addition to any disappointments of a pecuniary
nature that Dr. Hope experienced in his profession,
he had serious losses in his private resources.   The
full extent of these did not become known to him till
his father's death, in 1838.   On an occasion which
would have been so trying to most men, Dr. Hope's
predominant feelings were those of gratitude, that
these losses did not become known to him until his
profession had made him independent of his father's
fortune ; and that during those years when assistance
was absolutely necessary, and when the want of it
might have forced him to have worked for money
rather than for higher objects, he had been granted the
needful aid.

The following extracts from letters written to Mrs.
Hope in the autumn of 1822, prove, however, that his
submission to the Divine Will was not assumed only
when he was in a situation to be independent of pecuniary losses, but that in the midst of difficulties he was
supported by the same sentiments, and animated by

faith in Him who will never forsake those who trust in Him. The first extract is at the close of a letter written from the house of his brother, who had given him a very unfavourable report of the property.

" I grieve that you should receive a letter like this in my absence, but do not let it fret you. We are all doomed to a certain portion of unhappiness, and if it comes in this form, it does not come in some other perhaps more intolerable. Nor can I see that, while surrounded with friends, and cheered with good prospects, the want of a few hundreds is an overwhelming calamity. Possibly it may be the key to our greatest prosperity. Assure me in your reply that you are not unhappy in my absence, and rest confident that if we bear patiently the modicum of ills allotted to us, and honestly do our best to surmount them, we shall not be left unassisted by Him, who provides for the sparrow, and waters the flower of the desert."

The following was written a few days later from the house of his father, who had given a different version of the story, and, while deceiving himself, had inspired his son with his own sanguine hopes and expectations.

" Your letter indeed seems (as if in approbation of its tone, and as another proof that Providence lifts the burden which is thrown upon him,) to have changed the aspect of our affairs. Many might call me superstitious on this point; but I so constantly see a particular Providence connected with the blessings and visitations which befal us, that I have, practically, no doubts on the subject, while the highest authority teaches us to believe it."

In many points Dr. Hope resembled his father, to whom he was much attached. It was his constant habit to write him the most minute details of his plans, his hopes, and his success; and the old gentleman took a lively interest in all that concerned his son.

The following letter affords so beautiful a pattern of encouragement and admonition from a Christian parent, that we cannot refrain from inserting it in this place.

" October 27th, 1832.

" MY DEAR JAMES,

" The contents of your letter of the 15th instant delight me much, and I have full hope and trust in God that all your anticipations will, in due time, be fully realised. But forget not that man may plan with much care, foresight, and prudence, and yet in the result be disappointed, for God only gives success and increase; therefore, in God alone, it is duty and sound wisdom in man to place full trust and confidence. In the morning, on your knees, ask his blessing on your endeavours for the day; and, at night, with grateful heart, thank Him for the comforts you have found. From this habit fully settled and acted upon, you will find constant relief in both body and mind. Tell your wife that your last letter has given me an opening and peep into her heart, and perceiving it so perfectly in unison with that of the Hopes, I love her dearly, and hope, ere long, I may be permitted to tell her so in person. In the mean time and afterwards, go on as at present, hand in hand, and I fear not your united efforts and industry will be crowned with complete success. Occasional information of successful progress in your present bold undertakings will add to my comfort. With every good wish,

"I am, dear James,

"Your's most truly,

"THOMAS HOPE."

CHAPTER V.

Correspondence with Dr. Burder — Continued medical investigations —Election of a chaplain to St. George's Hospital.

IN a previous chapter we have said, that personal ambition had ceased to be the main-spring of Dr. Hope's actions; and that he now desired to devote all his talents, his professional eminence, and the influence accruing from it, to the service of religion. That we were warranted in making this assertion will be evident from a letter which he wrote on his election to St. George's Hospital. This letter, and those of Dr. Burder in connexion with it, show in what light professional preferment is viewed by the religious man.

On Dr. Hope's first arrival in town, he had been introduced by Dr. Beilby of Edinburgh, to Dr. Burder, the son of the pious and well-known author of " Village Sermons." A great similarity in talents and disposition, in refinement of sentiment and delicacy of character, drew these two excellent men together; and, at a later period, when they discovered in each other a unison of religious opinion, these feelings kindled into warm affection. Dr. Hope looked up to Dr. Burder as one who had been trained in religious principles, and who had always maintained a consistent conduct. While he respected him on these grounds, he felt Dr. Burder especially endeared to him as the only one of his professional brethren with whom he was in the habit of interchanging religious sentiments, or from whom he could ask advice founded on religious principles. What was Dr. Burder's estimate of Dr. Hope may be seen from the following extract from a letter to a friend. In reference to the early period of their acquaintance, he says, " Some years ago, before I was aware of Dr. Hope's religious principles, I had sometimes said to Mrs. Burder, after observing him narrowly, ' Well, if Dr. Hope is not a pious man, he is the most perfect man without religion I ever met with.' But the more I knew of him, the more anxious was I to discover whether *any* principles short of those which teach repentance towards God, faith in our Lord Jesus Christ, and an unreserved consecration of heart and life to His service, could have yielded such transparency of conduct, such humanity, disinterestedness, humility, guileless simplicity, and undeviating integrity, as I observed in him. At length, I learned that he lived ' as seeing Him who is invisible.' "

Shortly before Dr. Hope was elected assistant-physician to St. George's Hospital, Dr. Burder's health had obliged him to retire from London practice. On hearing of Dr. Hope's election, he wrote the following

G 5

letter of congratulation, which we introduce, not only
on account of its intrinsic merit, but because it is
closely connected with Dr. Hope's answer :—

"Tilford House, near Fárnham, Surrey,
"November 1834.

"MY DEAR SIR,

"I cannot refuse myself the gratification of offering
my sincere and hearty congratulations on your election
to St. George's Hospital. I expect it will prove an
epoch in your professional history. Your talents and
attainments are now sufficiently acknowledged to render that hospital very valuable to yourself and beneficial to others—especially to younger men requiring
an example, as well as instruction, in their medical
career. Among other advantages accruing to the students from such men as Chambers and yourself being
their directors, that of maintaining a high tone of
moral principle, and discountenancing every approach
to artifice and chicanery, every attempt at professional
trickery and cajoling, appears to me none of the least.
Whatever changes may take place in our 'order,' I
do hope that the leading physicians will always be
gentlemen and men of integrity. I earnestly wish for
you, my dear Sir, much health and prosperity in the
performance of your additional duties, if, indeed, I
ought to say 'additional,' for I presume you will
relinquish the infirmary, in which you never felt altogether at home. Will you allow a cautious friend

once more to say :—' *Do not work too hard, but pray secure intervals of repose, and a fair proportion of sleep.*'

*   *   *   *   *   *

" I do not, my dear Sir, venture to obtrude one important subject again upon your notice, because you have not particularly adverted to a former communication. Allow me, however, just to remark, that when in the midst of harassing engagements, *I* have often found myself in danger of being so absorbed by ' the things which are seen and temporal,' as to lose sight of those things which are ' unseen but *eternal.*' The device of the excellent author of ' Theron and Aspasio,' was ingenious and instructive. At the end of a long and almost tiresome avenue in his garden, a beautiful arbour promised the wished-for rest ; but on reaching the attractive spot, a plain surface was only found ; all was light and shade—a complete illusion, with the motto in the centre of the painting—' *In*-visibilia *non* decipiunt.'

" Believe me,

" Your sincere and faithful friend,

" THOS. H. BURDER."

To this letter, Dr. Hope sent the following reply :—

" 13, Lower Seymour Street,

" November 27th, 1834.

" MY DEAR SIR,

" Accept my sincere thanks for your most acceptable letter. Many have congratulated me on my recent success; you, alone, have made the occasion an opportunity of conveying a friendly and useful lesson. Such is the difference between worldly courtesy and the ever active principle of christian love. The last part of your letter, so delicately and kindly expressed, gives me a profitable hint of my former neglect; and I rejoice that you have given it, not only because I feel the subject to which you advert, to be the most valuable substratum of all your letters, but because it re-opens a portal, which my former neglect might have closed between us. Your communication, my dear Sir, was not thrown away. I read it often: I promised you an answer when at leisure to reply fully: mentally, I sent you many answers; but procrastination (perhaps I may say excessive labour at that time) prevented me from writing, till shame for my neglect made me silent. This further instance of the best kind of interest that you so kindly take in me, affects me much—and the more, as you touch the very chord which would have given the tone to my reply, had I written; namely, that the interesting nature of our profession, its very utility, is a snare; that devotion to it has exposed, and continues to expose me, to the constant danger of being absorbed by ' the things which are seen and temporal.' This danger is ever increased (without proper care, and aid from above,) by the reflection that it is a duty to labour with a view not only of acquiring a competent knowledge of our profession, but also of improving it. A work which I read some years ago, the memoir of Miss Graham, has always appeared to me to place this subject in a proper light; namely, that time, health, and the faculties of reason, are given to be exercised for useful purposes in our several spheres; but that every undertaking should have for its sole ultimate object, the glory of God, and should be commenced and prosecuted with prayer for His blessing.

"I have a strong practical belief in a particular Providence, and habitually regard every event or dispensation—especially chastisement—as a blessing. Remarkable circumstances in my own history, and that of my whole family—now, I hope, all brought to the Saviour's fold—have clearly taught me this. My promotion to St George's, therefore, I feel and regard, not as a matter of triumph, but of increased responsibility—a talent given to be improved; for I have seen for some years, that the extraordinary way in which apparently insurmountable obstacles have vanished, could only have been by the design of Providence to remove me to this new sphere. You will perceive, that to one who has been graciously permitted and enabled to entertain these views, your suggestions respecting St. George's must be no less acceptable than valuable. Give me your prayers that I may be enabled to act upon them.

* * * * * *

"Ever, my dear Sir,

"Your sincere and faithful friend,

"J. HOPE.

"P.S.—The device is beautiful. It pleased me the

more, as Sir George Staunton had recently practised the illusion on me at his seat near Portsmouth. Thanks for the cautious friend's advice. I now follow it, and enjoy excellent health."

This beautiful illustration of christian principle in its practical bearing on professional conduct and temporal prosperity, called forth the following answer :—

"Tilford House, near Farnham, Surrey,
"February 24th, 1835.

"MY DEAR SIR,

"Your last communication gave me a high degree of pleasure. I had before doubted whether *mere* moral principle could so influence the mind as to produce one *uniform* course of honourable, upright, and beneficent conduct : yet, had I not been apprised of the existence of a still higher and more vital principle in the friend I am addressing, I should at least have wondered that merely human motives could have achieved so much, even though acting in concert with a disposition naturally amiable. You will not suppose me capable of flattering ; but will receive the remark as a proof that I observed with great interest the development of my friend's character, and was not a little anxious to *know* that an all-pervading principle did influence the whole man. A high sense of honour and a keen desire of preserving self-esteem, may indeed effect much ; but my own observation would lead me to doubt if fallen man, essentially selfish, however that selfishness may be disguised and refined, does ever *persevere* in a self-denying course of active benevolence, *unaided by christian principle.* What is the boasted honour of a man of the world when no human eye is upon him!

"I rejoice with you, my dear friend, in the choice you have made; and that, while 'diligent in business,' you are aiming to be 'fervent in spirit, serving the Lord.' Your deep feeling of responsibility is, doubtless, leading you to 'the strong for strength,' and to the 'God only wise' for wisdom. Were I to resume my profession, I think I should be bolder in offering 'a word in season,' where I had reason to believe the care of the soul was neglected, especially in the prospect of a change of worlds. One need not fear the consequences of following out any line of duty; and, in truth, however men may *seem* to spurn at spiritual counsel, there is, we know, an internal monitor which silently responds, 'Thou art the man.' And if one should be the honoured instrument of converting even *one* 'sinner from the error of his ways,' it would compensate for a whole life of anxious labour. To a very small extent, I can attest the important influence which the well-timed hint of a physician sometimes obtains.

"With cordial esteem, believe me,

"My dear Sir,

"Your attached friend,

"THOMAS H. BURDER."

In the foregoing letter of Dr. Hope's there is an intimation that he had relaxed from his excessively studious habits. Though his health was excellent, yet he knew that the life which he had been leading for many years must eventually undermine the best constitution. While there appeared to him a necessity for such unremitting application, he had not shrunk from it; but to have continued it, and to have risked his health when that necessity had ceased to exist, would have been the extreme of folly. The happy proportion of Dr. Hope's character enabled him to perceive what were the occasions in which moderation was the greatest virtue, as well as those in which every energy was to be strained, and every sacrifice deemed trifling. He had now completed the works at which he had laboured for fourteen years, and, aware that they had made him a reputation which would eventually place him at the head of his profession, he determined quietly to wait till his turn should come. Strange as this phrase may appear to a non-professional reader, it is not misapplied. No man can rise suddenly to the head of a profession, but must wait till the casualties of life have removed those who have had the start of him; and this succession becomes more evident when he arrives near the goal than at the commencement of the race. Besides, a practice founded on professional reputation, is like the ramifications of the banyan tree. One patient who is pleased, recommends another, who, in his turn, does the same; and thus, spreading in all directions, the practice, like the tree, shoots out new branches, and throws down fresh roots. In one, as in the other, this growing process evidently requires time, and, therefore, every man must wait till his turn of practice comes.

From this time, he restricted his labours to the ordinary working hours of mankind, going to bed at ten o'clock, and rising between seven and eight. He seldom departed from this rule during the remainder of his life, and on such occasions, eleven o'clock or midnight was the extreme limit of his vigils. But, though his hours of occupation were fewer, the time allotted to labour was as industriously improved as before. His increasing practice, the lectures that he gave subsequently to the period at which we are arrived, and especially his patients at St. George's, occupied him so much that he had no leisure for any continuous study, yet he was always engaged in prosecuting medical investigations simultaneously with his attendance on patients. These observations were, for the most part, entered in his medical journals, which were always furnished with an index, by means of which he could, at any time, refer to his remarks, and the cases on which they were made. It was between 1832 and 1839 that he thus collected all the valuable matter which caused the third edition of the " Treatise on Diseases of the Heart" so far to surpass the preceding ones. He used always to keep on his table a copy of the first edition, into which were bound a few blank leaves. On these, on the margins of the printed pages, and on loose scraps which he fastened in, he scribbled the most abbreviated notes of any new idea which occurred to him, and references to the cases illustrative of it. From these notes, which were written at broken intervals of time, and were scarcely perceived to occupy him even by those who lived in his house, he made such additions to the third edition that he may almost be said to have composed the work anew. Nor was this the only subject which engaged him. He was much interested in diseases of the brain, and used deeply to regret that he should never again have ten years of leisure to explore them, as he had done those of the heart. He afterwards wrote a very valuable paper on inflammation of the brain, which is published in the library of practical medicine ; but this was far from being the sort of work which he desired leisure to write—a work which was to contain much original matter, and supply many deficiencies on the whole of that obscure subject. There were many other topics, chiefly connected with the treatment of various complaints, which he was revolving in his mind, and on which he hoped to write papers when he should have arrived at satisfactory conclusions. He was always slow at obtaining these, and, far removed from that spirit of charlatanism which would affect to found truths on the results of two or three fortunate cases, he required the experience of years and of many cases to prove the accuracy of any new theory. This is evident from his last production, a paper on chronic pleurisy, where he quotes thirty-five cases extending over four years, and in which, instead of considering his opinions as established, he leaves them on the approach of death, to be confirmed by the experience of others. In a paper on the treatment of acute laryngitis, which he commenced, but had not strength to finish, he refers back to the period of his residence in the Edinburgh Infirmary seventeen years before.

In looking over Dr. Hope's papers, one is struck with the great variety of subjects which occupied his mind; with his zeal in picking up knowledge from all sources, and with the remarkable deference which a man of such great talents showed to the opinions of others who were better informed than himself on individual subjects. Among others, there are notes of conversations on surgery with Mr. Henry James Johnson, lecturer on anatomy and surgery at the Kinnerton Street School, a gentleman, of whose moral qualities and intellectual attainments he had a high opinion, and whose observations he thought sufficiently valuable to be committed to paper. This humble deference to the opinions of those whom he had reason to believe superior, in certain points, to himself, pervaded his general character: it caused him to be always open to conviction, and made him the most reasonable antagonist with whom one could have to deal.

An opportunity soon offered for Dr. Hope to use his newly-acquired professional influence in the election of a chaplain to St. George's Hospital. Many years before a trifling circumstance had served to show him how great is the religious responsibility attached to the selection of such an individual. He had, at the request of friends, assisted a clergyman with whose character he was not personally acquainted, to obtain a similar office. Meeting this gentleman some time after, Dr. Hope inquired how he liked his new situation. " Very well," said the other ; " I like every thing very much, except reading and praying with the sick !"

On the present occasion, Dr. Hope was informed of the expected vacancy months before it took place ; and, instead of awaiting the chance of any candidate who might present himself, he lost no time in commissioning all his religious and clerical friends to seek a suitable person, in whose favour he pledged himself to make the most strenuous exertions. By means of this prudent foresight, the desired object was gained, and the election was secured to the Rev. William Niven, whose consistent and truly christian deportment gained him universal respect. He held the office for three years, when he was removed to the living of St. Saviour's, Chelsea, which he now occupies.

The following extract of a letter from him bears a valuable testimony to Dr. Hope's conduct on the above occasion, and during his connexion with St. George's Hospital.

" I became acquainted with Dr. Hope in December 1835, on the occasion of my becoming a candidate for the office of Chaplain to St. George's Hospital. His conduct at our first interview was particularly candid, and left an impression upon my mind of one whose actions were in full accordance with the principles which he professed. He expressed his deep sense of the importance of the appointment of a chaplain to the spiritual interests of the inmates of the Hospital, and his firm determination to be guided solely by the religious principles of the candidates. To this he strictly adhered, and he honoured me with his support on that occasion, simply because he reverenced the piety of those by whom I was recommended for the office. During the period of my connexion with the Hospital, I had many opportunities of judging both of his professional and of his private character. Of the former it would be unnecessary for me to speak, as he has the testimony of those far better entitled to pronounce a judgment than I am; but of the latter I may be permitted to say, that the influence of his high moral and religious character was most beneficial. He was, on all occasions, the firm and uncompromising friend of everything connected with the promotion of piety and virtue."

No reflecting mind can approach the death-bed scene of a fellow creature, without keen anxiety respecting the state which awaits the departing soul. If

he be a believer in revelation, he can scarcely silence
an inquiry regarding the past life and supposed fitness
of the sufferer for a state of happiness or of misery.
But if the beholder be deeply impressed with the
natural unworthiness of man to enter heaven, and also
feelingly alive to the joys which are prepared for the
true believer in Christ, this anxiety will be so power-
fully excited, that he will find himself loudly called
on to proclaim salvation through Christ, and to render
his mite of assistance in rescuing a brother's soul,
about, perhaps, to sink for ever into the bottomless
abyss. Dr. Hope acknowledged this responsibility,
and his frequent visits to the chamber of death were
far from deadening him to it. At the same time he
saw the difficulty of acting on this conviction. He
was aware that by judicious interference he should
only injure the cause which he meant to serve; and,
while he was alive to his own deficiencies in religious
knowledge and christian conduct, he shrunk timidly
from inculcating on others what he felt that he so
defectively practised. He determined to consult Dr.
Burder on the subject, and at the close of a letter to
him, he says, " Can your opportunities and experience
furnish me with some hints how to offer ' a word in
season' to those who are seriously ill?" This inquiry
called forth, from Dr. Burder, several letters, which he
was pressed by his friends to publish. They accordingly appeared in a valuable periodical of extensive
circulation, under the name of " Letters from a Senior

to a Junior Physician." On receiving them, Dr. Hope wrote the following letter.

" April 18, 1836.

" MY DEAR Dr. BURDER,

" Your letter, announcing the design of giving the public as well as myself the benefit of your answer to my queries, afforded me a great and unexpected pleasure. Though my expectations were high, the letters have fully answered them. To me, indeed, they are *perfectly* satisfactory, more so than I could have ventured to anticipate; for, having long been impressed with the feeling that the *effectual* addressing of ' a word in season' required great delicacy, and being apprehensive that this feeling was possibly the result of undue timidity on my own part, I am relieved, as well as gratified, at finding that you entertain similar views, and display a delicacy of the very highest order. The easy, natural, yet earnest manner in which you blend this quality with the gentle, evangelical spirit pervading the whole, constitutes to me, and I am much mistaken if it will not prove to others, the great charm of your letters. It gives a peculiarly happy and engaging tone to the religious principles inculcated, and is eminently calculated to counteract the idea that the interference of a physician beyond the immediate profession is impertinent. It places his interference in the most amiable point of view, as emanating from a sense of paramount duty, while it is disinterested, unobtrusive, and considerate. The letters strike me as being eminently in ' *good taste*,' and this is an important qualification in essays designed to disarm irreligious prejudice, no less than to stimulate religious zeal.

" You will anticipate that these remarks are a prelude to my urging you, which I earnestly do, to expand the letters into a small volume. If I may judge from the relief, the instruction, and the general satisfaction which they have afforded to myself, I cannot doubt that they will be useful to others : and I think, for the reasons above assigned, in addition to your medico-religious experience, and to the easy elegance of your pen, that you are singularly qualified for this task. Since, too, you are not permitted to prosecute your profession, you may, perhaps, feel called upon to devote your talents in this manner to the glory of God. I say, ' a small volume,' rather than a pamphlet, because I fear that the latter might be too short. The only disappointment which I experienced from the letters, resulted from their brevity. After reading each paragraph, I longed to have the idea developed in detail ; the *taste* was so palatable, that I yearned to indulge it—to dwell upon it. This is, I believe, a legitimate criterion : and hence I cannot doubt that your rapid sketch would, by more light, shade, and colouring, become a rich and valuable picture.

" As you may think it worth while to know what

kind of wants and longings occur to the mind of an ignorant and inexperienced person—wants which *you* must ascertain, not by feeling, but by imagining them or by recurring in memory to your own feelings when inexperienced, I will venture to give you the first crude impressions which have crossed my own mind.

" Give a few *instances* of the mode of ' connecting in an easy and natural manner some serious remark with his medical counsel.' Instances to illustrate this rule would, at once, make it *particular* and practical. Though one might, by practice, succeed in finding out suitable hints, yet a very few, already approved by your experience, would give confidence, and remove the anxiety attendant on the first attempts.

" Introduce a model of a conversation, with texts, for one who is dying—*i. e.* the special case.

" The attractive and encouraging promises of the gospel might be dilated upon—especially to show that no other religion—nothing but the gospel, can meet the exigencies of the sinner at the eleventh hour, and that, for him, it is all-sufficient.

" In order to give a ' word in season' one must be *ready* : one must have a little stock always available at a moment's notice. If this readiness is to be acquired by personal experience and reflection only, it will be acquired slowly, and used timidly at first. How much better to be provided with a type from the hand of a master !

H

" *Convalescence*. Give specimen of a conversation with a religiously inclined person, and with a worldly one. Show that illness is often sent, in mercy, to awaken, and how delightful to regard it as such.

" Recommend books and name a few tracts, and point out their adaptation to a few supposed cases of different ages, ranks, and religious proficiency.

" Believe me ever, my dear Sir,

" Very sincerely yours,

" J. HOPE.

" P.S.—Pray let the junior physician remain incog. He shrinks from publicity, lest he should injure the cause by being found unworthy."

Dr. Burder did not republish the letters, and their circulation having been confined to the subscribers to the periodical, they cannot be purchased by any one inquiring on the subject. Agreeing with Dr. Hope on the importance of giving publicity to them, and being aware that other professional men are not without feelings of anxiety as to the religious duty which attaches to them when attending a dying patient, we have applied to Dr. Burder for permission to republish the letters at the end of this work, and he has most kindly granted our request. He has intimated that, should health permit, they may yet be expanded, further illustrated, and published in a separate volume ; a design, which we cordially hope that he may be enabled to execute.

Before quitting this subject, we may state that Dr.

Hope was far from agreeing with many who think that it is injurious to the patient, in a medical point of view, to inform him of the probability or certainty of a fatal termination to his disease. On the contrary, his own experience led him to believe that when the communication is made in a judicious manner, and accompanied with the religious consolation fitting such a season, the effect is likely to be salutary, by calming the mind, and subduing that irritability of temper which so often accompanies and aggravates disease, and which, in many cases, may arise from unexpressed fears and doubts, which cannot but obtrude themselves on the mind of the patient.

CHAPTER VI,

Constitution of an hospital—Lectures on diseases of the chest—Lectures on forensic medicine—Experiments on the sounds of the heart—Religious and general reading.

FEW men have worked harder than Dr. Hope had done up to the period to which we have now brought this memoir. He was, however, frequently heard to say, that laborious as his studies had been, they were but child's play to the exertions he underwent during the next five years of his life, as assistant-physician to St. George's Hospital. What was the amount of those exertions will be best seen from a document which will appear in connexion with the circumstances which led to its being written: but the following fact will prove that Dr. Hope did not over-estimate his own labours.

The medical and surgical staff of St. George's Hospital consisted of eleven persons; and while ten of these saw about one-half of the patients, the other half fell to Dr. Hope's share.* It may be objected, that

* This statement is founded on the following data. A letter from

this estimate gives a fallacious idea of his *real* work, because the in-patients which were seen by the other officers, being acute cases, required more time and attention than the out-patients seen by Dr. Hope. This objection is so satisfactorily answered in the document above referred to, that it requires no further comment.

Dr. Hope had always attached great value to the Marylebone Infirmary as a sphere for the observation of acute disease; and he considered himself no less fortunate in the opportunity now afforded him at St. George's Hospital for treating chronic cases, that class which comprises the greater number likely to occur in private practice. He said, that the duties of the assistant-physician at the latter institution presented an unparalleled field for the scientific observation of the comparative applicability and efficacy of different medicines when given in a great number of cases; of the comparative prevalence of different diseases; of the circumstances by which they are most easily induced; and of many other facts which are not only very

---

the Secretary's office shows, that the out-patients during the five years that Dr. Hope was assistant-physician, were 29,842. Of these, upwards of two-thirds were medical, and it may be said, in round numbers, that Dr. Hope saw 20,000 of them. The printed annual report for the year 1837, states the in-patients to have been 2,402, which, multiplied by 5, will give a result of 12,010 in-patients during the same period. The total number of patients for the above five years must have been 41,852, of which Dr. Hope saw about 20,000—that is, nearly one-half.

valuable ·to the private practitioner, but also throw much light on the subject of statistics and public health.

Besides seeing the medical out-patients, which was the only duty necessarily involved in his new appointment, his desire to be on friendly terms with his colleagues, united to his activity of mind, led him to entail on himself the additional fatigue of lecturing— a task which it remained at his own option to undertake or decline, and from which several of the other physicians and surgeons kept aloof without incurring the slightest censure. As the public cannot be supposed to understand the constitution, if it may be so called, of the medical and surgical departments of an hospital, the following explanation may not be amiss.

At St. George's, as at most of the other metropolitan hospitals, the services rendered by the physicians and surgeons are gratuitous, so far as regards the governors, not being paid for out of the hospital funds. Instead of a salary, they are permitted to instruct students, each of whom, on admission, pays a fee for liberty to follow the physicians and surgeons in their rounds. These fees are divided among the physicians and surgeons. The assistant-physicians and assistant-surgeons at St. George's are excluded from any share in them, on the plea that their practice is not in general of a character to attract pupils; and their services to the institution are thus strictly gratuitous. Another source of emolument is open to the medical officers. A medical school at which lectures are given, and anatomy is taught, is always attached to the hospital. Each pupil attending the lectures or the anatomical demonstrations pays a fee, which is the perquisite of the lecturer or demonstrator. Some courses of lectures, as those on the practice of physic, surgery, &c., being attended by all the students, afford a handsome remuneration; while others, as those on botany, forensic medicine, &c., pay so badly as not to compensate a man whose time is of any value. They are only kept up to promote the general interests of the school, and are delivered sometimes by the junior physicians and surgeons, sometimes by persons unconnected with the hospital. Besides the foregoing lectures, a certain number of clinical or bed-side lectures are given by those who are best qualified to attract pupils, and for these no remuneration is received. The medical school is quite distinct from the official duties of the hospital, and, as before stated, it is optional with the physicians and surgeons to join it or not.

At the time when Dr. Hope became attached to St. George's, two medical schools were connected with it. The quarrels which had attended the appointment of an assistant-physician and a second assistant-surgeon, had led to the establishment of a new anatomical school, and the most strenuous exertions were made by the greater part of Dr. Hope's colleagues to support it. Dr. Hope could not personally be interested in this cause, for he derived no emolument from the pupils attending the hospital ; but selfish considerations formed no part of his calculations. He could not be in any way connected with a cause without giving it the most cordial support in his power. As soon as he was elected assistant-physician, his colleagues expressed a desire that he would give some lectures on diseases of the chest, and accept the office of lecturer on forensic medicine. The former being gratuitous lectures, and the latter being of that class which sometimes do not even cover the expenses incurred in delivering them, Dr. Hope had no inducement beyond the desire of serving and obliging others—unless, indeed, we except the sincere interest which he always took in the instruction of the students with whom he was placed in contact.

In compliance with the wishes of his colleagues, Dr. Hope delivered, in November and December 1834, twelve lectures on the diseases of the chest and auscultation. At the same time, he made preparations for the lectures on forensic medicine, which he gave on the re-opening of the medical session in January 1835. Forensic medicine, though a very elevated branch of the science, holds out but poor inducement to the lecturer as far as emolument is concerned ; for it has no tendency to increase the reputation of its professor as a practitioner, and not being generally required by the boards of examination, is little attended to by students : hence few persons give much trouble to the preparation of so unprofitable a course. A love of excellence, whether in small or great things, was, however, a very marked feature in Dr. Hope's character ; a sense of religious responsibility also urged him on every occasion to estimate his work, not by its value in a worldly point of view, but by the talents with which he had been endowed for its execution. Thus, prompted alike by inclination and by principle, he gave as much pains to the preparation of his lectures on forensic medicine as if his reputation had depended on them alone. The evenings of this winter were devoted to writing the notes for the thirty lectures which formed the course, and the succeeding summer was spent in adding to his large collection of drawings, such as were more immediately suited to illustrate forensic medicine.

Early on the morning of the 1st of October, 1834, Dr. Hope was summoned to Bexley to see the late Lady Say and Sele. It was before sunrise, and a damp sea-fog prevented his seeing a foot from his carriage window, or availing himself of the gray twilight which began to dawn. While thus shut out from all interest in surrounding objects, his thoughts were engaged with the sounds of the heart. His former experiments in 1830 had fixed these two sounds on the contraction and dilation of the ventricle, but had not gone far enough to demonstrate their immediate cause. Various theories were started by different writers, and Dr. Hope had commenced in 1832 a new series of hospital researches in connexion with the subject. In the course of these, he arrived at certain presumptions, but no experiments

had hitherto been devised to afford direct demon-
strative proof of them. On this morning the experiments which are described at pp. 77-80 occurred to him.
On coming home, he mentioned to Mrs. Hope the idea
that had entered his mind, and rejoiced at the discovery which it seemed probable that he had made. In
the course of that month, he made a preliminary trial
at his own house on a rabbit, poisoned with woorara,
being assisted privately and confidentially by Mr.
Henry James Johnson, lecturer on anatomy at Kinnerton-street, and one of the proprietors of that theatre.
The smallness of the animal prevented their appreciat-
ing satisfactorily the modifications of the sounds.

On the 1st November, 1834, the last of Dr. Hope's
articles in the Cyclopædia of Practical Medicine was
published, and it contained no allusion to the experiments in which he was engaged. All these articles,
as before stated, were written in 1831, previous to the
publication of the first edition of his Treatise on the
Heart, at which time they were submitted to the edi-
tors of the Cyclopædia. As the final article appeared
on the 1st November, it was in the press before the
first of this series of experiments, that with Mr. Johnson, was performed. Being a part of a work which
was the property of others, it was not in Dr. Hope's
power to retard its publication; and as no satisfactory
result had been gained from the experiments, it would
have been premature to express doubts which might
prove, after all, to be unfounded.

On the 3rd November, 1834, Dr. Hope repeated the experiments at Mr. Field's, veterinary surgeon, on an ass; but the woorara being exhausted, a hammer was used to stun the animal, and the results were unsatisfactory. To these experiments, Dr. Hope invited Dr. Thomas Davies, Dr. Williams, Mr. H. J. Johnson, and Mr. Field, who were all present. Actuated by feelings of friendship to Dr. Williams, Dr. Hope on this occasion gave him permission to publish the result of these experiments when completed, in an edition of his work on the lungs, which was about to be published, and the value of which would be increased by their introduction. Dr. Hope proposed to repeat the experiments as soon as possible, and Sir B. Brodie promised to supply him with woorara. Some delay was unavoidable, in consequence of the darkness of the mornings, at which time alone Mr. Field would lend his room. The Kinnerton-street theatre, at which the experiments were completed, and which Mr. Johnson and his colleagues had kindly offered to Dr. Hope, was not finished till January: and, finally, Dr. Hope's pressing engagements at St. George's Hospital occasioned a further delay of two or three weeks.

The total delay, however, was not very great, for at the end of January 1835, within three months of the former attempt, Dr. Williams urged Dr. Hope to complete them, and undertook to procure animals, and to make the other necessary preparations. On this occasion Dr. Hope consented to give Dr. Williams an equal share in the experiments.

The experiments were completed on the 17th February, 1835, and both gentlemen began to prepare an account of them for a new edition of their respective works on the lungs and the heart. Dr. Hope having lent his MS. notes to Dr. Williams, he sent to him for them. Dr. Williams had mislaid them; but after some delay, on the 13th March, he returned one half in his own hand-writing, with the following note :—

"MY DEAR HOPE,

" I have not succeeded in finding the original notes of the first experiment, but those of the second I send you.

" I depend on your taking care that they do not find their way to any printer's hands, for, after the trouble I have had, I am jealous of their being *published or otherwise pirated.* House full of company, so excuse haste.

" Yours truly,

" C. J. B. W."

To this, Dr. Hope sent the following answer on the evening of the same day :—

" MY DEAR WILLIAMS,

" Your letter has taken me by surprise, as I certainly considered myself entitled to, at least, an equal property in the experiments.

" As the subject is too delicate for me to venture

an opinion of my own on it, I would propose to submit it for arbitration to friends.

" I have seen Sir B. Brodie, who expresses himself willing to undertake the task. If you would name a friend, we could, perhaps, arrange a meeting tomorrow.

" You will, I trust, see the propriety of stopping the press till the question is decided.

" I regret this difference of opinion, and should be glad if it could be decided à l'aimable, which I think it might with equal advantage to both parties.

Yours, &c.

" P.S.—Thanks for your confidence in sending me your notes, which, of course, I immediately return unread."

Dr. Williams having declined choosing any other arbiter than Sir B. Brodie, the affair was confided to him. Dr. Hope submitted to him, as the subject for arbitration, the two preceding letters, accompanied by one to Sir Benjamin from himself, in which he appealed against the interdict of Dr. Williams, and claimed for himself an *equal* right of property in the experiments.

Sir Benjamin's arbitration was as follows:—

" 14, Saville Row, March 19, 1835.

" MY DEAR SIR,

" I understand from your and Dr. Williams's statements:

" 1st.—That you and Dr. Williams have been both engaged, for a considerable time, in researches respecting the pathology of the heart:

" 2nd.—That you formerly instituted some physiological experiments with a view to illustrate the subject, at which you invited Dr. Williams to be present:

" 3rd.—That since then you and Dr. Williams have been in the habit of discussing questions arising out of the experiments, and that you had contemplated making other experiments conjointly:

" 4th.—That Dr. Williams frequently urged you to proceed with the projected experiments, but that your various engagements prevented your doing so:

" 5th.—That at last Dr. Williams applied to Mr. Tatum for the use of the new dissecting-room, procured animals for the purpose of the experiments, asked several gentlemen to assist in making them, and invited you to them also:

" 6th.—In addition to all this, I am informed by some of the gentlemen who were present, that the experiments were made almost entirely under the direction of Dr. Williams.

" Now if these statements are correct, I own that I do not see that you can well complain of Dr. Williams for making use of the experiments in the new edition of his work now in the press: at the same time, I am opinion, that, in doing so, Dr. Williams should be careful to explain what share you had in projecting and planning the experiments in the first instance, and that he should acknowledge whatever assistance he derived from your suggestions at the time of the experiments being made.

> " I am, dear Sir,
>> " Always yours truly,
>>> " B. C. BRODIE."

The statements in clauses 4, 5, and 6, which Sir Benjamin assumed to be correct, were protested against by Dr. Hope, who was willing to produce witnesses to disprove them. They referred, however, to minor details, on which it was unimportant to insist, because the arbitration had given him more than he had claimed, and on this ground he accepted it. Not only did it declare the experiments to be conjoint, but it bound Dr. Williams to " be careful to explain what share Dr. Hope had in projecting and planning the experiments in the *first* instance"— by which, in connexion with clause 2, where Dr. Hope is said to have " formerly instituted" them, he is given the honour of the invention, the only circumstance worth contending for.

A reference to the foregoing letters which Dr. Hope had sent to Sir Benjamin, renders it evident that the arbiter had made a strange mistake in the question, and had arbitrated as if Dr. Hope had prohibited Dr. Williams from publishing, instead of the reverse, as was plain from the letters submitted to him. The morning after the receipt of Sir Benjamin's letter, Dr. Hope called on him to point out this oversight. Sir Benjamin candidly owned his error; but, on being urged to rectify it, he declined, on the grounds, of not wishing to be further troubled. He suggested that a third person should be employed to arrange the final particulars between Dr. Williams and Dr. Hope. Immediately on leaving Sir Benjamin, Dr. Hope went to Dr. Mac Leod, who consented to carry to Dr. Williams the following proposals from Dr. Hope, which we prefer copying verbatim, notwithstanding their imperfect form.

" Willing to acknowledge that the experiments were conjoint, he doing the same."

" To agree as to the original notes, though, as I have authentic notes, this is unnecessary to me."

" Not to anticipate Dr. Williams in publishing."

" If he wish, I do not object to his publishing when ready, whether I be ready or not."

These proposals are thus endorsed by Dr. Hope.

" Proposals of accommodation to Williams sent through Dr. Mac Leod, March 20th, 1835, to which Dr. Williams assented, leaving each party to publish when he pleased. This agreement he broke by not acknowledging them to be conjoint in his publications."

The facts mentioned in this endorsement are confirmed by the following letter from Dr. Mac Leod.

" MY DEAR SIR,

" I remember perfectly having called on Dr.
Williams at your request in reference to some points
connected with the results of your mutual experiments
You made certain proposals to him on a paper which
I carried, to which, according to my recollection, he
assented ; but I do not remember the details sufficiently
to say precisely what those details were.

" Yours very truly,

' R. MAC LEOD."

" Lower Seymour St.
June 12, 1839."

It might have been hoped that this arrangement
through Dr. Mac Leod would have terminated a misunderstanding which threatened to disturb a friendship
of above ten years' duration.   Not only did Dr. Hope
sincerely desire that it might be so, but he believed
that it was as he wished, and he therefore met Dr.
Williams as formerly, shaking hands, as had been
their custom.

The coolness between them was afterwards renewed,
because Dr. Hope was of opinion that Dr. Williams,
in the new edition of his work on the Lungs, departed
from Sir Benjamin Brodie's arbitration.   He felt that
by continuing an intimacy with Dr. Williams he
would have been tacitly relinquishing his own claim,
which he had advanced in the recent edition of his
work, to a share in the experiments—a claim which

was not admitted in that of Dr. Williams. A regard
to his own character for truth and integrity, obliged
him to break off all communication with Dr. Williams,
not on the ground of the original point in dispute,
but on that of a departure, by one or the other, from
Sir Benjamin's arbitration.

Dr. Hope was, however, far from cherishing any
vindictive feelings against Dr. Williams. Contention
was totally foreign to his nature, and anything approaching to it never failed so deeply to affect his
happiness, and even his health, that he was only too
glad to banish the hated subject from his thoughts.
Peace was what he loved and earnestly sought,
whether within his own bosom, in his family, in his
household, or in his communications with strangers.
The religion of peace which he professed, strengthened
this natural disposition, and grounded on the firm
basis of principle those feelings, which, when unconnected with religion, are, even in the best specimens of human nature, too weak and unstable to be
trusted as unerring sources of action. Proceeding
on this united feeling and principle, Dr. Hope
sedulously avoided the mention of the subject to all
except a very few whom he found to have been
prejudiced against him, and to whom he felt himself
bound to submit his version of the facts. So scrupu-
lously did he act up to this rule, that even the members of his own family were unacquainted with the
details of the dispute—some even with its existence. A

proof of this was given many years after, when, Dr. Hope's health obliging him to decline any further professional attendance in the family of his sister-in-law, that lady immediately sent for Dr. Williams, alleging to him as her reason, that "she remembered to have heard Dr. Hope speak highly of his professional talents."

Dr. Hope had, however, an opportunity of proving his amicable feelings by actions no less than words. In the summer of 1836, about sixteen months after the commencement of the misunderstanding, Dr. Hope was consulted by the gentlemen connected with the Aldersgate School of Medicine, on the appointment of a lecturer on the practice of physic. As Dr. Williams then, and for several years after, was unconnected with any medical school, Dr. Hope thought that this appointment might answer his purpose, and gladly seized* the opportunity to recommend him to it. Dr. Williams declined it; but the friendly act on Dr. Hope's part remained the same as if Dr. Williams had accepted it.

On the publication of the third edition of his work on the Heart, Dr. Hope felt himself justified in following the example which he conceived Dr. Williams to have set him, and claimed the experiments as solely his own. He affixed a note, in which he explained the circumstances which led him to adopt a different

* See certificate signed by Mr. Skey, p. 172.

course in this edition from what he had done in the
preceding one; but it was his sincere wish to abstain
from the use of any offensive, harsh, or hasty term,
and with this view there was no part of his work which
underwent so frequent and such careful revision as
this note.   In the summer of 1839, an arbitration
being proposed by a mutual clerical friend, the Rev.
W. Niven, Dr. Hope gladly assented to it; but after
some preliminary arrangements, Mr. Niven wrote to
inform Dr. Hope that Dr. Williams declined it.   Dr.
Hope from this time felt himself totally exonerated
from every imputation of want of charity in the continuance of the alienation.   In a letter to the Rev.
W. Niven, which he dictated a fortnight before his
death, he says :—

"I have arrived at the last stage of debility, and
feel incompetent to the task of going into the subject
again, even with a mediatory friend of Dr. Williams
on the plan you proposed.   I feel also that, however
successful the result, little circumstances might be
revived tending to create feelings ill-suited to my present condition, which ought to be one of undisturbed
peace and unbounded charity.   *   *   *   In conclusion, I can only assure you that I have, throughout,
gone on the principle of forgiving him, and that I
seldom neglect him in my prayers.   I have consulted
an excellent and judicious clergyman here, Mr. Ayre,

and he has advised me to the course which I have now adopted, and which accorded entirely with my own previous feelings.

> " Believe me, my dear Mr. Niven,
>
> " Yours faithfully and affectionately,
>
> " J. Hope."

" April 26th, 1841."

The same day he wrote to Dr. Locock, in reference to the same subject. His note contains the following expression :—

" I sincerely forgive all those who may have injured me, and I entertain no wish for them but that they may enjoy the same peace and joy which I feel in the prospect of my heavenly inheritance."

It may appear that the above particulars of a private quarrel have been given in greater detail than is called for in the memoir of one who has buried all animosities in the grave. The writer would be sorry to call up any angry feeling in the minds of others, and is far from harbouring any uncharitable sentiment. The circumstances have, however, been widely and industriously circulated by Dr. Williams's friends, and have been eagerly caught at by that class of persons who gladly seize upon any trifle, which may detract from an excellence which they find it more easy to depreciate than to imitate. As Dr. Hope's forbearance prevented the real facts of the case from being known, except to very few, the biographer feels compelled to vindicate the conduct of one who was too generous, simple, and confiding.

In the winter of 1835-6, Dr. Hope gave, at St. George's Hospital, a second course of lectures and demonstrations on diseases of the chest; and in the spring of 1836, he repeated his lectures on forensic medicine.

The summer and autumn of the year 1835, and the ensuing winter, were the most disengaged that Dr. Hope had known. His original task being completed, and his lectures on forensic medicine finished, he removed the injunction which he had laid on his reading newspapers and books of general literature and science, and once more he became an eager politician. Some persons have accused him of an inordinate ambition, which made him sacrifice health, ease, and every other enjoyment to his profession. That he did fall a sacrifice to his profession, none, alas! can deny; but it was not ambition which prompted his astonishing efforts, and which supported him through his long and unwearying labours. It has already been said that a high sense of responsibility for the use of his time and tatents, was one strong source of incitement to him. Another cause was his great natural activity of mind, which became most evident in his hours of relaxation and in the pursuit of non-professional studies. Though he might now be said " to have nothing to do" for many hours of the day, yet none who lived in the house with him could have perceived that he did much less than he had formerly done. His sense of the value of time still prompted him to turn every moment to account; and, indeed, his avaricious love of time can be compared to nothing but the miser's love of gold. His nephew, Mr. Unwin, was preparing for the university, and Dr. Hope undertook, during one year, to assist and direct his studies. He now rose about half-past seven, and from eight till ten o'clock he gave to dressing, to breakfast, and to the instruction of Mr. Unwin, an occupation which proceeded simultaneously with the others. From ten to twelve was given to seeing patients at home. As soon after twelve as he was at liberty from these, his luncheon was brought in, and while he took it, Mrs. Hope read aloud. He then went out, and did not return till six or seven. As soon as dinner was over, either Mrs. Hope resumed her reading till bed-time, or he read to himself, but he generally preferred the former.

His studies were of a grave character. Perceiving what unfathomable depths of unattained knowledge lay before him, he arrived at that rare wisdom, inculcated by the Grecian sage, a conviction of his own ignorance. He entertained a very humble sense of his attainments, and forgetting the way that he had already gone, he eagerly pressed forward with the feeling that he had scarcely begun the race. He was aware that his scientific eminence would eventually give him considerable influence with those around him, and he already found that in society much attention

was paid to what he said.   This moral influence he
felt to be but another talent committed to his keeping;
and to make it the more available, he sought to improve his information on those subjects which were
most likely to be started in general conversation.   His
object was not to dazzle but to convince.   He accordingly strove to combine the greatest accuracy with
the most extended knowledge of every subject on
which he spoke, and when thus supported by facts,
and the champion of what he knew to be the truth,
he forgot his natural reserve and timidity, and spoke
with a boldness and decision which were quite foreign
to his disposition.   He read general history not with
a view to facts only, but as a philosopher or statesman,
deducing principles from facts, and gaining wisdom
from the comparison of different ages and different men.
He pursued the same course with the study of Church
history, especially the history of the Church of England,
to which he was strongly attached, because he daily
discovered it to be more scriptural, more apostolical,
and more suited to the necessities of mankind, whether
viewed as individuals, or in the collective light of a
nation.   In proportion as he became more fixed in his
own religious principles, he sought more earnestly to
recall those whom he believed to be in error; and he,
therefore, laid up a store of those facts which served
to show most evidently to his own mind the superiority
of the principles which he advocated.   His knowledge
was very extensive and diversified; he was ignorant

alone on subjects of light and frivolous literature: there was no use to be made of these, and it was for profit not for amusement that he read. The book which afforded him what he called a greater treat than he ever had known, was Napier's Peninsular War. He read this to himself, because when read aloud he found that it proceeded too rapidly to allow him to follow all the movements of the respective armies. He not only read but studied this work, till he knew the whole with much greater accuracy than could have been expected from one who had not been an actor in the scene. His almost boyish recollection of the time " when he was a soldier," and exercising with the Cheshire troop of lancer yeomanry, never forsook him. He reverted to this period with much pleasure, and Napier's most interesting work reviving the early taste which had long been smothered in the dust of folios, and the atmosphere of anatomical schools and hospitals, he longed to be versed in military tactics, and obtained from his military friends a list of works which he proposed reading, when the approach of disease and death turned his thoughts to other subjects.

It was his custom to keep lists of books which were recommended to him by competent judges, generally affixing the name of the person on whose authority he proposed to peruse the book at a future time, when leisure and opportunity should permit. The solid character of the works so selected, and the extended range of information which they embraced, showed the work-

I

ings of a mind insatiable in its desire of knowledge. They also satisfactorily refute the supposition that ambition was his inducement to study   On the contrary, to study was but the gratification of a taste which was as prominent in non-professional as in professional pursuits; and it was only the prohibition to study which proved a restraint to him.

CHAPTER VII.

Lectures on the Practice of Physic at the Aldersgate School of Medicine.

IN the spring of 1836, Dr. Marshall Hall having resigned the lectureship on practice of physic in the Aldersgate School of Medicine, it was offered to Dr. Hope. This school is a large one, and though unattached to an hospital, it is one of the most respectable in London, and has furnished lecturers, whose names stand high in the profession, to St. Bartholomew's Hospital, and other public institutions; Dr Hope, therefore, felt that the acceptance of this office would not be a departure from his established rule not to associate himself with schools or institutions of secondary rank. He consulted several of his colleagues at St. George's, and they unanimously advised him to accept it, not only as a source of direct emolument, but as a means of increasing his reputation among students who, in a few years, would be converted into practitioners, and might send him patients from all corners of the kingdom. After some consideration, Dr. Hope accepted the situation, and once more parted for a time with that leisure which he had recently been enjoying. Some months later he had reason to regret the step which he had taken. The resignation of Dr. Hue, who had long delivered the principal lectures at St. Bartholomew's Hospital, to which the Aldersgate School of Medicine was considered as a rival, had brought Dr. Hope into collision with Dr. Latham and Dr. Burrows, whom he had long considered as friends, and to whom he never would voluntarily have opposed himself. It was July before he was informed of this change in the lecturers at St. Bartholomew's, and then, following the dictates of his friendly feelings, he at once resigned the lecture-ship. As this fact was doubted some years after, we subjoin the following statement, which was drawn up by himself, and verified by Mr. Skey, the proprietor of the Aldersgate School :—

" After having accepted the lectures of the practice of physic at Aldersgate-street, I sent in my resignation of them. I advised the gentlemen of the school, who demurred to this, to offer the lectures, among others, to Dr. C. B. Williams. They did so. He declined them. They then wrote to me, saying that they had failed to procure a substitute, and called upon me, *as the season was far advanced*, to fulfil my pledge. I could not honestly refuse.

" June 15, 1839.   " J. HOPE.

" The above statement is correct.
        " June 17, 1839.   " F. C. SKEY."

Having thus no alternative but to fulfil the promise which he had made to the other lecturers in Aldersgate Street, Dr. Hope called on Dr. Latham and Dr. Burrows, and explained the dilemma in which he was unexpectedly placed. They kindly received his apologies, and this circumstance in no way interfered with the friendship which had so long subsisted between them. Dr. Hope's early success was the means of exciting much professional jealousy, and in the later years of his life he had reason deeply to deplore the enmity of some—an enmity which could not retard his progress, but which materially injured his health and peace of mind. He, therefore, recurred with peculiar pleasure to the opposite conduct of these gentlemen, whose superiority raised them above all jealousy.

Dr. Hope commenced his lectures on the evening of the 1st October, and he felt more anxiety from this than from any preceding trial to which his talents had been subjected. He knew that the influence of St. Bartholomew's Hospital would be thrown into the scale against him; besides, the further a man advances in his career, the more does success become necessary to him; and Dr. Hope was by this time so generally known, that a failure would have been infinitely more mortifying than at an earlier period.

His usual success, however, attended him, and, notwithstanding the formidable opposition, he obtained a very large class.   A reference to his books shows it to have been above a hundred.   He did not write out his lectures at full length, but made very ample notes, which he read over on the morning of the lecture.   He made also a second set of notes, which were so brief as to be comprised on the two sides of a small piece of paper. This paper was all that he took into the lecture-room ; but he seldom had occasion to consult it.   His lectures had thus the agreeable .ease of extempore speeches, while they possessed the advantages of arrangement, perspicuity, and solidity, which can only be the result of study and careful composition.

Of his qualifications as a public lecturer we subjoin the following sketch from one who attended his course.

" He possessed all the highest attributes of a good professor.   The analysis and division of his subjects was clear, comprehensive, and precise.   During the entire series all the powers of his mind were brought into action, and the immense mass of facts and observations collected by himself were presented to his class, and placed in luminous apposition with all the leading opinions of the day.   He was gifted with a singularly pleasing elegance of language, and a remarkable precision and felicity of expression, which gave him a peculiar aptitude for tuition ; and with all these qualities he conjoined a generosity and amiability of disposition which won for him the collective admiration and affections of his pupils. The benches of his theatre were crowded every evening, and among his auditors were frequently noticed his brother professors and other distinguished members of the profession. There was one striking characteristic of his lectures which ought not to be passed by. Being himself a firm and devoted Christian, he never lost an opportunity of infusing christian principles into his lectures, and admonished his auditors, in his farewell discourse, that medical science, like all other science, was only the investigation of subordinate and minor causes and effects, all ultimately dependent on one first great cause, God. He implored them not to follow the fashionable insanity of the day, and for the sake of being styled *esprits forts* belie the sacred faith of Christianity, but with a solemn earnestness, which no description can paint, demanded of them first to examine those evidences which had carried conviction to the mind of a Bacon, a Newton, a Locke, a Descartes."

Besides the two prizes which are generally given by every lecturer on the Practice of Physic, Dr. Hope gave a third, for proficiency in Auscultation, which, as coming from him, was peculiarly valued, and was contended for with greater eagerness than any of the others. It was a stethoscope, ornamented with a band of silver, on which was engraved the name of him who gained, and of him who gave it, together with the date and all usual particulars. Three of these were given at Aldersgate Street during the three years that Dr. Hope belonged to that school, and one at St. George's. The total number being so small, owing to the premature fate of him who awarded them, their value is now very much increased. Dr. Hope frequently said that he never met with any students who showed more attention and talent than those in the Aldersgate School. Taking notes of the lectures was generally practised; and the prizes were so well contested, that he found it most painful to be obliged to judge between essays, each of which was truly entitled to a prize. On one occasion the young man who gained the prize had, some time before, been seized with an affection of the brain, brought on by hard study, and Dr. Hope had ordered him to read as little as possible. Notwithstanding, he went in for the prize, and wrote continuously for nearly thirty hours. His hand then became paralysed, and he was going to give up in despair, but one of the lecturers coming in procured him some refreshment, cheered him on, and after a short sleep he resumed and completed his task. Dr. Hope was not aware of this till after he had awarded the prize to this young man. He then found it necessary to interfere, and limit the exertions of the students on these occasions to a few hours, instead of allowing them, as formerly, to write as long as they pleased.

At the close of the first session the unusual compliment of an Address of Thanks was paid to Dr. Hope. It was signed by ninety-six names, and as it was not thought of till late in the session, when many of the pupils had left town, a still larger number would probably have signed it, had it been got up a few weeks sooner. This address was presented in form, at a very crowded meeting of the pupils of the school, and a complimentary oration was pronounced on the occasion by Mr. Bampton, the most promising student of the year, who had carried off two of Dr. Hope's prizes, besides several from the other lecturers.

The address is as follows :—

" Aldersgate School of Medicine,
" To Dr. Hope,   Session 1836-7.
      " SIR,
" We, the undersigned pupils of your class, feel desirous of expressing the deep sense we entertain of your great and unwearied exertions in this Session, and of the extremely useful knowledge we have thereby derived.

" We do indeed feel deeply sensible of your earnest anxiety to impart to us the results of your valuable researches, your great talents, and extensive experience. While we duly appreciate your generous solicitude to endeavour to render us acquainted with our profession, we feel likewise particularly anxious to express our fervent and unfeigned admiration of the gentlemanly affability, the urbanity, and kindness which have so peculiarly distinguished your demeanour to us all.

" In conclusion, we beg to tender you the tribute
of our most sincere regard, and to assure you, that
your exertions, your courtesy, and your talents will be
remembered and appreciated by us to the latest period
of our lives."

Dr. Hope held this appointment three years, and
resigned it in 1839, when he was elected Physician to
St. George's Hospital. His success as a lecturer was
so great, that he was subsequently offered the lecture-
ship of the Practice of Physic at many of the principal
medical schools which are unattached to hospitals. He
was told by the late Dr. Birkbeck, a leading member of
the Council of University College, that on Dr. Elliot-
son's resignation of the chair of Practice of Physic, it
would be offered to him, and he had thus the best
reason for supposing, that were he to volunteer his
services they would be accepted. He was informed that
the income proceeding from these lectures was about
£1000 per annum ; and, as he was not in a position
to render £1000 per annum a matter of indifference,
he consulted with some friends, especially clergymen,
on the propriety of profiting by the hint which he had
received of the favourable inclinations of the Council.
After deliberate consideration, he preferred sacrificing
£1000 per annum to doing what he deemed to be a
compromise of religious principle. Although religion
forms no part of the education at any medical school,
and in this respect University College is on the same

footing as the rest, yet he conceived that there was a great and essential difference in the fact, that the medical school of University College forms a part, and is the chief support of an institution which was founded on the openly asserted principle that *all* education may be conducted apart from religion—an opinion which he warmly opposed on every occasion that offered. He afterwards found that the income had been very much exaggerated; but as his choice was made before he was undeceived, it was, indeed, the golden bait of £1000 per annum which he refused.

Although religion does not necessarily form any part of a medical education, yet Dr. Hope felt that no concern in life should be prosecuted without a reference to the great First Cause and Lord of all. In his conversations with students he frequently combated the infidelity and materialism which are too often embraced by them, on the false notion that such opinions argue superior intellect. He never opened or closed a session without introducing religious allusions and motives to action, and animadverting on the irrationality of infidelity—a habit which is referred to in the preceding character, written by one of his class. He intended, at some future day, to write a book for medical students on this subject, and others connected with their moral and religious welfare. Death alone prevented his carrying this design into execution.

The following passages have been compiled from the

brief and hurried notes which he made of his introductory lectures. They are inserted as an illustration of fine, generous, conscientious feeling and high moral principle. Their sketchy style shows that they must have been enlarged when delivered.

The following is an extract from the commencement of the introductory lecture given in October 1836 :—

" The teacher of the practice of physic (and of the practice of surgery) undertakes a task of greater responsibility, I think, than teachers in other departments.

" The practice of physic is, as it were, the last and single link of the manifold chain of medical science.

" If this link be unsound, vain is the strength—unavailing the temper of the previous chain.

" You may be expert anatomists, profound physiologists, scientific chemists, learned botanists, experienced pathologists, adepts in natural science, elegant scholars—accomplished in every department of knowledge subservient to medicine ; yet, if your knowledge of the practice of physic be unsound—if that last medium which brings you in contact with your patient be unsubstantial, futile are your proud acquirements. You are no better than Horace's statuary, who could make the nails and the hair and other details, but was

' Infelix operis summâ, quia ponere totum
    Nesciet.'

You are a bane to society instead of a blessing—a walking pestilence, disguised as ministers of health.

" Great, then, is the responsibility of him who would teach you the practice of physic. Great, too, is your responsibility who undertake to learn this arduous science. Whilst competency and zeal are demanded on his part, concentrated attention and dogged perseverance are requisite on yours. Gentlemen, I feel this responsibility; I trust we mutually feel it. It is a wholesome stimulus, and the most substantial and durable guarantee for the discharge of our respective duties.

" In compliance with the dictates of this feeling, I think it proper to sketch to you the plan which I propose to follow in this course, and also to delineate to you the mode in which (according to my experience) hospital studies may be conducted with the greatest effect, the greatest ease, and the greatest economy of time. In this way, if you approve of my plan, we shall have the satisfaction of understanding each other, and acting in concert. If you disapprove, I shall, at least, have the consolation of having offered you the bill of fare before you have taken your meal, and afforded you the opportunity of getting a better dinner from any more accomplished caterer than myself.

" It will be an object which I shall hold primarily and constantly in view, to give you information up to the level of the existing state of medical science: to teach you the doctrines of what the public denominates ' the new school,' (a fortunate word, for you gentlemen, that word ' *new school*.' It evinces that the public have ceased to regard experience and

gray hairs as synonymous, and that it considers youth
with science as more worthy of its confidence and rewards.)

" The term ' new school,' however, though a popular phrase, is not a mere idle hallucination of public
prejudice. It is truly the expression of a great fact.
The strides which the medical profession has made
within the last twenty years, especially within the
last ten, are colossal! Greater by far than had
been made during the whole 18th century. And it
must be highly satisfactory to you to know that the
discoveries to which I allude, have not only added
power to the medical art—but also *simplicity*. They
have swept away an augean accumulation of obsolete
trash ; they have developed general principles ; they
have even given us a dawning glance into the great
enigma—the ultimate laws of vitality. They have, in
short, redeemed medicine from the opprobrious epithet
of Celsus—" ars conjecturalis," and elevated it to the
rank of a rational science—approximating even to the
nature of an exact science. A science which, I flatter
myself, I shall be able to exhibit as simple and intelligible for you to learn, and infinitely more satisfactory
to practise than it could have been within our own
recollection. Now all this is nothing more than the
triumph of rational over empirical medicine. And here
permit me to warn you : empiricism, I fear, is often
practised by other than vulgar quacks. Not many
years ago there was a wondrous rage for what were

denominated ' practical men' with small round grisly
heads, a dogged look, and perhaps knees, and long
black gaiters on ; who were assumed to deal in nothing
but facts and common sense, in contradistinction to
the theoretical tribe of juvenile innovators. Gentlemen,
permit me to hazard an opinion, that there is no tribe so
theoretical, so hypothetical, as these practical wise-acres.
Do not suppose that they have no ideas in connexion
with their measures. If you probe their minds by
conversation, or look into their writings when they
venture on the pen, you will find that they usually
have a reason for everything they do—but the difference is this : while the rational practitioner reasons
scientifically, the so called practical man reasons at ran-
dom ; any wild vagary, floating across the misty horizon
of his intellect, sufficing to satisfy his contracted and
illiterate mind.   If you would be true practical men, be
scientific—be rational practitioners. Science will teach
you to recognize what John Hunter said was the most
doubtful thing in nature—a fact. It will keep you
simple, true, and sound. I will now rapidly glance at
a few of the leading modern improvements, in order
both to exemplify the difference between rational and
empirical practice, and to show you how these improvements will fall into my present course."

Dr. Hope then dwells on the modern improvements
in medical science, explains the plan of his course, and
concludes as follows :—

" Gentlemen, a question has often been put to me

which I think it proper I should answer to you, *viz.*:
how it is worth my while, with engagements as a
teacher at my own hospital, and other engagements,
to come so far to lecture to you on the practice of
physic. It is sufficient to answer thus far. It is a
principle common to all human nature, that when an
individual has expended much pains on a subject, he
does not like his pains to be in vain. Now, I have
spent my medical life (nearly twenty years) in studying, and making specific preparations for lecturing on
the practice of physic. For the purpose of collecting
materials and qualifying myself, I resided two years
in the Edinburgh Infirmary as house physician and
surgeon; and two more I spent in the hospitals of
Paris, Heidelberg, Bologna, Florence, and Rome.
I have treated from 12 to 15,000 hospital cases in this
country; seen nearly 3,000 post-mortem examinations;
made 5 or 600 drawings, and written 30 volumes of
cases. Having done most of this specifically for the
purpose of lecturing, I do not like that my labour
should be in vain. Nay, I believe that Providence
assigns each of us our little sphere of usefulness, from
which it is culpable to shrink, and which it is our duty
to find out. As I have been blessed with opportunities, and health and strength, I think it is my
duty to employ them to the best of my humble
abilities. Though I have taught most facts of my
profession clinically, and lectured to practitioners on
the diseases of the chest in particular, neither the

Marylebone Infirmary, nor St. George's Hospital, have afforded me the opportunity of giving a complete course. Meanwhile, years steal on; one's best days flit rapidly by, and the business of life makes increasing inroads on one's time   The season is now or never. Here is offered to me a wide and honourable sphere in a large and flourishing school—and I have accepted it. I have thought this explanation proper in justice to you, gentlemen, lest you should think that I had no adequate motive for devoting my best efforts to your service; and this must be my agology for the rudeness of in any way adverting to myself. It will add much to my pleasure, that I shall meet you here, as a fraternity of which I am one; for *I*, also, am an alumnus of St. Bartholomew's, and much attached to your clinical teachers as men of science, and as esteemed personal friends. Let me add, that having spent much of my life in hospitals, and in constant connexion with students, habit has become a necessity to me; and the more you give me of your familiar confidence, the more gratified and obliged shall I feel."

The second year Dr. Hope concludes the introductory note in the following manner :—

" It is not inappropriate for a lecturer on the practice of physic to advert to the demeanour of the medical men in actual practice. Moral lessons come with best grace from the Nestors of our profession:

but, perhaps, even I may, without presumption, offer you a few simple remarks.

" I congratulate you on the selection of your profession. It is certainly arduous, and laborious, and responsible. But what profession has not its drawbacks ? The lawyer rises to eminence through a path infinitely more dreary, and tedious, and doubtful than yours. The merchant fills his coffers at the risk of reverses which may lay him irrecoverably prostrate. You have a profession to which the path is bestrewed with flowers—all its studies are delightful ; a profession which will support you in comfort and respectability with little risk ; a profession which is not surpassed in the pleasure which it affords by the energetic exercise of the highest faculties of the mind.

" There are two great sources of pleasure in the practice of our profession. One, and certainly the greatest, is the feeling of benevolence in connexion with, and greatly augmented by, the feeling that we are workmen doing the prescribed will of our great Master. Our profession is calculated above all others, except the clerical, to excite this gentle sentiment of benevolence. It is surprising how we get attached to our patients, merely from sympathising with them in their sufferings and their dangers. It is incredible what a glow of delight one experiences when a patient emerges from a state of imminent danger into one of safety ; after our every faculty has been long kept acutely—painfully terse in devising, and balancing, and watching the means of his safety—after our anxiety has been fed, beyond what others can understand, by every fluctuation of the symptoms — every alternation of hope and fear. And well it is that we do feel this intense excitement. I envy not those that are strangers to it. It is a wholesome excitement. Under its influence, the able physician feels his faculties invigorated, his reasoning powers sharpened, his resources increased : while the ignorant or apathetic man, overwhelmed by his difficulties, betrays a want of readiness, or calmness, or decision, and loses that to which he was never entitled, the confidence of his patient.

" The second source of pleasure is the exercise of mind—energetic exercise, with a great and adequate object. Every difficult case that you attend will summon into action the quick perception of the special pleader, the profoundness of the mathematician, the analytic and combining powers of the military tactician, the foresight of the statesman — all the faculties, in short, in the exercise of which superior minds experience intense, though exciting enjoyment.

" You have a profession of usefulness : one in which the benevolent feelings are especially fostered : one in which the temptations to dishonesty are as few, perhaps, as in almost any other.

" How are you to succeed in this profession ? You remember the story whipped perhaps into some of us

as school-boys—that when Demosthenes was asked
what was the first essential to make an orator, he
answered, 'Delivery.' What the second? 'Delivery.'
What the third? 'Delivery.' Now, important as
delivery was to Demosthenes, so ought application to
be to you, especially during your stay in London.
You cannot understand, nor will you, till you can
look retrospectively on your studies in London through
the vista of past years; you cannot understand that
perhaps not one in twenty of you will ever again enjoy
so many advantages as this most giant metropolis in
the world affords. Avail yourselves of them, and,
under Providence, your fortune is made. Sir Astley
Cooper used to say, in his lectures, that he had never
known a diligent student in London who did not
ultimately succeed. 'But,' says the clever fellow,
'I need not work, I may enjoy myself.' That is
just the man that ought to work! Even *selfishness*
indicates this ; as otherwise he throws away his
advantage, and reduces himself to ordinary mediocrity.
But it appears to me, and I doubt not to you equally,
that he neglects a moral duty. There is no doubt
that we are all mere stewards, and I will only remind
you of the parable of the talents.

" Superficial teachers are the very bane of science,
because they lead students to be superficial in their
mode of study. The superficial teacher, who imagines
that ability consists in quickness alone, and who is
therefore ambitious of being thought remarkably

quick, says at a glance, ' Oh, this patient has such a disease, you may be sure, from such a symptom ;' or, ' this patient is merely nervous, don't you see that she has a clean tongue ?' Such must either be ignorant or uncandid. Ignorant, if he imagines that he can unravel disease, with as much certainty as the present state of science enables us to unravel it, by an intuitive glance, and without instituting a complete analysis and comparison of the symptoms ; or he is uncandid, if he makes this analysis in his own mind, (and habits of analysis may enable him to make it with a quickness resembling intuition,) without confessing it to the student, and teaching him the steps of the process. These remarks do not apply to our profession in particular : they apply to the science of mind in its bearing on every branch of human knowledge. What says Dugald Steward on quick men ?

" ' By far the greater part of the opinions we announce in conversation, are not the immediate result of reasoning on the spot, but have been previously formed in the closet, or perhaps have been adopted implicitly on the authority of others. The promptitude, therefore, with which a man decides in ordinary discourse, is not a certain test of the quickness of his apprehension, as it may perhaps arise from those uncommon efforts to furnish the memory with acquired knowledge, by which men of slow parts endeavour to compensate for their want of invention.

" ' A man of original genius, who is fond of exercising

his reasoning powers anew on every point, as it occurs
to him, and who cannot submit to rehearse the ideas of
others, or to repeat by rote the conclusions which he
has deduced from previous reflection, often appears, to
superficial observers, to fall below the level of ordinary
understandings, while another, destitute both of quickness and invention, is admired for that promptitude in
his decisions, which arises from the inferiority of his
intellectual abilities.'

" And now look around, and see how this is borne
out. Look around, and see whether you find mere
quickness of perception to constitute genius. Look,
and see whether it does not require an adjunct before
it becomes genius—whether it does not require pro-
fundity—the faculties of concentration, of analysis,
of judgment. Sydenham was quick, but who doubts
his depth? Hippocrates—Bichât—Newton—Cæsar
—Napoleon.

" Then look at Andral, and Laennec, and Bichât,—
how did they study? By clinical medicine, morbid
anatomy, &c. While others were mere superficial
and distant gazers at the phenomena of nature, they
went as it were behind her scenes, and saw all closely,
noted her secret combinations, and marked her remote
relations; analyzed the occult connexions of cause and
effect, and unravelled her mysterious results. Hence
their works are graphic, and bear the very impress of
nature; hence they contain nothing that is uninteresting, and much that is original.

" It is thus that you are to study nature ; you, who propose to yourselves to extend the boundaries of medical science. It is thus that you are to study (though in a more limited degree), who, as simple practitioners, wish to acquire quickness without error, and the power of inspiring confidence in your patient by the firmness resulting from knowledge.

" I have dwelt on this subject, because in a life of connexion with great hospitals and students, I have noticed, that the tinsel of superficial talent has thrown a shade over those loftier powers of the mind, too often disguised by the opprobrious epithet of plodding industry."

We venture to give the opening of the lecture for the third year. Though the sentiments expressed are much like those of preceding years, yet they are dwelt upon more fully, and the very circumstance of their recurrence proves that they were not words got up to create an effect, but fixed principles, which he wished to inculcate successively on the fresh students who came each year to his lectures.

" Gentlemen, we are met once more, to prosecute together our mutual labours—the labours of our calling—the task of life. The meeting affords me sincere pleasure, yet not unmingled with a feeling of deep responsibility—a feeling which must and ought to be experienced by every teacher of medicine and surgery, since he starts at that momentous point towards which all your other studies converge ; he brings you in contact, as it were, with your patients for better or for

7

worse, and deals with what will hereafter be the actual business of your life. This applies more forcibly to the physician than the surgeon, for at least nineteen twentieths of your cases will be medical. He may do you and society infinite harm, by negligence or incompetency, or he may (Deo volente) do you some good. My best efforts, at least, to accomplish the latter shall not be spared.

" But a deep responsibility rests on you also. It is obvious that there is no profession or vocation, except the clerical, of which the duties are so arduous, and the results, issuing in life or death, are so important. Whatever be your talents, however brilliant, however profound, in the acquisition of a profession which involves so many, and so complex, and so ponderous considerations, they can never supersede fixed and sustained attention, untiring industry, and dogged perseverance,

" Nil sine magno
Vita labore dedit."

" Here, however, I shrink from stimulating you too far. I look back with a mixed feeling of admiration, alloyed by fear and pain, at the astounding efforts which were made at the last competition for prizes in connexion with this class. Far be it from me, gentlemen, to encourage you to write for forty hours without intermission, till your intellect is exhausted, your external senses benumbed, and your limbs almost paralysed. Study, gentlemen, but stop short of that point where your health begins to fail. Respecting the latter, you will always find me ready to give you all the advice and assistance in my power.

" As you have an arduous task before you, the prospect ought, at least, to be cheering. Let me, therefore, congratulate you on the profession you have chosen. The lawyer, it is true, has avenues to greater emoluments and higher distinctions, but his path is beset with fearful temptations, it is bestrewed by few flowers, and its commencement is obstructed by infinitely greater obstacles and impediments than encumber even your own. I was lately told that if the total receipts of a party of barristers on Circuit were counterpoised against their total expenses, the surplus would be nothing! Constantly does it happen that barristers of first-rate talents pass the ages of 35, 40, 45, 50, without ever meeting with the opportunity of displaying their superiority, till their faculties wane, their stores of learning become rusty, and they pass in disappointed obscurity off the scene of life, simply because untried. And when they rise to eminence, to be statesmen and patriots, what is their position? Battered by perpetual storms of envy and jealousy; their minds in a continual turmoil from conflicting passions and parties; a peerage perchance, but often tottered into with the same steps that lead them to the grave.

" ' He who ascends to mountain tops, shall find
   The loftiest peaks most wrapt in clouds and snow ;

K

He who surpasses or subdues mankind,
Must look down on the hate of those below.
Though high above the sun of glory glow,
And far beneath the earth and ocean spread,
Round him are icy rocks, and loudly blow
Contending tempests on his naked head,
And thus reward the toils which to those summits led.'

Childe Harold. Canto III. 45.

" Look at the merchant, again ! Huge fortune accumulated no doubt. But glance around at many whom you must individually have known. The crash in 1825, the Indian crash in 1832, the American crash this year, have laid thousands of the mighty low. The accumulated hoards of a lifetime may take unto themselves wings in a moment. Money gone, the sinews of the merchant are unstrung for ever ; he lies prostrate, and irretrievably so.

" How different is your profession ! It offers fewer temptations than any other. Nay, honesty is pre-eminently your best policy. You may not rise to great wealth nor high rank, but you have competency, and that competency exempt from risk ; for your sinews, under Providence, reside in yourselves. Your profession, moreover, gives the advantages of wealth, for it gives you a rank in society, otherwise only attainable by wealth, and it gives you a moral influence, which, in providing for your families, is often tantamount to wealth. The path of your preliminary and collateral studies, as you have already seen, is truly bestrewed with flowers, and surrounded

with fascinations. When you come to actual practice, though there are annoyances inherent in every vocation, you will find enjoyments of a still higher order. Your moral, benevolent, and religious feelings will be encouraged to their utmost degree of pleasurable expansion. Also it has been wisely ordained that there shall be an intense pleasure in the exercise of intellect. It is this which carries the speculative philosopher through intricate and abstract mazes of moral and physical science; it is this which fires the commander while he conducts the niceties and balances the contingencies of military combination; it is this which animates the lawyer, which is life to the statesman: but neither by the philosopher, the general, the lawyer, nor the statesman, is it enjoyed in a higher degree than by the medical man, for to him the life of a fellow-creature is an object worthy of his noblest efforts; and such efforts will often concentrate every power of his intellect; his sagacity, judgment, calculation, forethought and memory, into the most intense and anxiously pleasurable excitement."

He then proceeds, as before, to the plan of the course, and concludes as follows:

" Gentlemen, on taking my leave at the end of the last session, a particular circumstance caused me to advert in terms of reprobation to materialism. Shortly afterwards, I pitched upon the following passage in the Times paper:—' There is something peculiar in ' the professions of medicine and surgery. The sub-

' ject of study and observation in these professions is
' the human body—the most complicated of all God's
' works in the world, and one the most calculated, in
' enlarged and comprehensive minds, to inspire ad-
' miration and reverence of the all-wise Author—and
' yet there is probably no class of men in which there
' are so many sceptics, or even positive infidels, as
' among physicians and surgeons.'

"Some time before I had heard the same from a
pulpit. It is too true that we, of all men, have the
deepest insight into the phenomena of nature. The
human frame is indeed an aggregate of wonders. Its
great lineaments are wonderful; the minutiæ, only to
be scrutinized by the microscope, are surpassingly
wonderful. If we look through chemistry and geology
at general nature, from the giant Alp upraised to
heaven by vast volcanic power, to the impalpable atom
that dances in the sun-beam, all is regulated by immutable laws and definite proportions. If we look
through botany at vegetable nature, from the sturdy
monarch of the forest to the tender snow-drop which
droops over the coldness of its frozen parent, we find
the fluids circulate in all by laws as precise as those
which give mantling bloom to the cheek of youth and
beauty.

"How is it, then, that we are the blindest of the blind
to all this? I will read you the answer of the Times.
' The cause of this peculiarity is, perhaps, as follows :—
' There are no other works of God in which the

' different members and organs are so admirably and
' strikingly adapted to the purpose for which they are
' intended, and therefore ordinary understandings,
' having observed this wondrous adaptation, stop here,
' being unable to ascend from second causes to the
' great first; and the mass of mankind in every
' profession consists of persons of ordinary under-
' standings. Hence the frequency of religious doubt
' amidst the brightest evidence. But the really great
' masters of the heart of healing, the Harveys, the
' Meads, the Friends, the Boerhaaves, are among the
' firmest believers in the divine revelation.'

" I believe there is truth in this. But we have
scriptural authority for believing that the phenomena
of nature ought to be intelligible even to ordinary understandings.

" ' For the invisible things of Him from the creation
' of the world are clearly seen, being understood by
' the things that are made, even his eternal power and
' Godhead ; so that they (viz. the heathen) are with-
' out excuse.' Rom. i. 20.

" If this applied to the heathen, how fearfully does
it apply to us? Gentlemen, excuse me for throwing this
view of the subject before you ; and, if we have no
higher motives, do let us, for mere decency's sake, rid
our profession from such an opprobrium, and our
intellects from such a libel. That it would be our
personal interest I am sure ; since there are very few
who have not a lurking antipathy against the sceptic,

the atheist, and the materialist.   What I would entreat
of you is, that if these opinions should present themselves to you as students, suppress them till you have
ample time to reflect."

The subject of jealousy among professional men in
general, is one which is complained of, and in the
medical profession it is especially painful, as it un-
settles the confidence of the patient in, perhaps, both
practitioners, at a time when confidence and ease of
mind are peculiarly necessary to his welfare.   Let us
hear what Dr. Hope says on the subject.

" Let me touch on one point more.   When you
come to practise, be most careful to shun the habit of
depreciating other practitioners.   The reflection which
invariably flits through the patient's mind, is, that
envy and jealousy influence you, and thus you not
only degrade yourself, but the profession.   One who
indulges in this habit cannot have a fine perception of
the principle of justice.   We have no right to sit in
judgment on each other : each is entitled to his opinion.
And a slander, nay an insinuation, a look, a shrug,
may be as great an injustice as a direct robbery.   Our
immortal bard, always true to nature, says,

' Who steals my purse, steals trash ; 'tis something, nothing ;
'Twas mine, 'tis his, and has been slave to thousands ;
But he who filches from me my good name,
Robs me of that which not enriches him,
And leaves me poor indeed.' "

Dr. Hope acted up to what he taught.   We have

seen letters from apothecaries thanking him for the handsome manner in which he had spoken of them in their absence to their patients. The result proved that honesty *is* the best policy, He possessed the confidence of the practitioners with whom he attended, and he noticed that no man ever had occasion to call him in once, without repeating the summons whenever an opportunity offered. How little he was alive to this odious feeling, is strikingly evinced in the following anecdote. A patient of his once showed him a letter from the wife of a physician, upbraiding her for having selected Dr. Hope, instead of this lady's husband, as her medical attendant. After remonstrating on the score of long friendship, Mrs. ———, the physician's wife, entered into an account of the difficulties with which her husband had to struggle, and ended by saying that the conduct of her friend might have been the less grievous, had she not selected Dr. Hope, of whom, for many reasons, they felt peculiarly jealous. Dr. Hope was not aware that there was any cause for jealousy, and as the patient in question never had consulted Dr. ———, he was unwilling to believe that the physician entered into the feelings of his wife. He, therefore, laughed at the letter as the ebullition of feminine anger, and declared that the jealousy was confined to the breast of Mrs. ———, who, as a wife, might be excused for resenting the supposed slight placed on her husband by her friends. He did not, however, forget the lady's imprudent revelation of the difficulties in which her husband was placed; and as he had reason to believe that this might be true, he carefully took every opportunity of assisting him, not only by calling him into consultation, but by even entrusting to him the charge of his patients when he went out of town. With perhaps too confiding a simplicity, he also committed to him an important charge at the period of the St. George's election. Too late did he then discover that Mrs. ————'s letter had been true throughout. Dr. ———— betrayed the trust confided to him, and caused Dr. Hope much trouble in the canvass. Dr. Hope avoided all needless disputes, and therefore he did not upbraid Dr. ———— with his treachery, but satisfied himself with a resolve to be more cautious in future. It is probable that, at the present moment, Dr. ———— has not the least idea that Dr. Hope either saw his wife's letter, or that he was informed of his subsequent treachery, for there was no appreciable difference in Dr. Hope's conduct towards him.

One of the above extracts has given an interesting account of what were Dr. Hope's feelings when attending a critical case. There are not a few who can testify that his deportment in the sick chamber was but the faithful picture of such feelings. His extreme kindness, and the gentle tenderness of his manner, seldom failed to ensure him the affection of his patients, whether rich or poor, and some of his best personal friends date the commencement of that friendship from their own illness, or that of a relative. The secret of his success in gaining the affection of his patients, did not lie in any peculiarity of manner, but in the true interest which inspired it. In the earlier years of his residence in London, it was hi delight, and indeed his frequent custom, to spend the night at the house of a patient who was dangerously ill ; and though the increase of his practice rendered this impossible at a later period, yet he occasionally thus indulged himself even till within two years of his death. On such occasions Mrs. Hope naturally inquired how the patient was ; but such inquiries gave him so much pain, when he had only bad tidings to give, that he requested her to discontinue them. If the patient got well, he was sure to mention what afforded him so much joy ; but if the termination was fatal, it was only by the sudden cessation of his visits that his family knew the result, which was too great a disappointment to be mentioned by him. These attentions were not confined to the rich. There was a gentleman of large fortune whose dying bed he had thus soothed, and whose family avowed their deep obligations to him. Grateful as they were for that kindness to which the rich are so accustomed, that they almost deem it their prerogative, they were much surprised some time after, to find almost similar attentions lavished on a groom, who was seized with a dangerous complaint, requiring almost constant watching. After the most assiduous attendance on the part of Dr. Hope, accompanied by the Divine blessing, the groom recovered, and the family afterwards mentioned this circumstance as illustrative of Dr. Hope's genuine benevolence, uninfluenced by considerations of wealth and station.

The new regulations of the Apothecaries' Company having required the lectures on Forensic medicine to increase their courses from thirty to fifty lectures, and to give them during the months of May and June, Dr. Hope, in compliance with these regulations, delivered a course in May and June 1838. The fatigue of giving so many lectures at a season of the year when, town being full, a physician in any practice has least time, and the necessity of giving them daily in order to compress them into the time assigned for them, made the task too arduous to be accomplished by a practitioner of Dr. Hope's standing. He, therefore, resigned them at a meeting of the lecturers held in the beginning of June; but being informed that his resignation must be made to the Medical Committee, of which he was not a member, he gave Sir B. Brodie a letter to be laid before the Committee. Sir Benjamin advised his not sending in a written resignation, as being too formal, but promised himself to give it verbally. In order to prevent any appearance of disunion by thus seceding from the school which was supported by the greater number of his colleagues, Dr. Hope permitted his name to remain on the prospectus, and promised to give gratuitously the lectures

5

on Toxicology, which form the most difficult part of the course, a pledge which he redeemed the following spring. He had given these lectures for three years consecutively, and on averaging the profits and expenses of them, he found that for the three courses he had received 20*l.* And yet each lecture had cost him, besides the original composition, between three and four hours in the most valuable part of the day. Some disappointment was expressed that he should have given up these lectures, while he retained those at the Aldersgate School of medicine on the practice of physic. But such a sacrifice could not seriously have been required by any one who reflected on the comparative advantages of the two. Not only did the Aldersgate Street Lectures afford a handsome income, and increase the reputation of the lecturer, but being given in the evening, and during the winter, they did not interfere in the least with his private practice.

In the summer of 1838, Dr. Hope wrote the article on Inflammation of the Brain, which has recently appeared in the Library of Practical Medicine. His work at St. George's, together with his private practice, occupied him so fully at this period, that he could not find time to write during the day, and in the evening, after having seen perhaps 140 patients at St. George's, he was in such a state of nervous excitement that he was unequal to doing any thing. He managed to write this article on the brain by rising very early. At six he was at his desk, and from that

time till ten, he dictated to Mrs. Hope, not stopping
for breakfast, but taking it whilst he composed. He
adopted this mode of dictating, because he found that
it saved time by removing the distraction caused by
the manual labour of writing, and allowing his thoughts
to flow undisturbed. He composed with such facility
that Mrs. Hope was supplied with matter as rapidly
as she could transfer it to paper ; and with such accuracy, that this first copy, with very few corrections,
was sent to press.

It may not be uninteresting to mention what was
his mode of composing. In the first place, he rapidly
skimmed the writings of eminent men on the subject,
making brief notes of any parts to which he might
have occasion to refer in his own work, and carefully
affixing to each note thus made, the number of the
page from which it was extracted. His next business
was to revolve the whole in his own mind, digest and
arrange it, write down the heads of the chapters, then
the minor subdivisions, and finally fill in the whole
subject under these heads and subdivisions. The paper
which he thus covered, resembled the most minute
analysis of a finished work, rather than the outline of
one which existed only in the brain of its author.
While this method showed the strength of Dr. Hope's
intellect, and the clearness and vigour of his reflective
powers, it gave to his writings the advantage of a
remarkably distinct arrangement, and by preserving
the true connexion between cause and effect, and the

natural relations of things, it simplified the subject to the reader. How often do we not find ourselves at a loss to discover the meaning of an author for the very apparent reason, that he himself has not distinctly understood the idea which he wished to convey ? This plan of writing also caused a great economy of time, for when walking about, when driving in his carriage, when waiting for an appointment, or at any other unoccupied intervals, his mind was busy at his task, and though apparently idle, he was, in truth, composing a book or medical paper. It cannot be denied that what he gained in time was, perhaps, counterbalanced by the loss of recreation which most men find in these unavoidable intervals of leisure. But considering the constitution of his mind, and the great delight which he took in intellectual pursuits—a delight which he used thankfully to reckon among the chief blessings poured out on him by a gracious God—he cannot be blamed for the full exercise of those rare mental powers which were given him.

CHAPTER VIII.

Amount of duties as assistant-physician to St. George's Hospital—
Failure of health—Election to the physicianship of St. George's
Hospital.

In June 1839, Dr. Hope published the third edition of his Treatise on Diseases of the Heart. It was
illustrated by a few plates, which, like the Morbid
Anatomy, were drawn under his own immediate superintendence, and finished by himself, so as to ensure anatomical fidelity. This edition contained much additional
matter, derived from the constant investigations of the
author since the appearance of the preceding editions.
The intricate subject of diseases of the valves received
particular illustration, and the diagnosis of these diseases
was so simplified as to divest it of much of its difficulty. Dr. Hope offered to teach the diagnosis in ten
minutes to any person who had a previous knowledge
of auscultation. This offer having found its way into
the medical journals, was laughed at as an idle boast.
Dr. Hope, accordingly, selected six of the pupils of
St. George's Hospital, gave them his instructions

during ten minutes, and then left them with half-a
dozen cases which he had previously examined, and
of which he had written the diagnosis.   Every necessary precaution was taken to prevent the pupils from
holding any communication with each other.   Notwithstanding, their diagnoses, when compared, agreed with
each other, and with that of Dr. Hope.   The previous
editions of the Treatise on the Heart had been declared
to be the best on the subject hitherto written.   They
were completely thrown into shade by the present one,
which must confer lasting reputation on its author.
Soon after its publication, his modesty produced rather
a ludicrous mistake.   He never seemed to estimate it
above its predecessors; but when complimented by Dr.
Latham on its being a " great book," Dr. Hope, with
simplicity, began to apologise for the length to which
his subject had led him, and only feared that Dr.
Latham considered him too prolix.

In the earlier part of this work, it has been mentioned that Dr. Hope was descended from a family
remarkable for longevity, and he had reason to believe
that he inherited their constitution.   The laborious
life which he had led would have long since destroyed
a person of feeble frame: but his health remained
unimpaired.   In February 1836, he desired to insure
his life, and in the declaration which he was required
to send in, he says, that since infancy, he had never
consulted a medical man, except Dr. Chambers once,
for an attack of lumbago in 1833.   As some members

of his family had died of consumption, his chest was carefully examined by Dr. Mac Leod and Dr. George Burrows, and neither of these gentlemen could detect any disease. Hitherto he had never had a cough; but in May 1836, when he had begun to find his duties at St. George's too laborious, he had a slight cough and pain in his side, which yielded immediately to a blister, and he considered himself entirely re-established. In the spring of 1837, he had an attack of influenza, which settled on his chest, and from this period he was never free from a slight, hacking cough. It was an established maxim of his, that a cough, however slight, should not be neglected; and, therefore, from the first, he paid the greatest attention to the removal of his own. But he soon saw, that, so long as he had the charge of above 400 patients at St. George's Hospital, all medicinal remedies would be in vain. His health improved or deteriorated in exact proportion as the work at the hospital was more or less arduous. Occasionally he was obliged to absent himself altogether; at other times he succeeded, with the sanction of his colleagues, in obtaining assistance from the senior pupils: and, on these occasions, his health manifestly improved. In 1838, his symptoms were aggravated by the painfully excited state of his nervous system, which produced a distressing intolerance of noise, and great difficulty in fixing his attention to any subject. It has been shown how great had been his powers of abstraction; but the case was now totally reversed. When he came home the whole house was hushed into perfect stillness : the slightest sound was distressing—nay, he was sometimes obliged to take off his own shoes, because, as he moved in his chair, he heard them creak. In such a state of nervous excitement it may be supposed how painful was the effort of seeing 140 patients in rapid succession ; and yet his high sense of religious responsibility would not permit him to do his work negligently. A professional gentleman of considerable talent, who had many opportunities of noticing him, recently remarked, that, while there are many modes of prescribing for patients, varying according to the attention and ability of the practitioner, none but a superior mind could fully estimate the care, the science, and the intellectual labour which Dr. Hope expended on his out-patients at St. George's. Often, after remaining thus occupied for nearly four hours, he used to return home completely exhausted, and unable to call on any private patients.

In August 1838, he went to Scotland, and took the opportunity of consulting Dr. Abercombie, whom he happened to meet at Inverness. Dr. Abercombie gave a decided opinion on the necessity of avoiding study and fatigue ; but, not having examined Dr. Hope's chest by auscultation, he could not pronounce on the state of the lungs. After a month's relaxation, Dr. Hope returned to town considerably better ; but the

distressing symptoms were soon renewed by the recurrence of their exciting cause, the care of the numerous
out-patients of St. George's.   In compliance with the
entreaties of his family, he consulted Sir James Clark,
who examined his chest, and, forming an unfavourable
opinion, recommended his going abroad.   He told Sir
James that it was not in his power to do so, and he
was then desired to subject himself to as little fatigue
as possible.   No one who knew the particulars of his
position as assistant-physician to St. George's, and
the risk which he incurred, by absence, of losing his
election to the physicianship, could have urged him to
leave town.   He saw plainly that he must either
remain at his post, or abandon the idea of being
physician to the hospital, and with it the hope of
eminence in his profession.   It may be asked, with
some appearance of truth, what is a profession when
weighed against life ?   The answer is obvious—that,
to a man under 40 years of age, with a family, and
without an independent fortune, the loss of a profession involves the loss of much that renders life
dear.   After deliberate consideration, he saw no alternative but to continue as he was till the spring ; and
then, should his position remain unchanged, he made
up his mind to apply to the Board for regular assistance.   In expectation of being obliged to give the
Board an account of the nature and amount of the
work of which he complained, he drew up the follow-

ing document. This statement was shown privately to some of his colleagues, and, finally, laid before the Medical Committee.

" On my election to the office of assistant-physician at St. George's Hospital, in November 1834, the men and women out patients attended promiscuously on the same day; there was a constant rush at my door to obtain admission; the strongest succeeded, and the weakest were often long detained, to their great detriment and dissatisfaction. The patients' books were in boxes, out of which the physician had to hunt them, a process entailing great loss of time, especially from the frequent misplacement or absence of the books. These inconveniences did not, of course, exist when the patients were subdivided amongst four physicians. To obviate this, I arranged that the men should attend on Mondays, and the women on Fridays, and that such patients as required to be seen twice a week should take precedence of the opposite sex on their irregular day. Those who required to be seen thrice a week, were directed to take precedence of the new patients on Wednesdays. If any required to be seen oftener, I either made a special appointment, or referred them to the apothecary.

" I arranged that the porter should give a new ticket, bearing a number, to each patient on his arrival, by which he should be admitted to me in his turn, twelve being admitted into the room at once. By this means, all crowding was obviated, and detention avoided, as a patient could come at any time between half-past twelve and half-past two o'clock, and be sure of prompt admission.

" I further arranged, that the porter should deliver his prescription book to each patient on his arrival at the hospital, and that the patient should bring it to the physician, whose time would thus be economized.

" Finally, as the hospital pharmacopœia was obsolete, I constructed one for the out-patients, containing about one hundred and forty prescriptions, of as economical a description as was compatible with utility. By this, much time was saved to the physician, as he had merely to write the name of a prescription, instead of the prescription itself; and a still larger portion of time was saved to the dispensers in the shop, as standard prescriptions were kept in quantity ready-made. This was likewise a source of great economy to the Institution.

" I have invariably taken complete notes of the history and symptoms of every patient on his first admission, and have made similar notes in the progress of the case indicating new features, and accounting for any important change of the treatment. Of these cases, I have now upwards of 15,000 in my possession, ready for the inspection of the Board, and which will form a certain criterion of the degree of attention which I have paid to my patients.

" *Increase of the number of patients.*—It had been predicated to me by my colleagues that the number of out-patients would decrease, in consequence of there being the attraction of one physician only, instead of four. Under the above arrangements, however, the number not only did not decrease, but rapidly increased, amounting to 400 and upwards, more or less constantly on the books. This is a proof that the comfort of the patients was promoted by the arrangements, and that they were not dissatisfied with the attention which they received."

Dr. Hope here gives a calculation of the patients that he had seen, and which he estimates at several thousands below their real amount. We, therefore, prefer inserting a letter which he received a few days later, and which, being an extract from authentic records, places the matter beyond dispute.

" Secretary's Office,
" St. George's Hospital, 19th June, 1839.
" Sir,
" On the other side you will find an account of the out-patients for the years 1834, 1835, 1836, 1837, and 1838, according to your request. I beg to repeat the sense of obligation I am under to you for your kindness to my children, and to say, if I can be of any service at the ensuing election, you will not spare me.

" I have the honour to remain, Sir,
" Your obedient servant,
" RICHARD LOCKE."

		Out-patients on the books.	By letter.	Accidents.	Made out-patients.	Total.
1st Jan.	1834	776	2669	1919	588	5952
,,	1835	753	3059	1579	604	5993
,,	1836	769	3256	1552	561	6138
,,	1837	790	3135	1375	582	5882
,,	1838	787	2823	1692	575	5877

Total in five years 29,842

Dr. Hope concludes his calculation, by saying that of the out-patients admitted, upwards of two-thirds come under the care of the physician. The same assertion applied to the above statement, makes it evident that he must have seen about 20,000 patients during the preceding five years.

Dr. Hope thus continues :

" It may be objected that the above numbers (showing that nearly half the patients of the whole institution are seen by the assistant physician,) give a fallacious idea of his *real* work, for that in-patients are usually ' *acute*' cases, which require more time and attention ; also, that out-patients attend irregularly, which diminishes the number seen at each sitting.

" The reply is as follows :—The bulk of acute medical cases become either convalescent or chronic within a week to fortnight, and thus resemble those of out-patients.

" 2. The in-physicians receive new patients only once a month each. The total number of new patients admitted weekly is not great, (twenty on the average,) therefore the number of acute cases is not great; consequently, at the end of a fortnight, the in-patients are very much like out-patients, and the in-physician's work is light. Journals, indeed, are kept by the in-physicians, but this is a separate affair; they keep them for the students, and are paid for their trouble by them.

" 3. On the other hand, the assistant-physician admits from thirty to fifty new patients every week. Taking even thirty as a standard, this gives one hundred and two a month, which number yields a much greater *absolute* number of ' acute' cases (of all descriptions except low fevers) than is yielded to the in-physician by his twenty, or even thirty, new cases per month. The acute out-cases require to be seen twice, thrice, or more times per week, and also demand extra attention, investigation, &c. Now this compensates for the reduction of labour resulting from the irregular attendance of other patients.

" 4. The irregular attendance referred to, even assisted by a wet day, rarely reduces the patients below 100; and if a fine day follow a wet one, they run up even to 150 or 160. One hundred patients at 2 minutes each, gives about $3\frac{1}{2}$ hours: and 150 gives 5 hours. Allowing only $1\frac{1}{2}$ minute to each, the hours will be $2\frac{1}{2}$, and nearly 4; hence, in any point of view, the task is laborious—too laborious, according to my experience, to be efficiently performed by any one person.

" 5. Though irregular attendance reduces the total number seen, it does not in the same proportion diminish the time expended by the assistant-physician. For to meet the contingency of a full attendance, he is compelled to postpone his private appointments till a late hour; then, if the attendance happens to be slack, he loses half an hour or an hour in waiting and loitering. If he be tempted to appoint too early an hour, he runs the annoying risk of being too late all day through.

" *Aid received by the Assistant Physician.*—Two minutes each, is, according to my experience, the least average time in which medical out-patients can be efficiently seen—assuming that the physician gives them the advantage of stethoscopic, abdominal, and other examinations, (which I have uniformly done,) and allowing for occasional interruptions from students, unavoidable in an institution devoted to instruction.

" On entering office, I found the task more arduous than I had anticipated ; and in particular, the crowd on certain days, resulting from irregular attendance, compelled me repeatedly to avail myself of the kind assistance of Dr. Mac Leod, till I had got my arrangements, pharmacopœia, &c., in order.

" After doing this, I saw the patients without once transferring my pen for upwards of two years, *viz.* up to the year .1837, when the number having increased to the amount detailed, I engaged the assistance of Dr. Brown. I was sanctioned in this measure by the opinion of my medical colleagues, and of Sir. B. Brodie, as to the propriety of employing medical students for this purpose. I prescribed to. myself, however, the following rules :—1. Not to employ any but graduates, because the competency of others cannot be depended upon. 2. Not to employ any one for odd days, as I have observed that this is injurious to the patient, by giving instability to the practice. I consented to receive Dr. Brown's assistance on these principles, and nothing but illness has ever caused me to deviate from them for a day.

" Dr. Brown assisted me four or five months. A charge was brought against me before the Board, by the late Mr. Lockley, for having employed assistance. I appeared before the Board, acknowledged the fact, and expressed my readiness at any time to meet the charge, and give every information to the Board. The charge was withdrawn. The Board, therefore, sanctioned my conduct, and Dr. Brown continued in office a month afterwards.

" I did the duty alone (except during absence on leave in August,) up to the end of the year 1837; when illness, which had for some months been constantly induced by my hospital attendance, compelled me to leave for a fortnight. On returning, I wrote to Dr. Seymour, expressing my wish to apply to the

L

Board for an authorised assistant. This met with the general disapprobation of my colleagues, and, in acquiescence with their wishes, I desisted ; but, with their general approbation, I continued to avail myself of such assistance as I could get : *viz.*, that of Dr. Wilks, for about three months, but he was always late, having a lecture to deliver between twelve and' one o'clock.

" In 1838, a committee, consisting of the medical officers, the visiting apothecaries, and the chaplain in the chair, was appointed to investigate the manner in which the out-patients were seen. This referred especially to the surgical department, but I expressed my strong wish .to communicate to the Board all particulars respecting the assistance which I received. This wish again met with the disapprobation of my colleagues ; and I acquiesced, on the whole of the gentlemen round the table offering me a pledge, that if any objection should thenceforth be raised against the propriety of my conduct in availing myself of assistance, they would give me their conjoint support.

" From this time till October, I saw my patients unassisted, though in impaired health. Not being better for an absence from town on leave (during which, with the assent of my medical colleagues, Dr. Mac Leod and Dr. Nairne took charge of my duties,) I availed myself of the assistance of Dr. Thompson for about four months, ending in February 1839. From that time up to the present, I have seen the patients alone, except occasionally assisted by Mr. Hammerton, Dr. Nairne, and Dr. Aldis, when ill—for the excessive labour soon caused a severe recurrence of my former symptoms, under which I continue to suffer. Dr. Thompson has just recommenced assisting me one day a week.

" It may here be stated, that I have never permitted any one to assist me in receiving new patients on Wednesdays, except on a very few occasions, when compelled by indisposition.

" Thus, out of a period of four years and three quarters, I have been assisted little more than one—and that during two days in the week only: namely, about five months by Dr. Brown, four by Dr. Thompson, and three by Dr. Wilks: occasional assistance might make two months more.

" When unassisted, I have been at the hospital with almost undeviating punctuality at twenty minutes before one o'clock: when assisted by Drs. Brown, Thompson, and recently Mr. Hammerton, who could always attend at half-past twelve o'clock, I have been ten minutes later. On three occasions only (during this spring,) I have been as late as half-past one o'clock—once from sudden illness, and twice from uncontrollable medical contingencies.

" Private professional engagements have only once prevented my attendance at the hospital.

LECTURES, &c.—

1834-5. Twelve lectures on diseases of the chest and

demonstrations for two hours every Saturday during the winter. Also thirty
lectures on Forensic medicine.

1835-6. The same as the preceding year.

1836-7. Four lectures on chest ; demonstrations as
above. Also, fifty lectures on Forensic
medicine given daily. These first injured
my health.

1837-8. Eight lectures on Toxicology.

" I resigned the lectures on Forensic medicine by
the advice of Sir B. Brodie, and delivered to him a
written letter of my resignation, assigning as reasons,
that the increased number of lectures, (from thirty to
fifty,) and the necessity of giving them daily, were circumstances incompatible with the discharge of my duties to my patients. Sir B. Brodie, thinking a letter
too formal a mode of resignation, as involving a written
reply, offered and undertook to deliver the resignation
personally to the medical committee.

" The following year, I gave gratuitously eight lectures on Toxicology (a subject which I selected as
being the most difficult and laborious) in compliance
with the request of my colleagues on the occasion of
my resignation, for the purpose of retaining my name
on the prospectus.

" I was next compelled to relinquish my lectures
and demonstrations on auscultation for 1837-8, and
1838-9, but I substituted a prize, value 11*l.*, which

will perhaps evince that my interest in the school was not diminished.   This was so well received by the students, that I have actually taught more auscultation, &c., during the last two years than ever before, being habitually surrounded by a number of the senior students.   To afford them every facility, I keep a list of the best cases, and call them out as they are wanted.

" Independent of auscultation, it has always been the habit of a number of the senior and most intelligent pupils to ' attend my practice ' for periods of from three to six months.   Thus, though out of sight, I have not been a dormant member of the medical school.

    " June 13, 1839.   J. H."

On the 19th June, 1839, Dr. Chambers resigned the office of Physician to St. George's Hospital.   This was the first time that a vacancy had occurred in the physicianship of that institution, since the creation of the office of assistant-physician.   At other hospitals it was the established custom that the assistant-physician should succeed to the higher post, unless some charge of incompetency or neglect, should make an appeal to the body of governors unavoidable.   Not only does justice require the observance of this usage, but the welfare of the hospital demands it.   It is evidently the interest of the governors to secure the services of the first men in the profession, and how can such men be expected to accept a subordinate situation, unless it

be made the certain introduction to one more honourable and lucrative ? This applies the more strongly to
St. George's Hospital, where the duties of the assistant-
physician being peculiarly arduous and strictly gratuitous, they would necessarily be avoided rather than
sought, were it not for the hope of their leading to the
physicianship, and the impossibility of attaining the
latter without having passed through the former.   As
Dr. Hope knew that his conduct had been such as to
render any charge against him absurd, he was not a
little surprised to find that Dr. Williams, instead of
being a candidate for the assistant-physicianship, which
would become vacant by Dr. Hope's promotion, offered
himself as his opponent for the physicianship.   At
first, this unexpected opposition gave Dr. Hope very
little uneasiness.   He knew that the influence of the
physicians and surgeons of the institution, who composed the Medical Committee, would ensure the success
of the candidate whom they supported, and he had too
strong a conviction of the conscientious discharge of
his own duties, and too firm a reliance on their honour
and justice, to suppose that they would allow any
considerations to interfere with his claims.   He, therefore, quietly awaited the decision of the Medical Committee, which met on the evening of the 19th of June.
About midnight, Dr. Mac Leod handed him the following note from Dr. Seymour :—

" MY DEAR HOPE,

" I laid your papers* before the meeting, and return them to you.

" After much consideration, the meeting came to a resolution that they would not pledge themselves to support, collectively, any candidate for the present vacant office of physician to St. George's Hospital, but that each individual member will exercise his own discretion.

" I need scarcely say, that I, personally, regret this resolution; but give you my permission to use my name individually, as you may think proper.

" Ever, my dear Sir, faithfully yours,

" E. S. SEYMOUR."

Nothing could exceed Dr. Hope's astonishment at this communication. He could not understand that men who would not support him collectively, could support him individually; he did not suppose that that collective support would be withdrawn from one against whom no charge could be brought. He therefore, anticipated accusations before the Board of Governors, which, even if refuted, would leave a stain on a reputation which had hitherto been unsullied and unassailed. He foresaw opposition from, at least, a majority of the Medical Committee—an anxious contest—possibly a defeat. He had too much discernment not to perceive, that, while to Dr. Williams a defeat

* These papers were the documents which he had prepared to lay before the Board, and which we have inserted.

would be only the loss of an election, to him it would
be the loss of character, of fortune, of fame—of all that
he prized, and had worked so hard to attain. The
shock was too much for his already enfeebled frame.
He was immediately attacked with a spitting of blood,
and, while his family sat up through the night, occupied with preparations for the election, he himself was
obliged to go to bed.

The next morning, his first step was to call on his
colleagues and ascertain their intentions. He was
much relieved to find, that so far from having any
charge to bring against him, all, except one, were
ready to vote for him, and, as their conduct subsequently proved, to exert their influence in his behalf.
Thus assured of their support, his hopes began to
revive. Notwithstanding, as Dr. Williams had some
influential friends, and the issue of the contest still
appeared doubtful, Dr. Hope was urged not to relax
his exertions in canvassing the gove⁻n ns.

An election is an admirable occasion for showing
the natural character ; for detecting the moral coward
and unmasking who are the truly great and truly
little men, not in station, but in mind. It is not always
the highest professional rank and wealth which secures
independence ; nor, on the other hand, is independence
incompatible with rank and wealth. It is curious to
see how completely dead some men are to the very
notion of independence, to the difference between justice
and injustice ; when the man of low rank can gravely

affirm, that he cannot vote according to his conscience, lest he should offend so and so, who has given him a dinner; and the man of higher rank vies with his inferior in littleness and servility by unblushingly regretting that he cannot declare his sentiments lest an illustrious personage should take umbrage. Dr. Hope, at first, heard similar excuses from many who ought to have been above such conduct, and this embarrassed him for twenty-four hours. By that time, the circumstances of the election became generally known in the profession, and they rose almost in a body to support him. They considered it, not as a private question, but as one involving the just rights of every assistant-physician, and forming an important precedent in the profession. Strangers came forward to assist him. Many among his private and professional friends, were unwearied in their efforts; and more than one, who had been opposed to him on various occasions, seized this opportunity of showing that they knew the difference between justice and injustice, even towards one who was not a friend.

In five days, nearly 3000 letters left Dr. Hope's house, besides those sent privately by his friends. One lady wrote to say, that on applying to a well-known baronet for his vote, he had petulantly said, he was tired of hearing of Dr. Hope, in whose behalf he had already received thirty applications.

Nor were the students less interested in his cause. Although they had no influence among the governors, and could not canvass for him, yet they offered to write, to transcribe, and seal letters—to act, in fact, as clerks. His house was crowded with them, and he could, at all times, command more assistance from them than he needed. This decided feeling on the part of the profession, soon changed the aspect of affairs. The lukewarm became warm supporters, the timid were encouraged, and time servers found it to be their interest to go with the tide. On the morning of the 26th June, Dr. Williams retired from the contest, and on the 5th July, Dr. Hope was elected without opposition. The election was gained, his friends congratulated, perhaps his opponents envied him. But what was the price that he had paid—it cost him no less than life! The spitting of blood with which he had been attacked on the night of the 19th of June, the agitation and excitement of the ensuing week, the fatigue of the election, which caused him to work almost without cessation for five days and nights, were what he never could recover. From this time he dated the final breaking up of his health, which, thenceforth, progressively and rapidly declined.

Before quitting the subject of this election we would bear a pleasing testimony to the conduct of Dr. Seymour, because we know that Dr. Hope was in the habit of expressing most warmly his gratitude, for the open and bold support which Dr. Seymour gave him from the first. Dr. Seymour and Dr. Hope had never been united by the ties of personal friendship, and there were many points of medical science and practice on which their opinions were opposed : consequently, Dr. Hope had less claim on Dr. Seymour than on many others. He was, therefore, particularly gratified by a line of conduct which proved that Dr. Seymour acknowledged the broad principle of justice, and had the courage to assert it, without respect of persons. Dr. Hope highly esteemed him on this account, and took every opportunity of lauding that which he valued the more, because he could not flatter himself that it arose from private or personal considerations.

During this election, Dr. Hope did not depart from his old principle of observing Sunday. All books and papers were cleared away on Saturday night, and, engrossing as the subject of the election was, it was not permitted to be mentioned in his family. While he was justified by the Scriptures in expecting the Divine blessing on such conduct, the actual relief afforded by this day of rest from agitating and laborious employment was so great, that a similar course might safely be recommended to those who seek no blessings beyond those of this life. Dr. Hope also remarked, with much pleasure, throughout the election, the superiority of religious men in acting on principle, apart from interest, and the respect in which they are held even by those who do not agree with them. He noticed that those whose support he was directed especially to seek, were invariably religious men ; and he found that having gained these, their names carried more weight than he could have anticipated. So true is it, that a consistent religious conduct must call down the approbation even of those who cannot, or who dare not imitate it.

PERIOD IV.

FAILURE OF HEALTH—RETIREMENT FROM PRACTICE—
DEATH.

CHAPTER I.

Domestic life—Attack of pleurisy—Religious feelings.

THE day after Dr. Hope's election to St. George's Hospital, he removed his family to West End, a small village a few miles to the north of London, with the intention of joining them every evening, and thus enjoying a larger portion of relaxation and country air than he had hitherto allowed himself. The duties attached to his new office were such as to be scarcely felt by him, who, for ten years, had never had the charge of so few patients. The fatigues of a physician's private practice are also comparatively light, especially if, like Dr. Hope, he has laid himself out principally for consultation. At least, this was Dr. Hope's estimate of the labours of his profession, which now seldom occupied him except from nine or ten in the morning till six or seven in the evening. To one

accustomed to work for sixteen hours a day, the employment of only ten seems to border on idleness.
Feeling the shock that his health had recently under-
gone, he made the recovery of this prime worldly blessing his first object, and with that view, purposely ab-
stained from all study.

Dr. Hope had hitherto been so much engrossed by
professional objects, that the natural qualities of his
mind and heart had scarcely had scope to display
themselves. He was eminently fitted to be an agreeable companion, by the rich and varied stores of his
information, the lively and intelligent interest which he
evinced in all that was said, and still more by the unpretending modesty of his manners, and a well-bred
tact, which at once placed others, however inferior in
intellect, on a level with himself. Those who were admitted to his intimacy found his quiet evening conversations instructive, not merely in an intellectual point
of view, but on account of the tone and character of
feeling evinced in them. They savoured of his natural
gentleness of disposition, which was always considerate
for the feelings of others, and incapable of indulging
in uncharitable constructions. Finding that the ordinary style of London entertainments did not afford
him that interchange of thought, feeling, and sentiment, which is essential to society in its true significa-
tion, he every year withdrew more and more from
them, and threw himself into closer contact with those
whom he could call his friends. It was in this more

select circle that he peculiarly shone. He had also gradually given up attending all places of public amusement, and in expressing an opinion on the subject, he drew a distinction which evinced his candour towards others, at the same time that it did not compromise the superior holiness of the confirmed Christian. He allowed that many who are sincere in their religious profession, and conscientious in acting up to the knowledge which they possess, do frequent such scenes; but he believed that these individuals, in proportion as they make that progress in holiness after which all are to seek, and as their taste for spiritual things increases, will abandon them altogether, as unworthy of beings who have the desire and the capacity for loftier and purer pleasures.

Dr. Hope had always been an affectionate parent, tempering affection with judgment, and as he said, "loving his child too well to spoil him." He now took an active part in the education of his only son, and on the removal of his family to West End, began to instruct him in Latin during the time that he was occupied in dressing. This practice he continued till a few months before his death, when the boy was placed at school.

Dr. Hope's opinions on the intellectual training of children, are explained in a paper, which he wrote about six weeks before his death, and which is appended to this memoir. He acted upon them with respect to his own son, and the success answered his expectations.

While thus watchful over the development of his son's understanding, he was yet far more anxious that he should early be taught to follow and love his God. When the child was only two years of age he had seen the necessity for commencing the task of moral training, and curbing those ebullitions of temper, which so early proclaim in children the depravity of human nature, as declared in the Scriptures. He did not treat the faults of childhood as amiable weaknesses, but as the seeds of evil which must be eradicated from the first. He always taught the little Theodore to refer his actions to the law of God, and not to the arbitrary distinctions too often taught in the nursery, where a torn frock and soiled hands constitute the greatest crimes. All his precepts tended to imbue the mind of his child with the ardent and simple piety, which shed its constant influence over his own being, making him ascribe to a Divine hand every good and every ill with which his life was chequered, rendering him patient under all trials, and grateful for the slightest benefits.

Finding that her husband's health did not improve at West End, Mrs. Hope was very urgent that he should allow himself more complete relaxation by going to visit various friends in the country. He had long been in the habit of taking every year one month's

holiday : but this year, when he most needed such repose, his kind sympathy for a patient curtailed the
necessary recreation a fortnight.

A physician, on going out of town for his health
several weeks before, had consigned to Dr. Hope the
care of a patient in the last stage of consumption,
whose end was daily expected. She lingered much
longer than could have been anticipated, and she was
still alive when the time came for Dr. Hope to go out
of town. The physician who had originally had the
charge of her, was detained abroad by his own health.
The invalid could not bear to be transferred to a
stranger's charge, and entreated Dr. Hope to postpone
his departure till Dr. ———'s return. While seeking
during many weeks to relieve her sufferings, for of her
recovery he never dreamt, he had become too deeply
interested in her case not to consider her feelings in
the present instance. In spite of the urgent remonstrances of those who regarded his own health alone,
in spite of the conviction that he could be of no real
service to her, he lingered on till the return of her
physician.

It may not be out of place to introduce here a few
of Dr. Hope's opinions on the subject of the obligations, which a patient incurs towards his medical attendants. Loving his profession, and seeking ardently
to elevate it, he often spoke with warmth on this subject, as being one which, he said, was not generally
understood. It was once said in his presence by a

relative, that the patient is under no stronger obligation to the physician to whom he pays a fee, than to
the baker from whom he buys his bread. Such sentiments never failed to call forth his indignation, for
knowing what pure motives actuated his own conduct,
he felt anxious to elevate his profession to the high
station which, as exercised by him he felt it to deserve.
He maintained, most justly, that kindness shown by a
physician during illness, never can be repaid. The
physician is paid for his prescription, but he cannot be
paid for the interest which he has taken in the case,
and which formed no part of the contract. Besides,
in every serious illness, repeated visits are made in the
course of a day, and for many of these no fee is received. Though, on such occasions, Dr. Hope often
took no fee, he always maintained that he was *entitled* to one, and for such visits the patient was literally
indebted. It is, however, gratifying to know that he
seldom had to complain of his patients not entertaining
a grateful sense of his services. On retiring from
practice, he said that he had never met with more than
two who were not grateful, and, strange to say, they
were both under more than ordinary obligations.

But though willing to wave his own fee, and few
men, perhaps, have rendered so large an amount of
gratuitous services, he blamed, with great justice, the
custom of the profession in working without remuneration, when there is no real call on their liberality, as-
serting that their advice is always most prized when

best paid for. The unrequited labours of medical men at public institutions, and their declining fees in private practice, on grounds unrecognised in any other profession, are simply so many instances of mistaken liberality, for which their only thanks consist in the depreciation of their skill : where a man values his own commodity at nothing, the world is not apt to put a much higher price upon it.

With such sentiments, it naturally followed that while no one could have prized money less, or been less eager in its acquisition than Dr. Hope, he exercised great discrimination in the selection of those to whom he would give his gratuitous attendance. He was told that it was customary to decline fees from actors and public singers; but he would never consent to do so, because he considered that their gains were very large, and he disapproved of the mode in which their money was acquired. But, on the other hand, he gladly offered this advantage to subalterns in the army and navy, who were not possessed of private fortune; and more especially to such of the clergy as were in limited pecuniary circumstances. In favouring the latter, he was actuated by a higher motive than mere liberality, for he regarded them as the ministers of Christ, and felt that whatever assistance he was permitted to render them, was an oblation to Him whom they served. Many were the individuals and families whom, from a knowledge of their circumstances, he attended gratuitously; while in some cases, he took fees at very long intervals—a mode which his delicacy of feeling prompted as being more soothing to their feelings and inducing them to permit his attendance; whereas, had he refused all remuneration, they would have felt obliged to send for another, who might happen to have no mercy.   In the exercise of charity, his sobriety and judgment were apparent.   He sought to bestow his charity on the dictates of principle, rather than of his natural benevolence; but, at the same time, so feeling was his nature and so difficult did he find it to resist an appeal, that he has been seen to take to his heels, in order to avoid the importunities of a street-beggar, a class of persons to whom, on principle, he never would give.   A certain per centage was set apart from his practice and from all other sources of income, and he was most scrupulous that the whole of this money should be spent solely on objects of religion and charity.   Any sums that he might be induced to give to what he called " the gratification of his feelings," he insisted on not having included under the head of charity, even when he knew the recipients to be deserving and poor, though not in *want*.

But to return from this digression.

Dr. Hope at length left town, and derived so much benefit from the change of air, that in the course of ten days, spent at Finningley Park in Yorkshire, he gained 2 lbs. in weight.   Some may wonder that, at this period, when the obstacles regarding St. George's Hospital had been greatly removed, Dr. Hope did not try the effect of a winter abroad. Mrs. Hope had urged him to this course, but his medical opinion was against it. He had no faith in the efficacy of a warm climate except in the very early stages of the disease, when its existence may be surmised rather than asserted; and he believed that, to be of any use, a residence abroad must be extended to several years—a length of time which was impossible in his profession. He was persuaded that, in his own case, the time when such a step might have been of service, was past. Whatever hopes he had entertained of the rallying powers of his constitution, had now left him, since he found that the comparative repose and the increased portion of country air, which he enjoyed at West End, had not recruited his health, which, on the contrary, rapidly declined. Still, he possessed so much muscular strength, so much activity of mind and body, and such very cheerful spirits, that it was difficult for his family and friends to believe that he was seriously ill. The following is a part of a letter he wrote in October 1839, from Finningley Park, in answer to one from Mrs. Hope, urging him to go abroad for a winter.

" It will not do. I have no intention of committing the folly of rambling about for brief portions of time, which does no good, and is rather more expensive than convenient. If I am to convert 2 lbs. which I have gained since I left you into 2 stone, it must be by such care as I can take of myself in London. The only other alternative is, packing up and ' flitting for good'—which I do not fancy. So, dearest, be easy, and acquiesce patiently in whatever is the will of Providence.   *   *   *   *

" I have got entirely rid of my cold, and have walked six hours per day with more vigour than I expected, not having experienced the least stiffness or lassitude in the evening. The game-keeper was panegyrizing a gentleman, who leaped all the gates in the country with a gun in his hand : I surprised him by a similar feat after killing five brace of birds."

This improvement of health was only temporary. Almost immediately after his return to town his cough re-appeared ; but for some months he did not complain of illness, though he afterwards said that he had then had frequent stitches in his side.

On the 22nd of December, 1839, he was attacked with pleurisy on the left side of the chest. For a few days he struggled against the disease, and continued his practice ; but on the 26th, he was obliged to confine himself to bed. On the 2nd January, Dr. Chambers saw him, and two days later, Dr. Watson ; and, from the first, they took the most serious view of his case. The following week, Dr. Latham was called in, and from this period till his death, he was attended by Drs. Latham and Watson, with a kindness which, had he been their brother, could not have been exceeded, and which his family feel that they can never sufficiently acknowledge. His reasons for selecting these two physicians, and for recommending them, as

7

he afterwards did, to all his patients, was, that he had known them for fifteen years, and, during that time, he had reason to believe that they sought eminence in their profession by the same means as himself, the attainment of professional knowledge. Naturally gifted with good abilities, they had brought to the assistance of those talents, sound reasoning and patient investigation. They had long had great advantages in the acquisition of experience, by being attached to large public institutions, Dr. Latham being physician to St. Bartholomew's and Dr. Watson to the Middlesex Hospital. In Dr. Hope's case, as in all diseases of the heart and lungs, the advice of Dr. Latham and Dr. Watson was peculiarly valuable, because they were the most skilful, and, we believe, the oldest auscultators then in town. Their religious principles too, so much in unison with his own, caused him to feel additional confidence in the opinions of those, who, he might hope, would not only prescribe but pray for him, and to whom he could mention his feelings without restraint.

As soon as his illness became known, it was a very general inquiry, especially at St. George's Hospital, how one who had been so eager in his profession and so fond of occupation, could bear the confinement of a sick room? "Whether he was not fretting himself to death?" Little did such inquirers comprehend what had been the springs of his former exertions, and how these were equally calculated to produce energy in action or patience in suffering. Dr. Hope was now suddenly transformed. His activity was exchanged for the most placid composure; no irritability of temper was visible; a more than usual cheerfulness, and even playfulness, appeared in his manner; and, instead of struggling to be at liberty, he submitted like a child to his physicians, shutting himself up at home, laying aside all study, and consenting, should they require it, to go abroad, though in opposition to his own medical opinion.

The simple faith and unwavering hope which formed so striking a part of his religious character, prevented his mind from being agitated with doubts of his salvation. He knew that Christ had died for sinners, he acknowledged that he was a sinner. He read the invitation to all who thirsted for the water of life, to all who were willing to have it—he was willing—why, therefore, should he doubt? This firm confidence in God's truth was united to the deepest sense of his own unworthiness. Within himself he could perceive nothing but sin, and, therefore, it was only by looking at the Divine perfections that he could have the faintest glimmering of hope. Had he trusted at all to himself his unworthiness might have depressed him; but while resting on the promises of Christ, to the performance of which the Divine power and truth were pledged, no fear or doubt could shake him.

It was a remarkable circumstance in Dr. Hope's religious history, that his religion seemed, in the first place, to have been founded on his intellect, and through the instrumentality of his fine reasoning powers, his heart became interested. He heard a religious doctrine, examined it as dispassionately as he would have done a physiological fact; and, being satisfied of the evidence on which it rested, he received it as an acknowledged truth, placed it in his mind, of which, henceforth, it formed a part; and there, like the tree planted by the rivers of water, it brought forth its fruit in due season. To have doubted a truth so established, would have appeared to him as irrational and absurd as to have attempted to disprove a mathematical demonstration. It was a point settled; and he would as soon have thought of doubting the circulation of the blood or again examining its proofs, as of unsettling his mind by the reception of a specious argument against a religious truth, which had once been established to his complete satisfaction. He paid little attention to occasional feelings of depression, which, he said, depended mainly on the physical temperament, and originated, most probably, in a head-ache, an undigested meal, or the prevalence of an east wind. Indeed some of his religious friends were, occasionally, disappointed at his apparent indifference to the discussion of religious feelings, and his distaste for works of what are called " religious experience." With such views, the natural result was, that he talked very little of his own progress in religion: but the even tenor of his course, the conscientious discharge of his duty in every station of

M

life rendered it evident, while the unclouded peace of his latter days has silenced all objections.

He had often remarked how much misery is caused by the indulgence of temper, and how often a person destroys by caprice and petulance the effect of his otherwise amiable qualities. He noticed that when a trifle has discomposed such a man, or when, perhaps, his health is slightly deranged, all the innocent persons round, feel the unjust effects of that, of which they are blameless. It was, therefore, a maxim of his to guard against this unjust but most common practice. He valued peace at home, and never allowed it to be disturbed by annoyances from without. This command and gentleness of temper in domestic life, endeared him to his relatives and servants : and it became the more remarkable when he was attacked by consumption, a disease which is known to cause a peculiar irritability of temper, but the course of which, in him, was marked by increasing placidity, patience, and consideration for those around him.

It was proposed to send Dr. Hope abroad, but as the advanced season made it unsafe to risk the exposure and fatigue of a long land journey, and as he could never bear a sea voyage, this plan was abandoned, or, at least, deferred. He, himself, entertained little hope of his recovery ; he acknowledged that it was just possible, but far from probable. The great circumstance in his favour was, the excellent state of

5

his general health : he ate, drank, and slept perfectly well, and had no ailment beyond his cough. After a month's confinement, he was allowed to go out for a couple of hours daily, and as the spring advanced, he was permitted to resume his practice. Dr. Chambers had recommended him to decline family practice as much as possible, and, as this had long been his own wish, he found no difficulty in confining himself almost entirely to consultations. He now felt the great advantage of a practice founded on professional reputation alone, for it enabled him to act independently of his patients, and to consult his own health and comfort. He was invariably told that an absence on the continent for a year would not affect his practice, but that his patients would flock to him on his return ; and he had every reason to believe this, for he found that he did not lose one patient by the frequent interruptions now caused by slight attacks of illness and absence from town. On the contrary, his income increased as rapidly during the last year of his life as at any other period, and, notwithstanding these interruptions, he received more fees in the course of that year than of any other. Consultation practice afforded him also the advantage of greatly diminished fatigue. He sat at home for two or three hours daily to see patients, and during that time, he could make eight or ten guineas without leaving his easy chair.

Hitherto it had been his custom not to take out his carriage on Sunday, but to pay his medical visits either on foot, or in one of the public conveyances. The state of his health now requiring him to avoid fatigue and exposure to cold, the use of his carriage became a matter of necessity, and, as such, he did not scruple to employ it. He continued, however, his practice of avoiding, as much as possible, engagements on Sunday. If patients called at his house on that day, he frequently declined seeing them until he had ascertained that the cases were urgent, or that, for some substantial reason, they could not come on another day.

Although attendance on the sick on Sundays, is sanctioned by the example of our Saviour, and may be regarded as a work of mercy, by no means inconsistent with the sacred character of the Sabbath, some distinction ought, nevertheless, to be made between cases requiring immediate attendance, and those which are not affected by the delay of a day. Also many cases are seen at intervals of a day or two, or on alternate days, and in these, arrangements may be made to prevent the visit from falling on Sunday. These were points to which Dr. Hope paid great attention. If he was obliged to see a patient on the Sabbath, he considered it in the light of a duty appointed to him by the Master whom he served, and he cheerfully obeyed the call; but he carefully avoided all unnecessary engagements, which must be regarded, not as works of mercy, but as the pursuit of personal and worldly gain.

He also made his appointments for hours which did not interfere with his attendance at church. He always attended divine service once, and by stopping at any church near which his engagements might lie, he generally contrived to go again in the afternoon. He happened once to hear much praise bestowed on a gentleman in considerable practice, because he devoted every Sunday morning till one or two o'clock to seeing poor patients gratuitously. So far from joining in this commendation, Dr. Hope highly reprobated a practice which interfered with attendance on divine worship. He said, that he should certainly praise the same individual for thus sacrificing the morning of a week-day, or indeed any other time which properly belonged to himself, and was a source of emolument to him. But that in giving that portion of time which, in general, could not be turned to pecuniary profit, and which belonged to the service of God, he was acting on the principle of him who robs his neighbour in order to give to the poor.

CHAPTER II.

Letter to his Godson—Letter on tee-totalism.

AN incident in the spring of 1840, exhibited Dr. Hope's conscientiousness in the discharge of what are considered the minor duties of life, and the serious light in which he regarded a responsibility which multitudes are in the constant habit of taking lightly on themselves, and disregarding as lightly.

About nine years before, he had stood godfather to one of the children of Mr. William Heathcote, of Clapton. As the parents of this boy were alive, and qualified to give him Christian instruction suited to his years, Dr. Hope had not hitherto taken a part in his education, beyond occasional inquiries as to the schools to which he was sent. At this time, Mr. Heathcote proposed to emigrate to New South Wales, and as this removal would probably place Dr. Hope's godson for ever beyond the reach of his superintendence, it became incumbent on him to take some steps for his instruction in the doctrines and practice of our Church. For this purpose he selected a number of works, not indeed suited to the intellect of a child of nine years of age, but such as would be proper to guide and instruct him when he should be capable of examining these subjects for himself. He also requested that the boy might be permitted to spend some time in his house, and when, a few months later, this visit was paid, he took the greatest pains in catechising him, in instructing him from the Scriptures, and in making him learn those articles of our Church which were suited to his understanding, and which dwelt on the fundamental doctrines of Christianity.

In sending the books which he had selected, he accompanied the gift with a letter, which would serve as an explanatory index to the works themselves, when the boy should be able to understand them. This letter we insert, because it expresses Dr. Hope's opinions more fully than any other which we have been able to procure. It is as follows :—

"13, Lower Seymour Street,
May 22, 1840.

" MY DEAR CHARLES,

" I am your godfather. It is the common custom of godfathers and godmothers to make presents to their godchildren of silver spoons, corals, rattles, and other baubles, and to imagine that they have then performed all that is required of them. This is not the case; and I have made a point of never sending such things to you, lest I should countenance an error and assist to mislead you. The duty of a godfather is a very serious and responsible one.   It has nothing to do with worldly vanities, but exactly the reverse, as you may see by referring to your catechism.   Your godfathers and godmothers promised, in your name,— 1. ' That you should renounce the devil and all his works, the pomps and vanities of this wicked world, &c.—2. That you should believe all the articles of the Christian faith.—3. That you should keep God's holy will and commandments, &c.'   This promise, made by your sureties, ' You are yourself bound to perform, when you come to age.'

" Now, it is the duty of your godfathers and god-mothers, while you are a little boy and unable to perform your promise, to provide for you such religious instruction, as, with the blessing of God on the means, may enable and dispose you to perform your promise when you are old enough to think for yourself.   You are blessed with good and religious parents—a blessing of the first magnitude.   They have given you the requisite instruction during the period of your infancy, and no one is more competent to do it.   But now, when you are becoming a great boy and can read and understand, I, your godfather, can contribute my mite of assistance ; not, indeed, by speaking to you, for I have little opportunity ; but by sending you instructive books ; which, if you *wish* to learn, and will pray the Holy Spirit to give you an understanding heart, will infallibly conduce to the only interest which is of any real or vital importance in this world; viz., your translation to the world of eternal happiness. Little boys, it is true, cannot always understand this: they cannot comprehend that the present world has no more importance, when compared to the next, than a preface has, compared to a book; a prologue, to a play; a door, to a house; or an avenue, to any great, splendid, and happy mansion to which it may lead. Yet, it *is* so; and I hope that the books which I send, may contribute to make you comprehend this. You will then know that you have only one great, vital interest in life.

" I have not sent a Bible, because you, of course, have one; but I should strongly advise you to study it with the marginal references, and to do this as a settled habit, as Scripture is one of the best commentaries on Scripture. I send you however a ' *Bible Commentary*,'* taken from the most approved divines, because there are many facts and passages which might perplex you at first, and your studies would be expedited by an occasional reference. You must recollect, however, that the *Commentary* is for *you* —not for the Bible, the latter being all complete, and all-sufficient, if deeply studied with a praying spirit, and an understanding heart.

" You cannot advance a single step in the divine life without prayer. I therefore send you *Pietas Privata*, as a simple model.

* The Commentary published by the Religious Tract Society.

M 5

" Wilberforce's ' Practical View of Christianity' is excellent for showing the misconceptions of religion by worldly men, and for pointing out what are *really* the leading doctrines of Christianity. This was more useful than any other book at the time of the French Revolution, when infidelity was prevalent to a fearful extent, even in England.

" Venn's ' Complete Duty of Man,' enters more fully into practical details, and may be referred to for almost daily guidance.

" Scott's ' Force of Truth,' vividly displays the struggles of a powerful and honest, but enlightened, mind, slowly surrendering its prejudices before the irresistible force of truth. It affords a usefully humiliating lesson to those who trust to human understanding, in arguing against the revealed will of God.

" The life and works of John Newton, are those of a man who was brought slowly, and after much backsliding, to the knowledge of God, and who finally exhibited the highest degree of piety and Christian virtue.

" ' Bridges on the 119th Psalm,' is a devotional book of the first excellence. One of his short sections might be read daily, and made a subject of meditation.

" In these times, when the true Apostolic, or, ' Catholic,' Church of Christ is violently assailed by Romanists, it is desirable that every Christian man (especially those who have had the advantage of good education) should have a competent knowledge of Church history; so as to be able to defend his faith against the perversions and misrepresentations of those specious, but anti-scriptural, innovators. *Milner's Church History* demonstrates that the true evangelical Church, such as it was in the times of the Apostles, and such as it is in the Church of England at this day, has subsisted without interruption from the apostolic period, though it has often and long been obscured by the oppressions of the Papacy.

" *Peranzabuloe* exhibits the history of the Church of England in particular, and is full of interest and instruction. It furnishes a ready answer to that question so frequently put by ignorant Romanists or Protestants, ' *Where was your Church before Luther ?* '

" ' *Malan* on Popery,' is a controversial book, being an exposition of the principal errors of the Church of Rome ; and, though very brief, it is so lucid and complete, as to be conclusive to every unprejudiced mind. The monk who provoked the work by a challenge, was so overwhelmed by its success, that he left Geneva in confusion. As you are going, perhaps, into foreign lands, you may have even more occasion for knowledge of this kind than at home.

" I have not had the books bound, that you may neither be afraid of using, nor of lending them ; for your next duty, after reading a good book, is to lend it, and make it useful to others. Those who love Christ are always anxious to feed his sheep.

" I hope that you will pay me a visit of two or three

days before you leave this country, and I will communicate with your mamma for the purpose. Hoping and praying, my dear boy, that the books may be useful to you, and that you may be the means of making them useful to others,

" I remain

" Your affectionate godfather,

" J. HOPE."

In the autumn of this year, Dr. Hope received a letter from Mr. Barker, of Bedford, inquiring whether he had affixed his name to a tee-total paper, which was circulated with the signatures of eighty physicians and surgeons, including most of those of any eminence. As the necessity for the use of spirits and malt liquors is much agitated at present, and is ultimately connected with the physical and moral interests of the community, it may be important to show what were Dr. Hope's sentiments regarding it.   The tee-total paper in question is as follows :—

" An opinion, handed down from rude and ignorant times, and imbibed by Englishmen from their youth, has become very general, that the habitual use of some portion of alcoholic drink, as of wine, beer, or spirit, is beneficial to health, and even necessary for those subjected to habitual labour.

" Anatomy, physiology, and the experience of all ages, and countries, when properly examined, must satisfy every mind well informed in medical science, that the above opinion is altogether erroneous. Man, in ordinary health, like other animals, requires not any such stimulants, and cannot be benefited by the *habitual* employment of any quantity of them, large or small; nor will their use during his lifetime increase the aggregate amount of his labour. In whatever quantity they are employed, they will rather tend to diminish it.

" When he is in a state of temporary debility from illness, or other causes, a temporary use of them, as of other stimulant medicines, may be desirable; but as soon as he is raised to his natural standard of health, a continuance of their use can do no good to him, even in the most moderate quantities, while larger quantities (yet such as by many persons are thought moderate) do sooner or later prove injurious to the human constitution, without any exceptions.

" It is my opinion, that the above statement is substantially correct.

Mr. Barker's letter was as follows :—

" Bedford, Sept. 11, 1840.

" DEAR SIR,

" I trust you will pardon the liberty I now take in " inquiring if you have given your signature to a de-" cidedly *tee-total* certificate, discountenancing the " use, however moderate, of any stimulating liquor " whatever.

" Observing the printed name of one who ranks so

" high in our profession as yourself, appended to a
" certificate of this kind, and knowing that some of
" the signatures have been procured under false pre-
" tences, I have determined on thus troubling you.
" May I ask the favour of an answer?

" I am, dear Sir,

" Yours, most respectfully,

" T. HERBERT BARKER."

To this letter Dr. Hope returned the following
answer :

" 13, Lower Seymour Street, Portman Square,

Oct. 16, 1840.

" MY DEAR SIR,

" I received your two letters, but after date, as they
followed me on my journey. It is quite true that I
appended my name to the document with which you
have favoured me ; and, as I have the pleasure of being
acquainted with Mr. Julius Jeffreys, the inventor of
the respirator, and know him to be a most honourable,
upright, and philanthropic man, I cannot hesitate to
assure you of my belief, that in collecting the signatures to the printed ' testimony' (which was drawn out
by himself) he was incapable of resorting to ' false
pretences, trickery, &c.,' and that any error must have
resulted from a misunderstanding on the part of the
individual giving his signature. I will, however, with
your leave, transmit your letter to Mr. Jeffreys, and if

you will favour me with the names of those whose signatures you say you ' *know*' to have been obtained by false pretences, I am sure that he will be the first to rectify the mistake.

" After having been for twenty years in almost constant official connexion with six of the largest hospitals of this country and abroad, during which time I have habitually made statistical, and often numerical, observations with much care, I have a strong conviction that drinking is the grand curse of this country :—and, more especially, the notion, almost universally prevalent amongst the lower classes, that a *proportion* of stimulant liquors is *indispensable* for the maintenance of health and strength : under which impression, they take from two to four pints of ale per day, and think *that* moderation. It is admitted on all hands, that the old ' Temperance Societies' have signally failed, as the drunkard cannot partially abstain, and the sober cannot distinguish the line of demarcation between moderation and excess.

" I have especially studied the diseases and statistics of foreign nations—barbarous and otherwise—who have never had access to stimulant liquors, and I find their diseases almost as simple as those of animals, and their strength and endurance, under favourable circumstances of climate, food, and clothing, to be equal, and often superior, to the best specimens in this country. Add to this, the result of Sir E. Parry's observations, those of the Americans, &c., and it is, I think,

demonstrated that stimulant liquors of any kind, and
in any quantity, are unnecessary (except as medicines
under especial circumstances of delicacy or disease)
for the maintenance of health and strength, which is
the proposition broached in Mr. Jeffreys' testimony.

" The disease and destitution induced by drinking
are not more referrible to the direct effects of the drink
than to the *deficiency of wholesome* food, entailed by
the expenditure on what is called a very moderate
allowance of drink : say two pints per day. You will
be aware of this, as you have probably studied the
statistics of the lower classes, and compared their
dietary with that of the army and of parish poor-
houses.

" Now, I must admit that it seems cruel to deprive
the poor of the luxury of a little drink, assuming it
to be nothing better or worse than a luxury. I frankly
confess that I like a glass of wine or beer, though,
from finding that even the least quantities disagreed
with me, I have all my life been practically almost a
tee-totaller. As I can and do abstain, I have no intention of becoming a tee-totaller, nor would I urge
any one else to become one if he can do the same, and
is not misled by the false notion that stimulants are
essential to health. But when I see that the lower
classes cannot *partially* abstain ; when I see that they
are, almost to a man, under the false notion alluded
to ; when I see them suffer *directly* from disease, *indirectly* from self-inflicted, but ignorantly-inflicted, star-

vation, and resultingly from destitution in all its forms, and with all its miseries, I feel called upon to ask myself, not what would be the sentiments of the man of kindly feelings, who would indulge the poor with luxuries, but what would be the reflections of the patriot, of the philanthropist, and, though last not least, of the Christian. The patriot, I think, would rejoice in any measures which tended to increase the health, the happiness, the prosperity, the power of his beloved country as a whole, even at the sacrifice of the wishes and inclinations of a few—a principle which we see acted upon by our senators in every great measure of state policy. The philanthropist would participate in the same expansive feelings; and the Christian would hail a change which, though no foundation for religion, is, at least, an impediment out of its way.

"Such are the reasons which have induced me, without pledging myself to tee-totalism or anything else, to subscribe to the very judicious and circumspect testimony of Mr. Jeffreys, and I doubt not that in due time, it will be signed by almost every thinking and unbiassed practitioner in the kingdom. I am aware that prejudice may be created against a medical man by raising against him a cry of tee-totalism, but I should think this is a very unworthy reason for suppressing an opinion which I believed to be conducive to the public good. I have hitherto taken no part in the cause of tee-totalism, as my own engagements

render it difficult for me to turn my attention to subjects out of my province ; but if the question should
ever become a strictly medical one, I should feel it
due to my country, and to the cause of humanity, to
lend the aid of my feeble pen on the affirmative side.

           " I remain, dear Sir,

                " Yours, faithfully,

                      " J. HOPE.

  " P.S.—Though I do not see the name of Dr. Holland on the list, I have accidentally pitched upon the
following passage in his book :—

  " ' We have not less assurance that it (wine) is, in
numerous other cases, habitually injurious in relation
both to the digestive organs and to the functions of
the brain.   And it may be affirmed generally (as a
point wholly apart from the enormous abuse of spirits
amongst the lower orders) that the use of wine is far
too large for any real necessity or utility in the classes
which consume it in this country.   Modern custom
has abridged the excess, but *much remains to be done*
before the habit is brought down to a salutary level ;
and medical practice is *greatly too indulgent on this
point* to the weakness of those with whom it deals.'
Again, ' It is the part of every wise man once, at
least, in life to make trial of the effect of leaving off
wine altogether ; and this even *without the suggestion
of actual malady*.   To obtain them (the results) fairly,
the abandonment must be complete for a time—*a
measure of no risk even where the change is greatest.*' "

In justice to Mr. Julius Jeffreys and Mr. Barker, we ought to observe, that no trickery was used by the former talented and benevolent individual in procuring signatures to the tee-total testimony; and that Mr. Barker subsequently explained that he had formed such an opinion from finding that in some tee-total publications, the authority of the eminent physicians and surgeons signing the testimony, had been quoted as able advocates of tee-totalism—a fact which he could not believe, as he knew several of them not to be themselves tee-totallers. Dr. Hope's letter explained to Mr. Barker that this was not the proper interpretation to place on the testimony. Tee-totalism, in common with every other good system, has doubtless been injured in public estimation by the injudicious conduct of some of its supporters; but Dr. Hope, notwithstanding, thought the above testimony calculated to do so much good, that he purchased several hundred copies of it, and distributed them widely, wherever he found the opportunity.

The winter and spring passed without any material change in Dr. Hope's health. As he had not suffered from a return to his professional engagements, his family were full of hope that a longer residence in the country than usual would remove all fears of any serious mischief in his lungs. He left town in the beginning of August, and selected the Highlands of Scotland as a summer residence, because he had always derived great benefit from their pure and bracing cli-

mate.   During one fortnight which he spent at Loch-
indorb, he was sufficiently well to be able, mounted on
a Highland pony, to go out shooting for several hours
daily; but, with this exception, he was much worse
during the two months which he spent in Scotland.
His general health, which had, hitherto, been excellent,
now gave way. Enlargement and inflammation of the
liver were added to his former malady, and the great
aggravation of his chest symptoms, on his journey
homeward, led him to conclude that abscesses in the
lungs had burst.

CHAPTER III.

Feelings in the prospect of death—Preparations for death—Retirement
from practice—Amoun of practiec.

In the foregoing pages we have described the career
of a physician who seeks eminence by making it the
interest of the public to consult him. It has also
been our pleasing task to show that in the midst of
professional toils and temptations, religious principle
may be nourished, its influence avowed as the main-
spring of action, and its consolations experienced in
the reference of every trial and every blessing to a
Divine hand. Were we writing the memoir of one
whose greatest distinction lay in his professional and
scientific reputation, we might here lay down the pen,
for Dr. Hope had attained the objects of his ambition,
and his professional career was about to close. But Dr.
Hope was more than a physician and a man of science
—he was a Christian, not only in name and in profession, but in spirit and in truth. The genial influence
of Christianity had been evident in the public mainte-

nance of a course of integrity, honour, and usefulness, in the endearing family relations and in the social circle. But it was more evident in the trials of sickness and in the hour of death—that solemn hour which lays bare the weakness of human nature, exposes the sophistry of false philosophy, and tests the strength and sincerity, of a religious profession.

We now, therefore, turn to the closing scenes of his life, and we hope to show that in these, no less than in the fulfilment of his active duties, he furnishes an example which may be followed with advantage.

The sole earthly chance of Dr. Hope's restoration to health had rested on the benefits to be derived from the two months spent in Scotland He had now returned, and he could not disguise from himself that, instead of being improved, his health was much deteriorated. This was visible to all, though his great cheerfulness of mind would have deluded his friends into hope, had not his increased earnestness on religious subjects convinced them that he felt his near approach to eternity. It is very commonly said that illness is peculiarly distressing to medical men, because they see their own symptoms, and, agitated by conflicting hopes and fears, are disqualified from prescribing for themselves, and yet unwilling to submit to the direction of others.

The very reverse of this was Dr. Hope's case. He observed his own symptoms with as cool and accu-

rate an eye as he would those of another; he formed
a dispassionate opinion on them, and yet, without
abandoning that opinion, he was willing to submit in
all things to the directions of those whom he had in-
vested with the authority of his medical advisers.
His calm exercise of observation and judgment on his
own case may be attributed to the fact that he did not
fear a fatal result, while he could not hope for a
favourable one. His submission to the decision of
others arose from the sense of duty. He believed
that in choosing medical attendants he had thrown on
them the responsibilities of prescribing, and that it
was his duty to follow their guidance as implicitly as
he himself would expect a patient of his own to act
according to his.

Dr. Latham and Dr. Watson wished him to go to
Madeira for the winter. His own opinion was opposed to theirs, for he thought that so far from arrest-
ing the malady, a change to a warm climate would only
accelerate its termination. However, in accordance
with his prescribed rule of action, he determined on
obeying them, and made every preparation for his immediate departure. In order to facilitate the obtaining of leave of absence from St. George's Hospital, he
applied for a certificate of health to Dr. Chambers,
whose name would carry greater weight with the
governors than that of any other physician. Most
unexpectedly he found that the opinion of that eminent man coincided with his own. Dr. Chambers

strongly urged him not to leave England, and even flattered him with the hope of warding off any fatal results of the disease, by means of medical skill and great precaution in this country. This fallacious hope was totally disregarded by the invalid himself. He knew that of many thousands who are attacked with consumption, only one or two recover, and he said that it would be folly in him to reckon on being one of these rare exceptions. This discordance of opinion in his medical attendants left him at liberty, with equal propriety, to follow either, and it cannot be called a dereliction from his principle of obedience in the patient, when he preferred the advice of Dr. Chambers, which was in accordance with his own opinion. He, therefore, gave up all idea of leaving London, and resolved to remain in the post which Providence had assigned him, until he should be totally unfit to perform its duties.

Numerous are the promises contained in holy writ that God will never forsake those who trust in Him, and that He will be their God and guide even unto death. It cannot, therefore, be matter of surprise to any thinking mind that, in the prospect of death, and in its lingering approaches, Dr. Hope should have been strongly supported. There are, however, several features in his deportment which, while they furnish rich consolation to his sorrowing family, cannot but interest and instruct those who would imitate him in his death, no less than in his life.

The first point to which we would advert is the unwavering manner in which he always kept his end in view, and the deliberate and minute preparations which he made for his departure. Calculating from his medical experience, he concluded that he should not, in all probability, last more than nine months from the time when he believed the abscesses to have burst: that is to say, till the end of June, or beginning of July. He requested Mrs. Hope not to mention to him the possibility of his recovery, for such conversations tended to unsettle his mind, while his spirits were more cheerful when he took an opposite view of the subject. In the little domestic arrangements which were suggested to promote his comfort, he always used the expressions, " when I am thinner or weaker we shall do so and so," or " when such and such a symptom comes on ;" or " when I am confined to my bed," regarding these events as certain, and rapidly approaching. On his bed-room chimney-piece he kept a strip of paper, with which he used to measure the size of his leg, and as it diminished inch by inch, he used to smile, and to speculate on the probability of his going before or after July, the time which he had first named. He made preparations for death as he had done for every important step that he had taken during life. His family could find no more appropriate manner of describing his conduct, throughout the seven months that he still lingered, than that it resembled that of a man who, expecting to set off on a journey, puts everything in order before his departure, and makes arrangements to supply his absence. As to his own preparations for the journey he was about to take, they had been completed long before. When in health, he had frequently spoken of the folly of deferring a preparation for death to a bed of sickness. Even supposing that a man could be sure of having a long illness, he used to say, that few have any idea how much illness disqualifies the mind for thought; how many diseases, even at an early stage, take away the senses, and how very commonly a stupor precedes death. This subject had long been on his mind, and he had contemplated writing, at some future day, a book on the different modes of death, illustrating this religious view of the matter. During his illness he often exclaimed, " How could I now prepare for death!" and yet his was a disease peculiarly fitted for such a preparation, and his mind was to the last so clear, that he, if any one, could have done so. We have before spoken of the lowly opinion which he formed of his own merits, the simple faith with which he clung to the promises of the Gospel, and the lively hope which he reposed in the truth and love of God. In these were laid a fine foundation for the superstructure of his religion, and beside these, he needed no preparation for another world. But so long as he was in this world, he felt that he had duties to perform. He continued his practice, not from any interest he now took in it, but with a view of increasing the provision which he had made for his wife and son. The same affectionate solicitude for their future welfare, caused him to converse with Mrs. Hope about arrangements for her future life, and to give her advice and directions on the most minute points. He also entered into communication with the Rev. Charles Mayor, the tutor at Rugby to whom he proposed that his son should go at thirteen years of age, and from him he obtained an exact account of the books which should form his preparatory studies. These also he committed to Mrs. Hope with the most ample directions to facilitate her superintendence of the boy's education. Nothing could be more complete than were all his arrangements, both for his education and future advancement in life. As a professional man he remembered that there was much valuable information which he had amassed among the out-patients of St. George's Hospital, as well as in private practice, and that, with him, all this would be lost. When the voyage to Madeira was contemplated, he had made a list of several papers which he proposed writing during his absence, and which he used in joke to say, that he should publish under the name of, " A few Practical Results from 20,000 Cases." These papers were constantly in his mind, and though he was unable to attempt them while he continued in practice, yet he never abandoned them, and the hope of completing

N 2

them was one inducement for him to retire to the country when he did.

Another point to which we would refer was the remarkable peace and joy with which he was blessed. These were unclouded by even one fear or doubt; and he could not bear to see any tears shed for him. He loved to talk of his approaching departure, and of the glories which awaited him, and Mrs. Hope loved to listen; but if any involuntary tears escaped her, he always stopped and said, that he would never speak thus again if she wept. He told her that she must pray, not for his recovery, but for his speedy release from a life of suffering. In the same spirit he objected to having prayers offered in church for his recovery, as had been done frequently in earlier stages of his illness. One day, he met Dr. Chambers in consultation at the house of a patient, and having alluded to his approaching death, Dr. Chambers kindly answered " that he ought not to despond, for that he would be quite well yet." Dr. Hope stopped him, with an assurance that he needed not to be thus cheered, for that he was well aware of his condition; that, besides, the nature of Dr. Chambers' communication was not cheering, for he should be sorry to be detained long from his heavenly inheritance, and to exchange its prospect for the toils of his profession.

One day one of his sisters-in-law inquired, whether he found that illness enabled him to realise spiritual things in a greater degree. He answered, " Yes, when we approach the invisible world, it is astonishing with what intensity of feeling we desire to be there."

. She asked from what cause.

He answered, " Oh ! for the glories"—and then as if soliloquising, he spoke so rapidly that she could not hear all that he said. She caught the words, " The mercies that we have received."—And again, at intervals, " When we consider, too, what we now are ; how continually we sin—Pollution is in every thought —When we analyse our motives, we see sin in them.— I did this from such a motive—that, from such another—Charity is given with a feeling of self-complacency—The only way is to bring the burden to the foot of the cross, and tumble it down there, saying, ' Here I am,'—It is surprisingly how prominently the promises come out." After some time he said, " Were a reprieve now given me, I should acquiesce in the will of God, but I must confess it would be long before I could rejoice."

With all this joy and peace, this eagerness to depart and be with God, there was no enthusiasm or excitement visible in his words or demeanour. His imagination had always been kept in subordination to his reason, and now nothing could have exceeded his sobriety of mind. He drew his hopes and conclusions from the Bible alone. From that source he derived the joyful belief that in another world, his renewed

faculties and purified nature would enable him to love
God more singly, and to serve Him more actively,
than he had hitherto been able to do.   He had also the
most vivid anticipations of the reunion of friends : and
while, on the authority of the Apostle, (1st Thess. iv.)
and in obedience to his injunction, he comforted Mrs.
Hope with the prospect, it was to himself a source of
extreme joy and gratitude.   One day Mrs. Hope was
talking to him about another world, and asking him
if he could realise those things to which he was so
fast approaching.   He answered in the affirmative.
She then proceeded to question him on the nature of
what he realised, but he immediately checked her by
the text, " Eye hath not seen, nor ear heard, neither
have *entered into the heart of man*, the things which
God hath prepared for them that love Him ;" laying
great stress on the words which are italics.

One invariable accompaniment of an excited imagination is the unreasonable expectation that others
ought to enter into our feelings, and an intolerance of
all which does not harmonise with our own view of a
subject.   The following incident shows how far Dr.
Hope was removed from such a state.   One day Mrs.
Hope was talking rather eagerly on some worldly
subject, when suddenly checking herself, she said,
" How foolish you must think me—how mad, to be
thus occupied with things which are temporal, and so
quickly pass away !   How can you, who are occupied
with realities, with eternal things, how can you listen

to my idle talking?" " Not at all," said he, " I do not think you foolish. I do not think of these things, but such conduct in you is only natural. You are on one side of the screen, and I am on the other."

Through the winter his sufferings were very great. Notwithstanding, as a physician, he knew that many in his disease, suffered much more than he did; and, with the truest philosophy, that of the Christian, he remembered, not how much suffering he actually had, but how much he was spared. No murmur, no complaint ever escaped his lips. He insisted that his was a very mild form of the disease, and his only hope was that he might be spared a long confinement to his bed. This same feeling of thankfulness continued with him to the end. The last time that Dr. Watson called on him, a few days before his death, the conversation turned on the modes of death to be preferred. It seems natural to mankind to fancy that the present evil is worse than any other. So far from this, Dr. Hope repeatedly said that he should choose his own complaint, except perhaps in a few aggravated forms, quite distinct from what he suffered. And this, too, at a time, when, in addition to his previous ailments, he had been unable for several weeks to speak above a whisper, or to swallow any thing without extreme difficulty, in consequence of an inflammation of the larynx.

The following letter, which he wrote to Dr. Burder in the month of December, will show, in his own words, what was the tone of his mind.

" 13, Lower Seymour Street, Dec. 8, 1840.

" MY DEAR FRIEND,

" Your most kind letter has overtaken me in my disgraceful procrastination, and put me sadly to the blush. I can only plead guilty, without pretensions to mercy: and I am in the same predicament with my brother, who upbraids me with not having written to him for four months. To you, however, I was bound to write as a matter of business, to acknowledge the receipt of the invaluable and most acceptable volumes of your excellent father's sermons. I was leaving town for my summer relaxation when they arrived: we took them with us, and, as went to a shooting ground in a remote part of Scotland, far from any church, we had service at home, and concluded by reading one of the sermons, twice a day, to a large family party. Thus the work has been, and continues to be, useful, though the kind donor has been neglected.

" I have, I think, to thank you most sincerely for some patients who have introduced themselves with your name. I know not whether I should sorrow or rejoice at your account of yourself; but if spiritual blessings are bestowed through the medium of chastisement, we can only bless the mercy that holds the rod. You kindly inquire after me. I have been for some years aware that the seeds of mischief have been laid in my constitution (apparently by the immoderate labours of St. George's); but I *say* little, as there are plenty to exaggerate for me. I feel, however, like yourself, that any thing which tends to detach me from the ' things that are seen,' to which the flesh adheres most tenaciously, is a blessing in the form of a chastisement, and that it increases the share of happiness which is granted to us even here. I have indeed nothing but blessings to be thankful for. I enjoy a moderate share of health, without what is worth calling suffering of any kind—unless lassitude would fall under that head, and, morally, a deep and mournful conviction of the sin inseparable from the flesh.

" Mrs. Hope and my boy are well, and, join in kind regards to you and Mrs. Burder.

" Always your sincere, but unworthy friend,

" J. HOPE."

When a man has discovered that which is most conducive to his happiness, the natural feeling of benevolence leads him to proclaim to others how they may arrive at the same felicity. If this is the feeling of man in his natural state, how much more is it that of the Christian, whose religion has a peculiar tendency to enlarge the affections, and to warm the heart with brotherly love to all around. This was the character of Dr. Hope's religion, and it showed itself in his increased anxiety to proclaim to others those truths, of which he daily felt the consoling influence, and to elevate their hopes to those eternal joys which were dawning so brightly on his own spirit. He had always been desirous to promote the glory of God, and to advance the cause of religion, but now this desire was become much more intense.

An individual, in whose spiritual welfare he took an active concern, was his aged relative Mrs. Mary Hope, who was eighty-six years of age. Fearful lest she should think that, because she had been regular in the discharge of her religious duties, and had endeared herself to her friends and relations by her amiable moral qualities, she was entitled to go to heaven, he addressed to her a letter, which contained the following plain exposition of the means of salvation.

 * * * * * * * *

" And now, my dear old friend, how stand you disposed for the other world? For, at the age of eighty-six, your time necessarily draws nigh. I hope you are deeply convinced, with the heart as well as with the head, that it will avail you less than a straw to ' have been as good as your neighbours :' to have done no harm to any one : to have been regular and attentive at church : to have committed no great crimes : to have read your Bible, and said your prayers regularly. To depend on these things, would be to depend on your own good works. But what says God himself on this subject? ' There is none righteous, no, not one :' ' there is none that doeth good, no, not one.' So much, therefore, for your own righteousness. The explanation of this you, I

hope, know; namely, that it results from the original
sin entailed by the fall of Adam; whence no person has
power to come to God of himself, because ' the carnal
mind is enmity against God.' What, then, is God's
scheme for saving lost mankind? You know that
God said that sin should be punished: ' The wages
of sin is death.'—(Romans vi. 23.) He could not,
therefore, refrain from punishing it, without falsehood
But God, you know, is truth itself. God, however,
is love also; and He extended that love to fallen man,
notwithstanding his sin: for He devised a wonderful
plan of grace, by which His justice should be satisfied,
and yet a full, free, and perfect salvation be secured to
all who would accept it: namely, ' God so loved the
world, that He gave his only begotten Son, that
whosoever believeth in Him should not perish, but
have everlasting life.'—(John iii. 16.) That Son suffered agonies in the garden and on the cross, ' which
were a full, perfect, and sufficient sacrifice, oblation,
and satisfaction for the sins of the whole world.'

" But how can you get at this salvation, for, as stated
above, you cannot obtain it by any works or merits of
your own. He gives it as a free gift to all who
sincerely desire and pray for it. ' Ho ! every one that
thirsteth, come ye to the waters; and he that hath no
money; come ye, buy and eat: yea, come, buy wine
and milk without money and without price.'—(Isaiah
lv. 1.) You must, therefore, pray for more and more
of the Holy Spirit, to enlighten your understanding,

and enable you to see that you have ' no money,' and
' no price:' in other words, that your own righteousness is but ' filthy rags,' and that if you have nothing
else to depend upon, you are lost for ever.   This will
induce you to 'flee from the wrath to come.'   You
will take refuge in the Saviour: you will believe in
Him not only with your head, but, cordially, with
your heart.   You will receive Him fully, and acknowledge Him as your ' Lord and your God.'—(John
xx. 28.)   This constitutes what is called faith in
Christ; which when you once *really* possess, you are
from that moment justified before God and by Christ's
righteousness being imputed to you: your sins are
expunged, and you are already, in this world, a
child of God, and an inheritor of the kingdom of
heaven.   We are all the children of God, by faith in
Christ Jesus.—(Gal. iii. 26.)   ' The just shall live by
faith.'—(Gal. iii. 11.)   ' We have believed in Jesus
Christ, that we might be justified by the faith of
Christ: and not by the works of the law: for by
the works of the law shall no flesh be justified.'
—(Gal. ii. 16.)

 " But you will say, ' are good works of no use,
then ?'   Of none, in justifying you before God ; but,
after you are justified by faith, they are indispensable
to prove that you have really received faith.   As
Christ says, ' The tree is known by its fruit.'   Unless,
therefore, your tree yield fruit—that is, good works—
you may rest assured that your tree is unsound : that

is, that your faith is not genuine, and will not save you. If you have true faith, good works will be your enjoyment, and you will grow daily in holiness, and in fitness for the blessed enjoyment of God's presence.

" Lest you should suppose that I have been telling you any thing new, turn in the prayer-book to the thirty-nine Articles of the Church of England, and you will find all that I have stated in Articles ix., x., xi., xii., xiii. Thus, you see that this is the doctrine of the Church of England, transmitted pure from the times of the Apostles.

" What a blessed and easy salvation is this ! I trust, my dear old aunt, that if you have any dependence on yourself, you will cast it off, and be constantly praying for the Holy Spirit to enable you to have saving genuine faith in Christ. Never cease or despair, for Christ says, ' Ask, and it shall be given unto you : seek, and ye shall find : knock, and it shall be opened unto you.'

" Now I must say farewell, with a prayer that this letter may be blessed to you. I write in a state of great debility, and my only reason for writing to you is, that you may have all the enjoyments which I experience from faith in Christ, and the assurance that, through God's mercy, I am one of his adopted children. God bless you.

" Always your affectionate nephew,

" J. HOPE."

Slowly and sadly, to all but the chief sufferer, passed the winter. He continued to see his patients at home from ten till twelve or one ; he then visited St. George's Hospital, and drove about, seeing patients, till five or six. After that hour he peremptorily refused all calls, however urgent. He did not feel much fatigue while thus occupied, and he very much preferred this employment to the feverish restlessness of a day spent at home. In his carriage he always took some small devotional work, such as " Bishop Hall's Union with Christ," or a child's text book, called " Scripture Truths in Scripture Language." From the time that this book was given him by Miss Joyce, of Hampstead, it was his constant companion, and from it he chose texts, which furnished him with ample meditation during his drive.

In January, he had a more severe attack of pleurisy than usual, and for a few weeks he absented himself from St. George's Hospital. On his return thither in February, he had such difficulty in dragging himself up stairs, that his weakness was noticed by the students, and by all who saw him. Dr. Nairne, the assistant-physician, very kindly called on him with an offer to relieve him from duties which he was quite incompetent to perform. The offer was most gratefully accepted, and he never visited the wards again.

Dr. Hope's strength declined so very slowly that he sometimes expressed an opinion that he might last till the ensuing year—a reprieve of which the prospect was by no means agreeable to him.

This expectation of a protracted illness proved fallacious. Towards the end of February, some private occurrences of a distressing nature totally upset him, and so impossible did he find it to rally from the attack brought on by these unforeseen circumstances, that in less that a fortnight, he yielded to the solicitations of Mrs. Hope to retire from practice. This resolution was adopted on the 1st of March, and he made preparations for removing to Hampstead, the vicinity of which to town would enable him to see his friends, while he was sufficiently removed from the importunities of patients, who, so long as he remained in town, still solicited his advice.

On thus closing the account of Dr. Hope's professional career, it may be expected that we should give some idea of the amount of practice, to which a successful physician may attain, in the short space of twelve years from his arrival in London, with only one friend. Dr. Hope kept a regular account of every fee which he received during those twelve years, and we are, therefore, enabled to speak with the greatest accuracy. The first two years that he was in London he made £200 per annum, a larger sum than he could have anticipated, considering how small was his circle of acquaintances, and that he had then had no means of introducing himself to the notice of the public and the profession at large. The third year, the accidental removal of some families who employed him reduced his practice to £150. At the end of the third year, his work on the Diseases of the Heart was published, and he came before the profession as physician to the Marylebone Infirmary. For the first year after, his practice was little affected by these circumstances; but from that time, as his reputation became extended, his practice increased gradually : at first more slowly, but without the slightest retrogression, till, in eight years more, when he retired, he was making £4000 per annum. During the last twelve months his health was so weak that he refused to see any one after six o'clock, and he was often incapacitated from going out for several days together. Had it not been for these limitations of his physical powers, it is probable that his practice, before the end of the year, might have exceeded even the large sum of £4000.

He had so completely gained the confidence of his patients, that even after he had retired from practice, they insisted on consulting him. During the first three weeks after his retiring, he made £100, that is, rather more than £1700 per annum, in fees received from those who would not be refused. Even after his removal to Hampstead he might have been fully occupied with those who, having come from the country, did not hesitate to go a few additional miles for his advice. So late as the day before his death, he declined a visit from one of his former patients.

At the early age of forty, with an extended reputation, an unsullied character, much promise of increasing wealth; with domestic happiness, which alone, in his estimation, would have suffered for his enjoyment; with a temper and tastes calculated to make him happy in every situation of life, Dr. Hope might have been excused had he preferred the longer enjoyment of so large a share of earthly blessings—had he even cast one lingering look behind. On the 30th March he left town with the certain knowledge that he never should return. It was the close of his professional life, the termination of all those dreams of wealth, honour, and usefulness, in which he had once so ardently indulged. Such a day would have made most men moralize, perhaps rather sadly; but he was conscious of only one feeling—that of unalloyed pleasure. He was going to enjoy repose, imperfect indeed; but preparatory to that perfect rest to which he was hastening, and for the rapid approach of which he earnestly prayed. But if he regretted not the change for himself, did he not regret it on account of his only child, for whom, like other fathers, he had his plans of ambition? When speaking of his son, he observed, that had he lived, the boy would probably have been independent of a profession; " but," he added, " I am not sorry for the change, for then he would probably have been more a child of the world than, I trust, he may now prove to be."

Let us pause one moment to consider this remarkable change, and inquire into its causes. Can this be the same individual who, filled from earliest childhood with bright visions of earthly honour, wealth,

and distinction, so perseveringly struggled for their
attainment, and for nearly thirty years sacrificed every
personal consideration to gain those very treasures
which he now prizes so lightly? Strange, incredible
as it may seem, it is indeed he! Whence, then, this
change? Has the world frowned on him, and has he
learned, by hard necessity, to despise the smiles of
fortune? No—the world before him is brighter and
more inviting than it ever was before. Is it the madness of enthusiasm, or the sickly dream of an exhausted
brain? No, for his intellect is clear, his judgment cool,
and his present feelings, far from being the growth of
temporary weakness, date their commencement from
the time when health was unimpaired. The Christian
alone can discover the cause in the book of God. He
will there find that, through the Divine agency, man
becomes a new creature: old things pass away, and all
things become new. To the transforming influence of
the Holy Spirit alone can we ascribe a change of
sentiment and feeling which human motives would
have been too weak to have effected. The infidel
philosopher may nerve himself to regard with stoic
indifference the approach of death: he may reason
himself into a belief of the worthlessness of those joys
which he has found insufficient to his happiness: but
he cannot, like our christian philosopher, enter into
the feelings, and appreciate the blessings of this world,
and yet resign them joyfully, because there are within
his grasp richer treasures, surpassing honours, purer

joys, which shall never fade, never cloy, but endure for ever and ever. This higher excellence is reserved for him who, justified by faith in Christ, and sanctified by the Spirit, has fought a good fight, has finished his course, and knows that henceforth there is laid up for him a crown which the Lord shall give him in the day of his appearing.

CHAPTER IV.

Residence at Hampstead—Last days and hours—Post-mortem examination—Societies of which he was a member—Catalogue of works.

THE morning after his arrival at Hampstead, Dr. Hope was in almost boyish spirits as he sat down to breakfast in the cheerful drawing-room of the house which he had taken. The view from the window, embracing a rich meadow and a few fine trees, offered no beauty beyond that with which the return of spring clothes every landscape; but he was a passionate admirer of nature in every garb, and he continually expressed his delight at the cheerful prospect which he enjoyed, and his gratitude to the Giver of every good gift for bestowing on him so many blessings.

It is a very common error to suppose that the prospect of death changes the entire character of a man—his tastes, his habits, his desires. Not only is a death-bed regarded as affording the best opportunity to prepare for another world, but it is imagined that, by sudden and undefined transmutation, those feelings which have hitherto been at enmity with God, and devoted to the world, will suddenly change their direction : that the Bible and heavenly things will charm the taste : and that patience, love, and bene-volence will spring unbidden. Experience seldom verifies this expectation. It is true that God's mercy and love know no bounds, and that these divine attributes are occasionally displayed in the reconcili-ation of a sinner even at the eleventh hour. It has been happily remarked, that the occurrence in the Bible of only one such instance, while it forbids any to despair, justifies none in presuming on a dying hour. Daily experience bears out the truth of this observation, and, in general, a man's death cor-responds with his life.

A leading Medical Review headed the publication of the medical paper which Dr. Hope wrote on his death-bed by an observation, that the zeal for science which dictated this paper " was consistent with the character of the man, who died as he had lived, an accomplished physician and a good man." No obser-vation could have been more appropriate. The amount of his occupation was now necessarily limited by his failing powers ; but the desire to turn every moment to account, the eager endeavour to promote general usefulness, at the sacrifice of personal comfort, were still visible in the distribution of his time. With

characteristic method every part of the day had its
allotted employment, and each employment, according
to its relative importance, had its due share of attention. He had such difficulty in swallowing, that
breakfast occupied from one to two hours, and during
the greater part of his meal, Mrs. Hope read to him
several chapters from the Epistles. When he had
been refreshed by a short sleep, he took advantage of
that part of the day when his mental faculties were
clearest, to dictate the two papers which he wrote at
this period. In the afternoon he again listened to
Mrs. Hope while she read the Bible, or some
other religious book. If he felt pretty well, he sat
up for half an hour, and attempted to finish a very
beautiful water-colour drawing of Staffa, which he
had begun the year before, and which Mrs. Hope was
desirous that he should finish, if possible, as a precious
memorial of his great talent for drawing. This picture was a copy, from memory, of one which was
exhibited by Copley Fielding in 1839, and it was
remarkable how well Dr. Hope had succeeded in
carrying off the original in his memory. He succeeded in finishing it with the exception of a few sea
gulls and some lights on the water, and these were
inserted by Mr. Duncan, one of our first painters in
water-colours, who, with great feeling and kindness,
humoured the invalid, and drew under his guidance,
as if he himself had been a novice in the art of which
he is so accomplished a master.

Dr. Hope was obliged to take much opium in order to allay the cough, which, in the inflamed state of the larynx, caused him great pain. Consequently he slept much, and the waking intervals becoming shorter and shorter, he felt the increasing value of time.

He went out occasionally in a Bath chair, but a week before his death, he discontinued this recreation, because " it took up too much time," proposing to resume it when he should have completed some of the work which he then had on hand. A day later he relinquished his drawing, alleging that though he had been anxious to gratify Mrs. Hope by finishing it, yet that he must deem her gratification a consideration of minor weight than the good to be promoted by the completion of the medical paper, and he found that he should not have strength for both. Finally, four days before his death, the medical paper was brought to a close, and, though he had begun another on laryngitis, he would not continue it, because his increasing weakness making him sleep except for a very few hours, he judged that his Bible had the greatest claims for the brief waking intervals. So conscientiously did he, to the very last, weigh all his actions, and so nicely did he discriminate between the gratification of feeling and the welfare of his fellow creatures—between the service of man and that of God!

It has been supposed by some that Dr. Hope's health had suffered from an undue anxiety to advance rapidly in his profession. The foregoing narrative proves that no idea could have been more erroneous. If we see him taking as great pains in the acquirement of general and religious, as of professional, knowledge—if we find him bestowing the same labour on the preparation of a course of lectures which could never increase either his practice or reputation, as on another which would do both—if we perceive him giving the same careful and laborious attention to his numerous hospital patients as to his private ones—if, after his reputation was established, we discover him taking notes of 15,000 cases which could answer no end beyond the advancement of his own knowledge—if, finally, when so reduced by illness as to be unable either to read or write, we behold him devoting the few best hours of his last days to the dictation, not of a brilliant composition which might increase his fame, but of rough and broken notes, in order that others might profit by his experience, and reap the reward of his labours :—if we see all this, we may, perhaps, say that he was too eager in the pursuit of knowledge—too devoted to the alleviation of human suffering—too conscientiously strict in turning every talent to the best account in the service of his Creator; but it can never be believed that he fell a victim to the desire of self-aggrandisement.

After removing to Hampstead he never went out in his carriage but once, and that was to Highgate Cemetery, where he intended to be buried. Without indulging unmeaning fancies on the subject of his interment, he gave directions for it as for any other ordinary affair. Mrs. Hope having hinted the possibility of her attending the funeral, he seized the idea with joy, and eagerly entreated that, provided it did no violence to her feelings, she would be present. Regarding the funeral service as an ordinance of the Church to which he belonged, and was much attached, he deemed it improper to throw disrespect on it by the absence, in conformity with custom or fashion, of female relatives. Entering, too, into the spirit of that beautiful service which the Church designs for the living and not for the dead, he looked upon it as a means of imparting consolation and hope; and he was unwilling that the mere circumstance of her sex should deprive of that consolation and hope, her who would stand most in need of them. So long as a funeral is not made an occasion of display, and is attended only by true mourners, there can be no real impropriety in the presence of female relatives. Indeed, did they more frequently attend, they might possibly be the means of banishing unsuitable pomp from a scene, at which, of all others, it is the greatest outrage to good taste and feeling. Dr. Hope's wish was complied with.

By some Roman Catholic divines consumption has been termed the death of the chosen, because so long a period of preparation is allotted, and because the intellect frequently remains unimpaired amid the crumbling fabric of the body. This sentiment was expressed to Dr. Hope in a letter from a Roman Catholic gentleman. He was much pleased with it, and in his own case it was especially applicable. His intellect remained so clear that even two hours before his death he prescribed for himself, and made observations on his own state. His temper was so sweet and child-like, his faith so simple, his joy and peace so perfect; he was so grateful for all little acts of kindness and attention; so unlike most invalids, who are occupied solely with themselves and their ailments, that it was a most pleasing occupation to attend upon him.

Dr. Latham, the last time he saw him, inquired if he felt quite happy. "Perfectly so," was Dr. Hope's answer. "I have always been a sober-thinking man, and I could not have imagined the joy that I now feel. My only wish is to convey it to the minds of others, but that is impossible. It is such as I could not have conceived possible."

He was particularly anxious to convey a cheerful idea of death, and his own happiness in the prospect of it, to the mind of his son, who was at that age when all impressions sink deep into the mind. He often talked to him of his great gain, and used sometimes to say, "You see, Theodore, what a lucky fellow I am. You have your fortune to make, but mine is ready made for me. I am going to my heavenly inheritance. You know how hard I used to work formerly to get fees for you and mamma, but all that is over now; my toil is at an end."

Immediately after Dr. Hope's death, Mrs. Hope, who was the only witness of the last few days of his life, wrote an account of them for his family. This account possesses the graphic fidelity, which can attach only to the narrative of an eye-witness while the scenes described are fresh in memory, and we therefore transcribe it.

" Sunday, May 9th. He slept much during this day, and in the morning I occupied myself in reading a chapter of the ' Pocket Prayer Book,' which is designed as a preparation for death, and contains several heads of self-examination for a dying person. To these I especially turned my attention, and, as I proceeded, I answered the several questions, to the best of my judgment, in the name of my husband. I gave satisfactory answers to all, except to that which related to repentance for sin. On this subject a painful doubt flashed across my mind, for, though I had frequently heard him insist on the general depravity of human nature, I could not remember to have heard him speak of his own individual sins, and lament them; except on one occasion, when he was, indeed, deeply humbled. On the other hand, he had never been in the habit of speaking much about his inmost feelings; and as I perceived him to enjoy remarkable peace and hope in Christ, I had every reason to suppose that he had experienced that deep conviction of sin, which alone can make a sinner prize Christ as a Saviour. Thus the doubt in my mind was speedily removed, but remembering that it might recur with increased bitterness at some future period, when I should not have the power of clearing it up, I determined to seize the first opportunity of ascertaining the truth from himself. When he awoke, telling him how I had been engaged, and what had been the result, I explained how great would be my satisfaction at hearing him express his feelings on the subject. He looked up for one moment, and then casting down his eyes and his head, he remained silent for a few minutes, during which time deep, strong, and painful emotions apparently struggled in his breast. At length, in a voice scarcely articulate from agitation, he said, ' I always begin my prayers with the mention of my sins, and generally with tears—I always have a deep sense of my own unworthiness. Even now, I find all sorts of worldly thoughts and feelings carrying me away from God, and polluting my mind. I cannot say what a grief this is to me ; and it shows me more than ever, that all my righteousness is but a filthy rag. And when I think, on the one hand, of the numberless offences which I have committed ; and on the other, remember the blessings which I have enjoyed—oh ! it is enough to bow one down to the earth !"—These words are in themselves strong expressions ; but the earnestness and deep feeling with which they were uttered, made them doubly so.

" After an interval, he renewed the conversation of his own accord, and repeated what he had already said.   He added, ' I have often taken a practical chapter of the New Testament, such as the winding up of one of the Epistles, or the sermon on the Mount, and have determined to act up to it during the day; but, alas! I often forgot it altogether, and when I did remember it, how miserably did I fall short of it! This, more than any thing, showed me the original sin in my nature, and threw me on the promises of Christ. I found it was useless to rest too much on details, but I took fast hold upon the grand, leading truth, that Christ is an all-sufficient satisfaction for sin.   I think also that I had a great fear of God, but I feared Him as one fears a parent.'

" On hearing him speak so decidedly, I expressed the pleasure that I derived from it, adding, that when I remembered how fully he had looked to Christ, especially since Christmas 1839, and what peace he had enjoyed in the anticipation of death, I could not think that Christ would have allowed him to remain in error on any vital point.   He immediately answered, ' Long before the time you name, I think I was in the way of salvation—even so long as ten or twelve years ago.   When I attended Mr. Howels' chapel, I learned the saving truths of the Gospel, and, although I was a most imperfect creature, I believe I might have come within the pale of salvation, because I had then the evidence of the Spirit working a change within me.' He explained that by the evidence of the Spirit he meant 'love to the brethren,' zeal for the promotion of Christ's kingdom,' 'an ardent desire to serve Him,' and 'a *craving* to be permitted to be His soldier militant.'

" I remarked that the last feeling had not escaped my notice, and that it had evinced itself in the desire he showed to use his influence and his powers of conversation in the service of Christ. He said that he would have spoken more if he had not felt how insufficient was his knowledge of the subject, and had not feared to do more harm than good. Actuated by this feeling, he had not always intruded the subject; but when he had spoken, he had done it in a bold and uncompromising manner. After some further conversation, he added, ' I cannot express my grief and humiliation at not having been able to keep my attention fixed at church. If Satan had a malicious or wicked thought to suggest, he chose that time. An exciting sermon might, indeed, rouse my attention; but, the prayers—oh!—the prayers. And when I think of the blessings that I have enjoyed, is it not enough to grind me down to the dust!' He then spoke with much warmth and gratitude of the many blessings that had been vouchsafed to him. He noticed that though God had not thought fit to give him affluence, yet he had always had enough. He dwelt with special interest on the large share of intellectual enjoyment that had been granted him—

more he believed than to most men—and ' this blessing ought to be taken into account.' He next turned
to his great professional success, and here the conversation, which was beginning to be discursive, was
terminated by the entrance of Mr. Evans, surgeon, of
Hampstead, who very kindly called on him from time
to time. The whole had been uttered with deep
emotion and much solemnity.

"On Monday, finding him much weaker, I said,
' I think that one week will do great things for you.'
' Do you think so, indeed?' answered he, very quickly,
and with a radiant smile; ' Very well, whenever God
pleases, be it soon or be it late, so that I go off in such
a way as not to frighten you. I think, however, that
you are very much mistaken. I must get weaker yet,
and take to my bed.' On this day a cast of his face
was taken, and he did not complain of fatigue in consequence.

" On Wednesday morning he was much weaker, and
I said that I thought my words in about a week would
come true. ' Do you mean about my dying in a week?'

" ' Yes,' I answered.

" ' I think it is very likely, as this *tugging* at my
chest is very distressing, and gives me a sensation of
faintness.'

" His departure, and all the tokens of its approach,
were constant subjects of our conversation; and one
never feared to depress him by noticing the progress
of his disease. The effect was always the contrary:

and, as I had never been with an invalid, he frequently called my attention to the symptoms of declining strength, and commented on them medically.

" During this day he was very restless, but betrayed no symptom of impatience. His bed could not be made to his satisfaction, but he seemed to be perfectly aware that this arose from his own feverish state. Instead of evincing annoyance at the repeated failures to promote his comfort, he only praised the patience of the attendants in making and re-making it so often. The most common services were exaggerated by his grateful spirit into acts of extraordinary kindness, and he frequently lamented the trouble which he feared that he was giving to all around him. He slept during almost the whole day; waking, however, every ten minutes or so, and asking me to read to him. This I did, first from the Bible, and then from ' Leighton on St. Peter.' As soon as I began he fell asleep, but, whenever he awoke he regretted that he had not heard anything, and begged me to ' give him another trial. He had often said that, though unable to follow the connected thread of my reading, he never failed to pick up what furnished him with delightful meditations.

" It was evident that he was worse, but neither of us apprehended any immediate danger. When awake he continued, however, to take an interest in our ordinary occupations. He directed me to put some lights into a drawing which I had finished some months before ; and even so late as half-past six o'clock he told me to put up his own drawing of Staffa, in order that he might look at it.

"At half-past eleven at night, the thermometer having fallen considerably, I shut the window, and told him my reason. In a minute he called me to his bed-side, told me to keep a good fire for myself, but to open all the windows and doors *as much as I could bear*. He then complained of great embarrassment in his respiration, and expressed a doubt whether he should get through the night.

" I made some parting observations. He rejoined, ' I will not make speeches ; but I have two things to say.' The first was an affectionate farewell to myself. In reply, I reminded him of the superior satisfaction which he possessed of having promoted my happiness, not only in this world, but, also, as I trusted, in the world to come.

" He answered meekly, ' It was not I.'

" Here he was interrupted by coughing. When he was again quiet, I reminded him that he had another thing to say, and begged him to take the earliest opportunity of doing so. He then added,

" ' The second is soon said. Christ is all in all to me. I have no hope except in Him. He is, indeed, all in all.'

" I quoted, ' Though I walk through the valley of the shadow of death, I will fear no evil: for thou art with me ; thy rod and thy staff they comfort me.'

" He said, ' They *do* comfort me. There is no darkness. I see Jordan, and the heavenly Joshua passing over dry-shod.'

" Throughout the night, when awake, he was perfectly calm and collected. At his request I read the fifteenth chapter of 1st Corinthians, and, at a later period, he begged me to repeat texts, which I did from time to time. He frequently asked whether I was cold or tired, made inquiries as to whether I was adequately clothed, and proved, in various ways, that he retained his faculties, and his characteristic solicitude for others. He also directed me what medicines to give him, how to prepare them, altering the quantities, and making medical observations from time to time on his state.

" At ten minutes to two, he said, ' You see it will not do,' and repeatedly urged me to go to bed, ' as I must be tired ;' promising to waken me when he came to the last.

" At ten minutes past three he left a parting message for Theodore, directing him always to pray to God.

" He then begged me not to make him speak, as it would cause him to go sooner. A minute after, he said in a quick, lively tone and with a smile of joy,

" ' I am going now. I shall soon sleep.'

" ' And you will wake again.'

" ' Yes.'

" I quoted, ' Those which sleep in Jesus will God bring with him.'

" ' He will.'

" Thinking he was going immediately, I said, ' Lord Jesus, receive his spirit.'

" This he repeated after me three or four times, and also some other things, of which I only caught the words, ' God,' ' Christ,' ' Triumph.'

" Day beginning to dawn, he looked out of the window, and I remarked,

" ' What a glorious day is dawning on you, my dearest.'

" He assented with a look of joy.

" I said, ' There will be no sun and no moon there, for the Lamb will be the light thereof.'

" Looking fixedly before him, he murmured ' Christ,' ' angels,' ' beautiful,' ' magnificent,' ' delightful ;' and then turning to me with a look as if re-assuring me, ' Indeed it is.'

" At one time he said, ' This suffering is little to what Christ suffered on the cross.'

" I quoted, ' But our light affliction, which is but for a moment, worketh for us a far more exceeding and eternal weight of glory ; while we look not at the things which are seen, but at the things which are not seen : for the things which are seen are temporal ; but the things which are not seen are eternal.'

" A few minutes after he said, ' I thank God,' and these were the last connected words which he spoke.

" I also said several texts, to which he assented, either by word or sign. I continued to do so at intervals, so long as he breathed, but he soon ceased to respond, though he must have heard them, as he gave the following sign of consciousness.

" At ten minutes past four, being tired of standing, I removed to the opposite side, and sat down on the bed. He missed me immediately, and following the sound of my voice as I continued repeating texts, turned his head with great effort towards me, and, grasping my hand, gave me a dying look.

" His hold relaxed almost immediately, and he gave no further sign of consciousness, except occasionally turning his eyes to me. He continued to breathe till twenty-three minutes past four, when he slept in Jesus."

The foregoing narrative requires no further comment than that which is furnished by the Psalmist. " Mark the perfect man, and behold the upright : for the end of that man is peace." That clearness of intellect which enabled him to exercise his professional knowledge to the very last, attests that his remarkable joy and bright anticipations of the glory into which he was entering, were not the result of delirium and decaying strength ; while, in contemplating the delightful manifestations of Divine support to the dying saint, we may take comfort from the assurance that his God is our God for ever and ever, and will, if we desire it, be our guide even unto death.

During Dr. Hope's residence at Hampstead, he had received the ministerial visits of the Reverend J. Ayre, minister of St. John's Chapel, Hampstead, from which he derived much comfort. On receiving the particulars of Dr. Hope's death, Mr. Ayre wrote the following letter to Mrs. Hope.

"MY DEAR MADAM,   May 24th, 1841.

"I thank you very much for the most interesting account that you have given me of Dr. Hope's last hours, and I also thank God that he so graciously supports you under your trial, and enables you to rejoice in the testimony your beloved husband gave to the power and faithfulness of the Redeemer. You have, indeed, strong consolation. You have seen how death, to the believer, is a conquered foe, and your own hope and humble confidence in Christ will be established.   *   *   *   *   *

*   *   *   *   *   *   *

"It is needless for me to add any confirmation of mine to the evidence you have in regard to Dr. Hope; but I can truly say that I was much struck with the perfect calmness with which he contemplated the approach of death. He let me, at once, distinctly see that he was trusting entirely to the merits of the Saviour, and he evinced a peace, which I never saw exceeded, in the assurance that, even to his last hour, that Saviour would not leave nor forsake him. He told me how long he had, from his medical knowledge, been aware that his disease must terminate fatally. The tender affection with which he regarded you, was, he said, his strongest tie to earth; but he could trust you, when he was taken from you, in the hands of a kind Father. He mentioned to me one or two matters in which he was pleased to find that my opinion coincided with his own; and he added, that he should put away further thoughts respecting them: he had done with this world for ever: the days of his appointed time he would patiently wait till his blessed change should come. There was no excitement, not the slightest tinge of enthusiasm in his manner or expressions; but just that meek and holy calm which evidences a spirit at peace with God, through the blood of the eternal covenant. I dwell on these details, my dear Madam, for, believe me, they are very pleasant and refreshing to my own mind. So frequently are ministers called on to attend in a sick chamber, where they see more reason to fear than to hope, that it is a blessed encouragement to them to behold, from time to time, the power of Divine grace smoothing the bed of death, and the sheep of Christ's flock peacefully and joyfully gathered into the immortal fold. The last evening I saw Dr. Hope, I read to him the twenty-third psalm. That, he said, was one of his favourite meditations: he loved to look at Christ in the character of a shepherd; the good shepherd who gave his life for his sheep; and he expressed his simple trust that he should, indeed, find, while traversing the valley of the shadow of death, His rod and His staff to comfort him.   *   *   *   *

*   *   *   *   *   *   *

" I congratulate you, my dear Madam, while I sympathize with you, and pray for you, that you, too, washed in the Redeemer's blood, may, one day, rejoin him from whom you are now parted : oh, it is but for a little—a very little while—among the blessed company of saints made perfect. Sorrow not then, as those that have no hope ; receive meekly the stroke with which it has pleased God to visit you, and it will yield you the peaceable fruit of righteousness. Believe me, my dear Madam,

" Your's, very faithfully,

" J. AYRE.'

Dr. Hope's will commenced by expressing an opinion that a physician should set a good example in causing his body to be opened, and, therefore, he directed that a post-mortem examination should be made ; and, in case there should be any specimens worth preserving, the medical men employed should be at liberty to make any use of them they might think fit for the benefit of science, merely suppressing his name.

An examination was accordingly made by Alexander Shaw, Esquire, surgeon to the Middlesex Hospital, under the direction of Dr. Latham and Dr. Watson, and the following was the result.

Upon examination of the body of Dr. Hope, thirty-two hours after death, the following morbid appearances were found :

" The epiglottis was thickened, and the membrane, covering the arytenoid cartilages, was rough and slightly ulcerated. The internal lining of the larynx exhibited numerous small points of superficial ulceration, mixed with minute granular depositions.

" The lungs adhered extensively to the pleura on both sides. The adhesions were chiefly at the posterior part, except in the situation of the upper lobes, of which a small portion only in front was left free. The adhesion of the upper lobe, on the left side, was so strong, that, in the attempt to separate it, a large cavity was ruptured. This cavity had evidently been formed by several smaller cavities running into one. This was the only cavity found in the left lung; but it was everywhere so thickly beset with small granular tubercles, that not the smallest particle was free from them. It was also throughout loaded with blood and serum.

" The upper lobe of the right side contained four large separate cavities, and several smaller ones. The rest of this lung was as largely beset with granular tubercles as the other, and equally loaded with blood and serum.

" The heart was flaccid; the liver was healthy, but

loaded with blood; and the gall-bladder was much distended with bile.

"P. M. LATHAM, M.D.
THOMAS WATSON, M.D.
ALEXANDER SHAW."

On the 18th of May, 1841, Dr. Hope's mortal remains were deposited in the cemetery at Highgate.

The details of the foregoing Memoir copiously illustrate the general features of Dr. Hope's character. Thinking, however, that a sketch drawn by a professional friend, who had been associated with him in habits of the closest intimacy, and relating to the period of his studies in Edinburgh, might not be devoid of interest, we have printed in the Appendix a letter from Dr. Julius, of Richmond, to Mrs. Hope.

In June, 1832, Dr. Hope was elected a Fellow of the Royal Society.

On the 5th of August, 1839, he was made a corresponding Member of " La Sociedad Medica de Emulacion de Guadalajara."

On the 2nd April, 1839, he was made a corresponding Member of the "Kaiserliche Königliche Gesellschaft der Ærzte in Wien."

Diplomas were also sent him from several French societies, but as these were not gratuitous honours, like the preceding, he never attached any weight to them, and none of the diplomas, except that of " La Société Statistique," can be found among his papers.

The Medical and Physical Society of Bombay passed a vote that their transactions should be regularly sent to Dr. Chambers and Dr. Hope, and as the list of their members includes none but those who belong to the East India Company's service, this vote was the greatest honour which they could confer.

Dr. Hope was also an Extraordinary Member of the Royal Medical Society of Edinburgh, of which he had formerly been President.

It was not till July, 1840, that he was elected Fellow of the London College of Physicians, and this diploma bears a later date than any of his others. He felt much disposed to decline an honour which he did not consider as such when given so tardily. On second thoughts he accepted it; saying, that it was not worth refusing, and he did not wish to make enemies of a body of men, which comprised some of his kindest personal friends. At the commencement of the year 1841, he was appointed to deliver the Gulstonian Lectures at the College of Physicians in the following May; but foreseeing what would be the state of his health, he declined the honour.

The only other society to which Dr. Hope ever belonged, was a small private one, called the Harveian, of which he had been one of the Presidents, but which he quitted many years before his death.

The Works published by Dr. Hope, during his life, were :—

1. Dissertatio Medica Inauguralis de Aortæ Aneurismate. *Edinburgi*, 8vo., 1825.

2. A Treatise on the Diseases of the Heart and Great Vessels. *London*, 8vo. The first edition of this work appeared in 1831 ; and the third, in 1839.

3. Principles and Illustrations on Morbid Anatomy. *London*, 8vo. This came out in parts, and was completed in 1834.

4. The following articles in the Cyclopædia of Practical Medicine :

> Aorta, Aneurism of.
> Arteritis.
> Dilatation of the Heart.
> Heart, Diseases of the.
> Heart, Fatty and Greasy Degeneration of the.
> Hypertrophy of the Heart.
> Palpitation.
> Pericarditis and Carditis.
> Valves of the Heart, Diseases of.

5. The article Inflammation of the Brain, in the Library of Medicine.

6. The following papers in the Medical Gazette :—

> On the Diagnosis of Aneurisms of the Aorta, by General and Stethoscopic Signs. August 22nd and 29th, September 5th and 12th, 1829.

Strictures on an essay by Dr. Corrigan, on the Motion and Sounds of the Heart. July 31st and August 31st, 1830.

Experiments and Clinical Researches on the Physiology of the Heart's action. September 18th, 1830.

Refutation of the Various objections to Dr. Hope's Theory of the Action of the Heart. December 25th, 1830.

On the Connexion of Apoplexy and Palsy with Organic Disease of the Heart. February 28th, 1835. (Read before the College of Physicians.)

A reply to Drs. Graves and Stokes' Remarks on Dr. Hope, in Reference to Auscultation. October 1838.

On the Diagnosis of Diseased Valves. March 16th, 1839.

The following papers have been published posthumously :—

1. Remarks on Chronic Pleurisy. Printed, *extra limites*, in the sixty-ninth number of the Medico-Chirurgical Review. This was written by Dr. Hope after he retired from practice, and finished only four days before his death.

2. Remarks on the Pulse in Diseases of the Heart. Medical Gazette of May 20th and 27th, 1842.

3. Remarks on Classical Education. Written after he retired from practice, and appended to the present Memoir.

REMARKS

ON

CLASSICAL EDUCATION.

BY JAMES HOPE, M.D. F.R.S.

It has long been known by metaphysicians, and
has been equally noticed by a class of philosophers
who certainly have the merit of very close and accurate observation, (I allude to the phrenologists,) that
the faculties of man are developed, not simultaneously,
but in succession; and it has been agreed that this
successive development is the mode best calculated to
bring the intellect of man to its highest state of cultivation. The order of development is regulated according to the wants of the several periods of life.
Thus, in the earliest period, it was requisite that the
infant should, as speedily as possible, become acquainted with language, and the external phenomena
of nature. Accordingly, the faculties of observation,
memory, and attention, to which, perhaps, curiosity
may be added, are developed in the highest degree.

These continue in operation, though with some varia-
tion in their respective powers, through the long period
during which it is necessary that the mind should
acquire stores of facts, and knowledge of every kind,
eventually to become the subject of the operation of
the higher intellectual powers.

These latter powers are developed rather late, and
there are differences, perhaps, in different individuals.
Some boys exhibit incipient powers of reflection, cau-
sation, analysis, synthesis, comparison, discrimination,
and judgment, at the age of thirteen or fourteen, but,
in general, these powers are feeble until some years
later.   In all cases, however, these intellectual faculties are progressively developed—in this respect differ-
ing widely from the perfect, and, as it were, instinctive
development of the faculties of childhood; and they
never attain their full perfection until the period of
manhood.

This subject has a very important bearing on education, in reference to health, and its consideration,
therefore, falls within the province of a physician;
not only as a philosopher, who is bound to scruti-
nize all the remote causes of deterioration of the
public health, but as a practitioner, to whom such
applications as the following are perpetually made by
parents :—" At what age shall my child begin to learn
to read ?"   " When shall he go to school ?"   " What
may he study without fear of injury ?"   " When may
he begin Latin, Greek, &c. ?"   For most parents are

aware that if education be improperly conducted the health may be impaired. Were we not acquainted with the order in which the faculties are developed, and with the object of that order, we should have great difficulty in answering these questions. But we we can now answer confidently, in general terms, that if those faculties only are exercised by education which nature has in the fullest operation at the time, and if that exercise be not carried to fatiguing excess, no injury to the health will be sustained, since we are only doing nature's own work, slightly modifying the direction of it. If, on the contrary, we attempt to anticipate the order of nature, and to draw out faculties which do not yet naturally exist, the utmost detriment to the health, no less than to the future intellectual powers, may be expected to occur. The case of the precocious child will at once suggest itself to the mind of every parent. A child exhibits considerable talent, as it is supposed, and, perhaps, a great propensity to reading. It is decided to be a little genius. Undue efforts are made to cultivate its mental powers, and this cultivation is not confined to the faculties proper to youth, but as it occasionally exhibits reasoning powers, every effort is made to cultivate these ; or, in short, more or less of the class of intellectual powers. The mind is now strained, the general health is impaired, and he who was so bright at nine or ten, is stupid or an idiot when he comes to maturity.　　　　　　　　　　7

Assuming these facts to be true, what, then, are the principles on which early education can be safely and efficiently conducted ?

Let us first examine how nature manages this matter, and let us take the instance of learning a language. You place a child with a French nurse, who cannot speak English. The child gradually picks up a number of words, and ascertains their meaning by the corresponding signs and actions of the nurse. His progress is daily more and more perceptible, and in a year, or less, he begins to chatter French very prettily. Now do we stop this, exclaiming that the child is learning too many words, with their meaning, and that he will never be a sound French scholar unless he immediately learn the grammar ? We do no such thing, but let him proceed and acquire the utmost facility in speaking the language that he is capable of, until he has attained the age of seven or eight, when a simple grammar may be put into his hands. Does he find the acquisition of the principles of this grammar more difficult from his previous knowledge of the language ? Certainly not. On the contrary, he finds it greatly expedited; for in every article, substantive, adjective, verb, he recognises an old acquaintance. And when he meets a rule, he readily understands and recollects it, because the examples illustrative of it are already familiar to his mind. In short, the grammar, so far from being a dry and irksome task, is comparatively easy, and even interesting.

Now we never hear of a child's health being injured from his learning French from a French nurse. Nature's mode is, therefore, perfectly safe, and for the simple reason that no faculties are called into operation, but those in full vigour at the time; namely, observation, curiosity, and the extraordinary memory for words which children possess, independent of reflection. It is, properly speaking, the memory of the ear.

Let us next examine the mode in which Latin was taught, according to what was called the old-school-system—a system which boasted that it gave a strong foundation and great superiority of accuracy, and which has only of very late years gone out of repute. At the age of seven or eight, a boy began Latin. Nothing like nature's process was adopted. There was no preliminary teaching of words and their meaning. The boy began with his Eton grammar, and learned this by puny fragments at a time, and much like a parrot, as he was generally left to do all for himself without explanations. This most dry and irksome task might have gone on for a year or more, by which time he might possibly have gone through the syntax, nominally construing it, but really understanding little or nothing of it. A Delectus is now put into his hands, and he is told to learn so many lines, perhaps five or six. But how is he to do this? The art of construing is the most difficult part of the language. He has been given no instructions respecting the order

P

in which words come in a sentence, and respecting
the, to him, irregular position of Latin words. He is
expected to know this from having learned grammar,
because the syntax says that the nominative comes
first, the verb next, the accusative after that, and so
on. But, unfortunately for him, the grammar was
only an unintelligible jargon. How then, I repeat, is
he to construe ? It can only be accomplished by a
powerful action of the higher intellectual faculties,
analysis, comparison, judgment, &c. But these faculties are not in existence at that early age ! The result,
therefore, is what might be anticipated. The child returns to his master—after turning out all the words in a
dictionary, and selecting the wrong meanings to a
great majority—incapable of translating a line. After
all, he has to be taught the whole. But never mind,
this tends to constitute " a strong foundation and
superior accuracy." The same process has only to be
repeated day after day, and the happy result will show
itself at last. This is not nature's mode of teaching,
for memory and the observing faculties are scarcely
called into operation. Meanwhile what is the effect
on the boy's health and spirits ? He hates Latin, and
entreats his parents to let him leave it off. He ar-
raigns the Romans for folly in not putting the words
straight forward as they are in English. He dreads
the hour when he has to go to his construing, and
still more when he has to appear before his master, to
undergo a suitable objurgation for not having done

that which was impracticable. His spirits become depressed. He is overwhelmed by a sort of calamity, and his general health, not unfrequently, becomes sensibly impaired. In this way, boys linger on almost interminably in the lower schools. It sometimes happens that an usher of superior capacity and intelligence greatly improves this state of things, but I speak of the average; and it will generally be found that boys, at the age of eleven or twelve, are incapable of construing the easiest books with any facility. A further evil attends this system. When boys are placed together in classes, it occasionally happens that one or two have more talent, or are more advanced, than the rest. These boys learn to construe the lesson, and, for fear that they, in common with the whole class, should suffer from the ignorance of the others, they construe the lesson to the class before going up. Henceforth, therefore, all the attempts by the others to learn construing for themselves, are abandoned. Such boys would eventually come under the head-master alone at the age of fourteen or fifteen, and would then be rapidly pushed through a number of the best books; but it is too late to acquire any considerable amount of well-digested knowledge, and after all, they would go to the universities at best but crude, indifferent scholars, often incapable of any honours. I have observed, indeed, that the boys who do take honours are very rarely the alumni of the public school itself, but others who, at the age of thirteen or fourteen,

have come from preparatory schools, with their minds
and memories much better stored, and, perhaps, specifically prepared to take a particular class, form, or
position in the school. A striking instance, on the
largest scale, of the total failure, at the universities, of
the old school-system, has been presented by the
Charter House since 1825. Scarcely anything but
grammar, exercises, and verses, was done up to the
age of fourteen, when few could construe Virgil and
Homer, from mere ignorance of the meaning of
words, and the choice years for verbal memory were
gone by. While myself residing near Charter House
Square, as a student of St. Bartholomew's Hospital, I
had full knowledge of the facts, as a number of my
young friends were pupils at the school.

Let us now contrast with this slow, irksome, injurious, and abortive school-system, what we will call the
" *natural system*," because nature adopts it in teaching young children.

No Latin and Greek *bonnes*, or nurses, unfortunately are to be had; nor has the master time to
officiate entirely as their substitute. What is to be
done? A literal translation is the only alternative,
and this answers the purpose almost as well as can be
desired. I fear to mention the word Hamiltonian
translation, as disrepute has, not without cause,
attached to this system, in consequence of its having
professed to teach Latin thoroughly, instead of being
a mere stepping-stone, preliminary, almost, to the

serious commencement of Latin. However, as there are few others which are literal, these may be used, care being taken not to abuse them.

About a year or so before the child would properly begin Latin, let one of these books be put into his hands. The Gospel of St. John, the first Hamiltonian book, is, perhaps, objectionable, as being a portion of the Bible. "Historiæ Sacræ" answers very well. In a week or two he will learn to translate word for word, half a page, and may say his lesson to his mother, or any one not acquainted with Latin. In three or four weeks more, he will do a page, and eventually two pages. Half an hour a day, at one or at two lessons, is abundance; as great care should be taken not to fatigue the attention of a young child. At the end of a year, he will have gone two or three times through the book, and, such is the extraordinary memory for words at this age, that the child will generally be able to give the English to any Latin word named, and will often quote the passage in which it occurs. I may take this opportunity of remarking, that this memory is independent of reflection; it is a memory, as it were, of the ear, singularly strong in early infancy and boyhood, sensibly diminishing towards the age of ten or eleven, and becoming so feeble at manhood, that the acquisition of words and abstract facts then becomes very irksome. As an illustration of this memory of the ear, there are persons, advanced in years, who have utterly forgotten both Latin and Greek, yet can repeat whole passages of both. Any one, indeed, who has in early life been in the habit of learning verses, may satisfy himself that, in later years, he repeats by the ear; as he can do this without any effort of the memory, or attention, and can even repeat them while thinking of something else. There is, undoubtedly, also a memory of the eye, to which I shall advert later, when speaking of geography, &c.

To return from this digression. A boy learning the book named, Historiæ Sacræ, meets with nearly 20,000 Latin words. I leave each to form his own opinion as to how many should be deducted for repetition of the same words; but I think it probable that the total number of words learned would amount to three or four thousand. Now, this is no contemptible vocabulary for a boy to have acquired in a year, and with absolutely no strain on his intellect. He now seriously begins Latin, that is, the grammar, and, of course, the Eton. On being put to learn the articles, substantives, &c., he finds these to be old acquaintances, and chuckles to discover that their inflections are quite familiar to him. A very little explanation suffices to make the meaning of the cases intelligent to him, because he has types of most of them in his mind. He, therefore, learns with cheerfulness, and even pleasure. The same may be said of the remainder of the grammar. It is not a dry task committed to memory like a parrot, for, from his

previous knowledge, he finds it, with a little explanation, more or less intelligible throughout. I shall
here digress again for a few minutes for the purpose
of explaining the most expeditious and efficient mode
of learning the grammar. This is, by invoking the
aid of frequent repetition, at short intervals, before the
first recollection has failed. This constitutes, as the
late Dr. Butler, of Shrewsbury, practically said, the
pith of the art of teaching and learning. The boy
should go over the substantives alone, six, eight, or
even ten times in succession, until he can do the
whole with the greatest readiness, either backwards or
forwards, indifferently from the English or the Latin,
and understands equally the intermediate remarks
This is done expeditiously, because the latter repetitions require very little learning. Netwithstanding
that the substantives have been thus *completely* learned
for the time, they will fade from the memory, even
several times over; but still the impression on the
memory will be incomparably stronger than if the
same number of repetitions had been made in the
usual way, *viz.*, of going so many times straight
through the grammar; in addition to which, the
latter process is incomparably slower, as the second
repetition scarcely receives any assistance from recollection of the first, and so on, though in a diminishing
degree, through the remainder of the ten. The
adjectives should be treated in the same way. The
pronouns require even more repetitions, and the verbs

still more. The latter should not be left until the boy can be dodged in every conceivable direction, and until he thoroughly understands the principle and formation of the several tenses. This may generally be accomplished in from nine to twelve repetitions. The irregular verbs will require rather less attention; and the defective verbs may perhaps be omitted at the first going over.

As to syntax, twenty or thirty only of the leading rules should be selected; since nearly half the rules are scarcely ever used in actual parsing, and they, therefore, would, at this early period, be a useless encumbrance on the memory. The twenty or thirty should be thoroughly learned by the same mode of repetition, and equally in English and in Latin. At a later period, additional rules may be added as required.

A boy may, to my knowledge, learn this amount of grammar, that is, up to the end of the useful rules, in less than a year, and even be able to repeat the whole from one end to the other with tolerable success; whereas, the old-school system would have required several years for the accomplishment of the same object. The Hamiltonian process should be carried on during the whole of this time, but in a book of better style, as Cesar, or Cornelius Nepos, though the latter is rather too difficult, were his elegance not a temptation.

Meantime, the boy should not have been wholly

unoccupied with translation. After the verbs have been learned, a Delectus may be put into his hands. The exercises, up to the end of the verbs, may be dispensed with, as his previous exercitations on those parts have superseded the necessity for their use. He may proceed to construe the short sentences. It has already been shown, that construing is the most difficult part in the acquisition of the language; that a boy cannot learn it wholly for himself, because that requires the intervention of the higher intellectual powers, which are as yet undeveloped. He must be *taught* to construe, and this can easily be accomplished. Let him take his book to his master and begin, or try. The master will tell him that, with the exception of any little adverb or particle, the nominative comes first in the sentence; that the verb comes next; that the accusative follows, and so on. The boy tries, and finds sense to come out of his sentence. If their be two words looking like nominatives, as a feminine in *a*, and a neuter plural in *a*, he tells him to examine the verb and see with which word it agrees in number and person, that word being the nominative. He explains, with reference to the position of words in a sentence, that a verb may generally be looked for either at the end of a sentence, or towards the beginning (the special reason for which it is yet premature to explain); and adds, that the word governed is generally placed before the word that governs it. He also explains, that in a sentence comprising several clauses, the boy may often diminish the complexity by postponing to translate parenthetic clauses, isolated by a comma, on each side, until he has done the direct or primary sentence. He likewise explains particular idioms and elegances, and gives him the correct meaning, whether primary or figurative, of every word which he does not know. He subdivides all compound words into their primitives, and explains the force of particles, prepositions in composition, thus rendering the acquisition of words much more easy, and their meanings more definite. He also carefully explains the difference between allied words, as paries, murus, mœnia. By gradually developing a variety of rules of this kind, and practising the boy upon them by cautious leading questions; by then sending him to learn the whole over again by himself, and by making him finally repeat it as a lesson, with a proportion of parsing, as about three lines for every ten construed, together with any remarkable words, or any bearing directly on the grammar recently learned, he will enable him to construe Delectus—a decidedly difficult book—with considerable ease, in the brief space of six or eight months.

It must be distinctly understood that each of these lessons must be learned by the boy with the utmost attainable degree of precision and accuracy. Here the master shows himself. If he be indulgent or slovenly, the boy will rely on being assisted, and will not concentrate his attention. But if the master turn down often, and connive at no mistakes, the boy will likewise be attentive and accurate, for accuracy cannot exist without attention. This latter quality, it is needless to say, is at the very foundation of talent, both in boy and man. In the genius it bears the name of concentration, and no man can be a genius without it.

Let us now, for a moment, compare the results of a single lesson done in the manner above described, with one done by a boy on the old school-system. The former is put in possession of the entire knowledge of the master on ten lines, including the teaching of words and the time of turning to a dictionary saved. This knowledge is, by repetition, so impressed on his mind, that it does not easily fade, and he imbibes no mistakes to unlearn again. The pupil of the old school, on the contrary, leaves five or six lines only, loses half his time in blundering with a dictionary, and acquires no more than he can puzzle out for himself at a period when he has no powers of reflection and excogitation—plus so much information as the varying talents of the usher, under the favourable circumstances, perhaps, of a large class, can impart. The result of such a comparison is almost too obvious to require comment.

There are, however, it must clearly be understood, limitations to this system of a boy's being taught his lesson by his master. When the master discovers that he can translate the simple book in hand with perfect facility, he then directs him to learn his lesson by

himself, and say it to him in the usual manner. But
if the boy be promoted to a higher and more difficult
book, as, for instance, to a poet (Ovid's Metamorphoses), the same process of being taught by the
master must be resumed, as the master can explain
to him that the stringent necessities of versification
render the prose arrangement of words impracticable;
that the verb must not be looked for towards the end
or beginning of the sentence; that the word governed
must not necessarily be expected before the word that
governs it, and so on: consequently that he must
depend almost entirely on a good knowledge of grammar and parsing, in order to discover the arrangement
of the words by their governments. He will also
explain a variety of other little circumstances and
devices peculiar to verse, which no ingenuity of a
boy could possibly excogitate. The boy may continue
to be taught the Metamorphoses by the master till he
can construe them with little difficulty: when another
and more difficult book may be substituted; and this
plan may be continued in successive books, so that the
boy shall always be learning some *one* book direct
from the master until he has attained the age of ten
and a half or eleven, or, in other words, until the
master find him in possession of such a stock of words,
and such a knowledge of the principles of construing,
both prose and verse, that his further assistance
becomes superfluous. It is obvious that this plan of
being taught by the master is equally applicable to a

class, as to an individual; as each boy would say a little, one would assist another, and the master's explanations would serve for all.

With respect to the selection of books for children, I am far from thinking this a matter of so much indifference as is commonly supposed. They learn words and phrases by the memory of the ear, independently of reflection, as already explained. They will therefore pick up exactly such a vocabulary and phraseology as is presented to them. I have witnessed a child change its pronunciation and much of its phraseology thrice, under three different foreign nurses. It is desirable, therefore, that boys should be confined to the best models of the Augustan age, if these can supply a sufficient number of easy books for the earliest studies,—which they certainly can be made to do by the selection of easy passages. The same remark applies to books of exercises, the examples of which may always be thus selected. Ellis's Exercises are admirable in this respect, as they are exclusively from Cicero, and the best selections. Thus, at the age of twelve, a boy's mind is stored with nothing but elegant Latinity—well-selected words, and the best phrases, idioms, and modes of expression. How important this is with reference to the all-engrossing subject of writing elegant Latin, at a later period, needs no comment.

It must now be stated that, in order to conduct even this *natural* mode of study with ease to the boy, and therefore perfect impunity to his health, it is absolutely necessary that his lessons be numerous rather than long: that they be diversified, and that the easy and attractive be judiciously intermixed with the more difficult. If we sit and watch a-child of four or five years old, making its own observations about a room, we notice that it does not dwell long on any one object, but roams quickly from one to another. The same obtains, though in a gradually decreasing degree, with boys. They require variety, and if the attention be restricted too long to a small number of subjects, it becomes wearied and enfeebled, instead of exercised and invigorated. It is of the utmost importance to obtain the opposite result, as it has already been stated that the power of commanding the attention is at the foundation of all knowledge. Let us take, for instance, the three hours of study which, at most schools, intervene between nine and twelve o'clock, and which is a considerable time during which to maintain the attention steadily fixed. The most difficult Latin lesson of the day might take precedence, while the faculties are fresh and vigorous after breakfast and the play which generally succeeds it. Let a Greek lesson, which is easier than Latin, follow this, and let it be the easier of the two Greek lessons of the day. Let the mind now be relieved by a transition to a totally different subject; for instance, a lesson on some branch of natural philosophy, as mechanics, astronomy, &c., subjects which children usually delight in and pick up with avidity.* A lesson of history may finish the morning. A boy, knowing that he has these four lessons to do, will so measure his time as to get each into its proper place, which, of itself, involves an act of sustained attention—it is working against time; and the decreasing difficulty of each lesson, and their increasing attractiveness, would amuse rather than weary his mind, and make the whole a pleasure instead of a toil. The same general plan will obtain before breakfast and after dinner; and with these precautions, a boy will bear with impunity six hours of work per day, exclusive of about an hour out of school, devoted to learning by heart and other preparation for the next day. Latin verses are particularly difficult, and therefore disagreeable to boys. Two sense verses per day, increased to four, according to the boy's facility, will generally suffice to teach them adequately before a boy goes to a public school. The principal supposed use of Ovid's epistles is to teach versification, but I doubt whether it is of much use to little boys, as the beautiful point and antithesis of that elegant writer are scarcely perceptible to the youthful faculties.

I think that the labours of the day ought to com-

---

* When boys have reached the age of nine, easy books on the subjects, avoiding technical terms, are not desirable; for, as these terms must sooner or later be learned, the sooner the better, as the ear picks them up more easily at this age than later. Joyce's scientific Dialogues is one of the best works of the kind that can be used.

mence at six o'clock in the morning, so as to terminate by four or five in the afternoon, and that nothing should be done in the evening but voluntary work, as both body and mind are now fatigued from play as well as study, and the faculties are incapable of further action without being strained.

I lately had the pleasure of conversing with a highly intelligent lady, who has long maintained a well-earned reputation for educating boys from the age of six to ten, or occasionally eleven, with unparalleled success, not only in Latin and Greek, but in all departments of general education.   I inquired whether, on a boy's first beginning to construe Latin, she left him to do it for himself, or taught him any rules of constructing by assisting him orally at the beginning. She replied, that she left him to do it for himself.   Why ? Because she had already taught him the grammar so thoroughly that he was in possession of the information required ; also that she should not have time to teach all the boys ; finally, that it was requisite to make them depend a good deal on themselves, in order to fix their atten-tion ; " but," she smartly subjoined, " I do not do the same with Greek."   " What then ?"   " I tell them every thing, absolutely every thing ; they recollect it, and they come to say it to me as a lesson."   " And why do you adopt this system in Greek and not in Latin ?"   " Because my boys generally leave me at the age of ten, and there is not time to teach them the grammar first.   But I can assure you that they often go away, knowing as much Greek as boys of eleven or more. You would be surprised how rapidly they learn it." Thus, the zeal of this lady that her boys should leave her well qualified in Greek, had actually induced her to take upon herself the task of a literal translation, with which, as I have observed, the learning of languages is most naturally and most successfully commenced. This practical result to which so intelligent an individual had come by mere observation, independent of theory, affords one of the most irresistible proofs that can be obtained of the soundness of the principles which I have been advocating. As to her remark in reference to Latin, that boys require to be left a good deal to themselves in order to fix their attention, I do not think this objection very material; because, if they learn a lesson which has been taught them, and which is, of course, longer than one which they would learn for themselves, and learn it with the parsing, as well as they ought to do, they will find ample employment for their attention.

Let us now institute a brief general comparison between a boy educated in the manner I have described, and another who has gone through the drudgery of the old-school system. Let us assume the age of the two to be twelve.

The former has had his memory, observation, attention and curiosity carefully cultivated, without being strained, from the age of seven, or even earlier. The natural results have been produced. His mind is as well stored as it is capable of, with all the facts and knowledge which have been submitted to it. He is master of the meaning of at least fifteen or twenty thousand words (the whole language being computed to contain about twenty-three thousand). He construes Virgil, part of Livy and Cicero, Ovid, and even portions of Horace, with considerable ease and accuracy, and often betrays a little pride in his willingness to betray his acquirements. His health is unimpaired, and he has his natural flow of spirits, evincing that the mind has been in no way over-strained.

The boy educated on the opposite system has never had his youthful faculties elicited and exercised. He is, therefore, correspondingly deficient in the facts and knowledge of which he ought to have been master. He knows not half the number of words, because he has not done half the *quantity* of Latin, and he understands them less perfectly because they have been less perfectly explained. He construes the above books with difficulty, and often is incapable of construing them at all, especially if he has trusted to the more clever boys of his class construing the lesson, instead of attempting to do it for himself. He has a disgust at classics, because they and hardships are an identical idea in his mind. If he have been a studious boy, and have done his best to accomplish impossibilities, his health has, not unfrequently, been impaired. But if he have been an idle boy, he has most probably contrived to evade nearly all his tasks, and has reached the age named innocent of almost all knowledge.

The remarks made upon Latin apply, of course, equally to Greek.

Were I now to stop at this point, under the supposition that the advantages of the system which I have advocated are confined to the learning of mere languages, I should stop short indeed, as they apply equally to a great variety of branches of learning in general.

Youthful memory is equally greedy and tenacious of the facts of natural philosophy in all its branches, history, chronology, geography, chemistry, &c. A sound elementary knowledge of the leading facts of all these, together with the technical vocabulary, may be attained almost insensibly by boys before the age of twelve, a very little done each day sufficing to obtain the result. When we reflect how much these have to do with the actual business of subsequent life, we must be forcibly struck with the importance of acquiring them in early life; for, if they are postponed to the period of manhood, when memory, together with all the youthful faculties are greatly impaired in vigour, it becomes exceedingly irksome to acquire them, and the intellectual powers, now mature and ready for re-production, are often exceedingly distracted, and their usefulness curtailed by encountering, at every turn, a want of that fundamental knowledge which ought to have been acquired in youth. It may be objected that the sciences alluded to cannot be perfectly attained in youth. This is true. But when the mature intellect meets them again in manhood, it encounters them as familiar subjects, and by digesting and working up the whole, soon brings it into order.

I forbear to say anything on the subsequent parts of education, as these depend entirely on the talents and application of the boy, and the competency and zeal of the master. The same principles, modified according to the age of the boy, may, however, be kept in view.

APPENDIX.

Letter from Dr. George Julius, *of Richmond,*
to Mrs. Hope.

————We became acquainted on the first day of our
arrival in Edinburgh, and for four years I there enjoyed
the uninterrupted privilege of being his constant, and, I
believe, most intimate friend. To me the value of such
companionship was peculiarly great, for being some years
my senior, he led me by his example, and infused into me
a desire to emulate his diligence. From the outset of his
career, it was evident that he had determined on a severe
course of professional study, that he had formed rules, and
with a far distant object in view, had laid down fixed
principles by which he resolved to attain it. From the
earliest days of our acquaintance he spoke of his ambitious
hopes of eminence, at some future period, in London. He
had calculated the labour, the cost, and the probabilities of
success. Gathering information from the most various
sources, by rigid inquiries and impartial investigation of
the prospects held out, he satisfied his own mind that the
end he aimed at was attainable; and having done so, he
entered at once upon a systematic exertion of those means
by which alone it was to be gained. Having once made
up his mind to do a thing, however arduous, however

remote the accomplishment, nothing could check, or interrupt his course. Every energy was bent towards that one object; he never lost sight of it; every daily task had a direct reference to it; every occupation bore upon it; every attainment was regarded but as a step towards the honourable prize he held in view. It was this loftiness of aim that gave a largeness to his design: he rejected all competition for mediocrity: nothing short of success, and eminent success in the highest sphere, would satisfy his desires. He would occasionally allude to the proposals made by his friends and family to settle in Manchester, or in the neighbourhood in which they lived, where, by their interest and connexion, he might, with ease and certainty, acquire considerable practice; but he would never, for a moment, entertain the project. "Aut Cæsar aut nullus," "If we are to work, George, let us work for something worth having," was the usual conclusion of his reply to all such solicitations. Nothing but a consciousness of power would have justified his frequent refusals to lower his expectations or change his plans of life. Had he not felt his own capabilities, and been thoroughly acquainted with the indomitable strength of his own perseverance, he would never have rashly rejected offers so promising; but he *did* know them, and he had read the world and history too observantly not to have learnt that all things are possible to the strenuous will. Relying on these, he made his decision and unhesitatingly abided by it. In this he was by no means misled by a sanguine temperament (the constitution of his mind was decidedly of an opposite character): it was the result of mature deliberation, and his resolution and ambition rested on a foundation which much reflection convinced him to be both just and reasonable. In looking back upon my departed friend's life and tracing its course, I lay much stress on this proud motive of action, for it accounts for the extraordinary efforts he made from the very commencement of his studies, and his perseverance in a system of mental exertion apparently excessive and uncalled for. Nothing was light or unimportant in his estimation; he brought his whole mind to bear upon everything he was engaged in; what to many of his fellow-students was simple and easy, to him was a stern task; he would receive nothing superficially; but, subjecting all he heard and saw to a severe scrutiny, he excluded from his mind everything that was valueless. To facilitate this mastery of every subject, he confined himself, as much as possible, to a single department at a time. Many of his contemporaries had a far wider and more general knowledge of the profession than he had, but it formed no part of his system to hurry through the schools, and the object he had in view needed a severer application. At times, so laboured appeared his progress, and so difficult his attainment of *general* information, that many were led to question the existence of those talents of which there was no display, and to doubt the opinions of those intimate friends who so highly appreciated and extolled them. There was always an air of abstraction about him which favoured the doubt. He was exceedingly absent, and failed to catch, readily, the passing current of conversation which frequently conveyed much useful intelligence, professional and otherwise. He was, too, " a dull hand at a joke," asking, amidst the loud laughter of others, some grave question of explanation, which ensured him a hearty quizzing for his obtuseness. This did not arise from any deficiency of the sense of humour, or the soul of wit, both of which he possessed richly when he chose to draw upon them for amusement, as many of his letters to myself abundantly testify, but from an inaptitude for the frivolities that flashed about him. His thoughts were otherwise engaged; his mind was too ponderous for these flitting vanities, and disinclined to rouse itself to entertain them. He had, moreover, made it a rule, on which he uniformly acted, never to discuss any subject with which he was not deeply and thoroughly acquainted—a practice which imposed silence upon him amidst the forward volubility of others, much his inferiors in acquirement. He was so fond of reducing all things to first principles, that I often told him he ought to have lived in the Academic Groves, so much had he the spirit of the old heathen philosophers; he would, indeed, have proved the apt pupil of a Socrates or a Plato; but herein lay the basis of all his future success. In his transactions with the world, as well as in professional pursuits, the same system regulated his conduct, and formed a character remarkable for its consistency and equality under any variety of circumstances. He was slow in forming a friendship, but once formed it was stable and undeviating. I remember an instance where he had met with the most ungrateful returns from one who owed him much gratitude, and was, in many ways, indebted to him. No change was perceptible in his conduct towards him; he was not insensible of his friend's neglect, but he palliated it, excused it, and never uttered a harsh word of reprehension, but rather sought to win back by the

5

forgiving kindness of his manner, a friend who had so ungraciously treated him. Other friends of the individual alluded to, forsook him as unworthy of their regard; for few were blessed with the faithful excellences of my departed friend.

There was not, I think, anything worthy of particular notice in the plan of study he pursued. He took the usual course, attending the same lectures as his fellow-students. It was during his third year of residence that he first turned his attention to the collection of drawings of morbid anatomy. Guided by the same logical principles which always influenced him, he saw that, to attain a perfect knowledge of disease, he must lay the foundation in an exact acquaintance with the *structural* changes produced by it. A course of lectures delivered about this time by Dr. Thomson, which he attended, and where he had the opportunity of seeing a collection of, perhaps, the largest and best-executed drawings of morbid anatomy then extant, strengthened him in his resolution to pursue it as a specially important branch of medical education. His talents as a draftsman and colorist enabled him to do so with facility, and to publish, at a future period, the valuable results of his early labours.

About this time, also, the stethoscope was first introduced into the British schools. It was lightly regarded by most, and ridiculed by many. Hope, with his usual far-sightedness, foresaw in it an instrument of such utility in the diagnosis of pectoral disease, that he at once advocated its use and strenuously insisted on its merits. Notwithstanding the indifference with which it was treated at that time by some, even of the Professors of the College,

Q

he from the first declared that it could not fail, ere long, to be universally regarded as an essential means of detecting thoracic disease; often saying, that "it behoved every student to make himself master of it *now*, lest by-and-by he should find himself alone in his ignorance." So fully was he convinced of its importance, that he, without hesitation, laid aside the subject which he had selected for his thesis, and on which he had expended much labour and time, and decided on making the stethoscope, and its application to the discovery of diseases of the heart and large blood vessels, the subject of his inaugural dissertation. He now found a new encouragement towards that great end which (as I said before) he always held in view, eminence in London. He often spoke of the promising prospect which a good stethoscopist would have before him if he settled in London, and the advantages he would enjoy above others imperfectly acquainted with the use of the instrument. To any objection I might raise, by saying, "that time was necessary to introduce it, that professional fashion, ever slow to changes, and the dislike of patients to its use, were to be combated, and could only gradually be overcome," he always answered—"Depend upon it, George, the intrinsic value of the instrument is so great and self-evident, that in a very short time you will no more see a physician without his stethoscope, than you would fifty years ago have seen him without his gold-headed cane, or a major without his boots." How far he was right in his opinion, has been sufficiently shown by his success and eminence in London. He lived to verify his prediction, and reaped richly the rewards of his sagacity.

The life of an active student admits of little leisure for

social recreation. Hope knew this, and, as he told me, purposely declined letters of introduction to many families in Edinburgh, through whose civilities he feared he might be led into a too great dissipation of time and mind. Saturday was, at College, permitted by common consent, as a partial day of rest; the only recognized holiday of the week; on it he generally spent the evening at Professor Monro's, either at his residence in George Street, or, during the summer, at his beautifully-situated country seat, Craig Lockhart; here he was always an acceptable visitor. The Doctor respected him for his talents, which he often employed in his service by procuring from Hope drawings of various morbid specimens for his museum During the vacations, he joined with two or three friends in tours through various parts of the highlands, where he completely unbent his mind, and entered into the full enjoyment of these pedestrian excursions. His rod and sketch-book were his constant companions. As an angler he was the most expert I ever met, and was thoroughly in love with the craft. From a boy he was always an enthusiast in the sport, and maintained the *dignity* of the science (for so it became in his hands), by constantly enumerating the host of worthies who were its devotees, and clenching its defence by an axiom which he heard Sir Francis Chantrey once advance at my father's table, " that every man of genius was born a fly-fisher." In sketching from nature he was very successful, filling his portfolio with beautiful drawings of every scene which presented subjects worthy of his pencil. In addition to these sources of amusement, he was always provided with a pocket edition of some of the standard classics. I have in my possession a Horace and a Euripides, which were his fellow-travellers, for many years, both at home and abroad. The education he had received under an eminent tutor, and his subsequent studies at Oxford, rendered him equal to the literary enjoyment of these authors. He was learnedly conversant with their works, and indulged in their perusal as an elegant mental relaxation. He was, in every respect, an accomplished classical scholar—his latinity remarkable for its fluency and purity. I have often been astonished at the rapidity with which he would strike off, " currente calamo," whole pages of Latin composition of the most finished elegance, replete with all the graces of diction and critical niceties of idiom. These productions were admitted, by highly-competent judges, to be of the highest order of excellence.

I have now, my dear Madam, given you a rude sketch of the prominent features of Dr. Hope's character, as displayed during his residence in Edinburgh. I have done so in much haste, and under a confusion of circumstances which has altogether precluded due attention to methodical arrangement. I have mentioned just what occurred to my mind at the moment, nothing more. If what I have written is considered by you at all illustrative of my departed friend's early character, pray make what use you please of it. With every sentiment of regard and christian sympathy,

I remain, my dear Madam,
Yours very truly,
G. JULIUS.

Lahinch, November 26, 1841.

LETTERS

FROM

A SENIOR TO A JUNIOR PHYSICIAN,

ON THE

IMPORTANCE OF PROMOTING THE RELIGIOUS WELFARE OF HIS PATIENTS.

LETTER I.

ON THE DIFFICULTIES OF THE UNDERTAKING.

MY DEAR FRIEND,

You were pleased to desire me to send you the result of my observation and experience on the deeply interesting subject of endeavouring to promote the spiritual welfare of the sick committed to your care. I cheerfully accede to your wish, although I can scarcely hope to offer any suggestions which have not already occurred to your own reflective mind.

If the soul of man be immortal, and if the state of the soul, at the moment of its separation from the body, determine its happiness or misery through endless ages, with what deep solicitude should every Christian approach the bed of a fellow creature, who, to all appearance, is about to undergo the momentous change, yet unprepared " to meet his God!" If we saw a human being proceeding blind-fold towards a tremendous precipice, even already at its brink, how eagerly should we try to snatch him from the threatening destruction! And can we, my friend, remain insensible to the spiritual danger of the dying man, who seems about to " take a leap in the dark" into the gulf of inconceivable—irretrievable ruin? How often, alas! are we called to witness the appalling scene, unalleviated by the presence of a Christian minister, or any pious relative, who might direct the helpless sufferer to Him, " who is able to save to the uttermost !"

I am aware, indeed, that those alone who, like ourselves, have felt the weight of medical responsibility, can fully estimate the difficulties to be encountered in attempting to advance the *highest* interest of a patient, while conscientiously discharging our primary duty, in the exertion of our utmost efforts for the restoration or relief of his bodily frame. Even to those, who, by habits of early rising, punctuality, systematic arrangement, and calm dispatch, have been able to allot a sufficient portion of time to each appointment of the day,—how often does it happen that some unexpected emergency, some sudden complication of disease, the alarming sickness of another member of the family, some anxious inquiries of the patient or his friends, or other unforeseen circumstances, have more than consumed the allotted time, and in justice to the indispensable claims of other cases, rendered an immediate departure necessary : thus affording no opportunity of even alluding to " things unseen and eternal."

Another difficulty is often found to arise, from the almost exclusive occupation of the physician's mind by the diseased condition of the sufferer, the relief of which is, of course, our primary and incumbent duty. In order to give to each symptom, as well as to the whole assemblage of symptoms, a close and discriminating attention, and to adapt, with equal care, a corresponding treatment in medicine, diet, and general management; to do this within a limited space of time, requires a concentration of all the energies of the mind in a degree scarcely compatible with attention to any other subject. Under such circumstances, it is difficult in the extreme, to dispossess the mind of the engrossing anxiety just described, so as to leave it sufficiently free for availing itself of any suitable moment for introducing, with needful delicacy and tenderness, the all-important subject of eternity. How frequently too, have we found that by the time we have completed our medical inquiries and directions, the patient has become too much exhausted to render any further exertion safe or practicable!

In addition to the obstacles already specified, you have probably, my dear friend, sometimes encountered opposition from the mistaken kindness of the patient's relatives, who have deemed it next to madness to endanger the comfortable serenity of one " whose goodness of heart," they persuade themselves, " must secure him a happy hereafter." Generally, however, the confidence reposed in the kindness and discretion of the medical attendant, will soon allay such a feeling of alarm, and afford the assurance that nothing will be attempted of a doubtful or hazardous character.

But the most formidable hindrance, I apprehend, exists *within ourselves.* I refer to the prevailing impression among us, that the religious welfare of a patient is foreign to our province; that to aim, in any direct manner, at promoting it, is superfluous, if not also obtrusive; and that the attempt might be regarded, moreover, as an unbecoming interference with the sacred office. The *sedative* influence of this opinion is often rendered still more paralysing by a consciousness of not possessing the facility and tact supposed to be essential to the success of the effort. Hence, opportunities for speaking " a word in season," are scarcely looked for or desired. The mind, at length, rests satisfied with an abandonment of the matter, as hopeless and impracticable, not duly considering *whose cause it is,* nor recollecting the divine promise that " strength shall be made perfect in weakness."

Such, my valued friend, are among the difficulties in our way; great, indeed, we must allow them to be, yet, happily, they are not insurmountable.

Assuming, for the moment, that the duties and qualifications of the medical practitioner do not impose upon him a higher degree of responsibility, relative to the spiritual good of his patient, than attaches to every other well-informed Christian, in reference to his neighbour, I may safely assert that the profession of medicine does in no wise release its member from a duty common to all Christians—that of embracing every opportunity to testify their gratitude to the adorable Saviour, and their anxious desire to extend the blessings of redeeming mercy to those who " are ready to perish." But the assumption itself is incorrect; for it would not be difficult to prove that the favourable opportunities and peculiar facilities possessed by the physician do proportionably *augment* his responsibility, and the consequent amount of obligation. Nor can this fearful responsibility be evaded, by a general impression of our unfitness for the task, unless we can conscientiously affirm that we have tried to the utmost—that we have done all that we were able to do.

As regards the alleged interference with the ministerial office, I may truly say that, to the extent of my own observation, the apprehension is entirely groundless. So far removed, indeed, are the judicious, well-timed suggestions of the physician, in relation to the immortal interest of his patient, from anything like interference with the sacred function, that, in the instances in which they are most needed, they may be strictly regarded as *precursory* and introductory to the more direct instructions of the minister ; as opening a way for him which would otherwise be closed, as removing ill-founded objections to his assistance, and enkindling a desire for his spiritual counsel. In many other instances, the Christian physician proves a powerful *auxiliary* to the faithful minister of Christ, especially by facilitating his visits, pointing out at what time, under what circumstances, and to what extent, the patient may be likely to attend, with safety and advantage, to " the things which make for his eternal peace." I have good reason, indeed, to believe that the enlightened ambassadors of the Saviour, so far from entertaining a feeling of jealousy, do really hail with cordial satisfaction such auxiliaries, in their trying visits to the bed of sickness and death ; persuaded that none can feel a deeper interest than a Christian physician, in the well-being of *the whole man,* bodily and spiritually in reference to eternity as well as to time. And how can jealousy be felt? Is not the glory of his Divine Master in the salvation of immortal souls, the supreme object of every pious minister's pursuit? If so, even the feeblest attempt to subserve the same cause must gain his hearty concurrence. Happily, the un-scriptural, un-Protestant notion of religious instruction devolving exclusively on the clergy has become obsolete. As well might the Bible itself be read and studied by them alone. The very constitution, indeed, of our most efficient religious institutions speaks a contrary language; especially that of the visiting and district societies, in which the principle of lay co-operation is clearly recognised, and the obligation thence arising is fully avowed. In truth, it requires but little sagacity to predict that, in the noble enterprise now in progress for evangelizing the world, the zealous exertions of Christians generally will be more and more called forth. Such an active and pervading influence seems evidently implied in the prophecy of Jeremiah, as cited by the apostle of the Gentiles, alluding to the period when " they shall not teach *every man* his neighbour, and *every man* his brother, saying, ' know the Lord;' for all shall know me, from the least unto the greatest." We have yet, indeed, to realize the happy day when, even comparatively, *every* man shall seek the spiritual good of his neighbour; but we are surely authorised to expect it, as well as bound to hasten it, by earnest prayer and vigorous endeavour. We are even encouraged to anticipate the more distant and glorious period, when the omnipotent Saviour shall have given complete efficiency to the universal labour of love, and when " He shall be all in all."

7

Not to weary your patience further, I will here close my letter; hoping, in a second communication, to present a few *encouragements* which may serve to cheer you under the difficulties we have been considering. I shall endeavour also to add some practical suggestions, in reference to the most eligible *methods* of introducing the subject of religion to persons dangerously ill. Of the power of executing the latter part of my task, especially, I cannot but entertain much self-distrust.

I remain, my valued friend,

Your's, with sincere regard,

T. H. BURDER.

Tilford House, Jan 1st, 1836.

LETTER II.

ON THE ENCOURAGEMENT TO BE EXPECTED IN THE ATTEMPT.

MY DEAR FRIEND,

In my former communication I placed before you the considerations which had most impressed my own mind, in reference to the *importance* of aiming to promote the spiritual welfare of the sick. You will have observed that, far from concealing, I fully admitted the difficulties attendant on the effort, while I endeavoured to show that they were by no means insurmountable. I am now desirous of presenting to your attention a few of the *encouragements* which the physician is warranted to expect in pursuing this " work of faith and labour of love." Such, I apprehend, will be found to arise from THE PECULIAR

FACILITIES WHICH THE PROFESSION AFFORDS; FROM THE
DIVINE BENEDICTION WHICH MAY BE HUMBLY, YET CON-
FIDENTLY, ANTICIPATED; AND FROM THE SUCCESS WHICH
HAS ALREADY CROWNED SIMILAR EFFORTS.

1.—No one who has witnessed the respect and confidence
with which the suggestions of a conscientious physician
are received, can doubt of his possessing an almost unlimited influence in the sick chamber. He has become, in
truth, the attached friend of the family, to whom they
freely unbosom their sorrows and their fears, particularly
such as appear to be inducing or aggravating any existing
or threatened disease. Hence the medical adviser, having
gained an important acquaintance with the mental constitution of his patient, its individual peculiarities and tendencies,
and with the varying complexion of thought and feeling
which bodily disturbance has been wont to excite, is already
prepared to introduce with delicacy and address, such
incidental remarks in reference to his highest interests
as the peculiar condition of the sufferer may naturally
call forth; and in the way best adapted to interest and
impress, while least likely to endanger that general
quietude, on the maintenance of which his recovery
may materially depend. Being aware, moreover, of the
different aspect in which other topics of practical importance have at various times appeared to his patient, or to
persons under similar circumstances, while viewed through
the distorting medium of disease, he will not be surprised
if the momentous subject of religion should also share (so
far as natural effects may be permitted) in the obliquity or
indistinctness of the mental vision. The same previous
knowledge will often enable him to calculate, with tolerable

precision, the degree of influence, whether exciting or depressing, which an allusion to the realities of eternity may be likely to exert on the patient's bodily frame; and thus to attemper and apportion his suggestions to the particular exigences of the case.

2.—Among the *facilities* to which we have adverted, I cannot but regard as one of the most valuable, that arising from the numerous opportunities possessed by the physician of connecting, in the most easy and natural manner, some serious remark with his medical counsel. So intimately, indeed, is the mind united to the body, and so generally does the one sympathize with the sufferings of the other, as constantly to demand a considerable portion of the physician's vigilance and discrimination. He cannot but observe the baneful influence of agitating and corroding emotions, in thwarting every healing expedient; and being constrained, therefore, to inculcate the importance of tranquillity, acquiescence, and cheering hope, he is led by the most gentle transition to trace those virtues to the true source of " every good and perfect gift," and to the surpassing value and efficacy of the Saviour's peace, and of the " hope that maketh not ashamed."

You have often, my friend, observed in the moment of danger, with what eager, anxious attention the patient listens to every word that falls from his physician. He knows that his friend and counsellor is deeply concerned for his well-being, and can have no interest apart from his. He is aware of the value of professional time, and has experienced the unwearied assiduities which have been exerted for the preservation of his life. Should, therefore, the physician appear to overstep the precise boundary of his province while touching upon the concerns of immortality, the patient, I am persuaded, will usually regard the solicitude thereby evinced, as an additional and gratifying proof of genuine friendship. The sick man has also the tranquillizing conviction, that nothing is likely to proceed from his judicious adviser which would either aggravate the disease, or interfere with the salutary operation of remedies. Hence, no alarm, no perturbation is induced ; while two or three well-adapted hints are gaining a quiet admission into the mind, and affording useful materials for private meditation and self-inquiry. Now, my dear friend, if such be the advantageous position of a humane and Christian physician in the chamber of sickness, and I am sure your own observation will verify the statement, how deep must be the regret that such 'vantage ground has ever been lost, yea, lost for ever! That where the sick man's anxious eye betokened confidence, expectation, desire, we should have allowed so fair an opportunity to pass away, without affectionately and urgently directing him to " Behold the Lamb of God!" I will not again expatiate on the serious responsibility which these facilities involve, but I respectfully entreat my professional brethren to be on their guard, lest timidity, apathy, or worldly policy should deprive them of the exalted privilege of being instrumental in saving a soul from death, and thus adding another jewel to the Redeemer's crown. It may still be said, that the afflicted patient will not be disposed to listen to the *religious* advice of his physician, considering it as altogether foreign to his department. I believe, on the contrary, that such advice, when tendered with kindness and discretion, will generally be regarded the more highly because it is *not* professional, because it is *not* a matter of course, but springing spontaneously from the lively interest which the physician feels in the entire welfare of his charge. This view of the subject seems to me quite · compatible with the sincerest respect for the labours of a Christian minister in the time of sickness. "His invaluable instructions have the weight and sanction of official character; while, from the aptitude afforded by kindred studies and pastoral duties, they may be expected to possess an appropriateness not otherwise attainable. They are held, moreover, in high estimation, because they are regular and ministerial; whereas the religious hints of the physician, as I have before remarked, acquire much of their interest and influence from the very opposite consideration,—from the fact of their being occasional, unexpected, and spontaneous.

3.—The powerful incentive arising from *an humble expectation of the Divine blessing,* appears to me fully authorised. If I have adequately shown the importance of the endeavour, and have satisfactorily proved that the peculiar facilities afforded to the physician, involve a proportionate amount of obligation (in those cases, at least, which have not and perhaps cannot have, the advantage of ministerial instruction,) it will follow, as a necessary consequence, that in performing a Christian duty of such moment, we are warranted to implore and to expect the special aid of Omnipotence. The object at which we aim is nothing less than the glory of the Divine Saviour, in the salvation of an immortal soul, and how cheering are the assurances of infallible truth,—I will make my strength perfect in weakness." " Him that honoureth me, I will honour!" " He that converteth a sinner from the error of his ways, shall save a soul from death, and hide a multitude of sins."

And let not my valued friend be discouraged at the difficulty of the undertaking. The cause is God's. He hath all hearts in his hand, all events at his disposal, and is often pleased to effectuate the greatest designs by the most feeble instrumentality, in order to show that " the excellency of the power is not in man, but in God" alone. Far be it from me to depreciate the value of prudence and discretion in an attempt of such importance; but I am bound to confess that the danger has not generally arisen from the neglect of cautionary maxims, but from permitting them to obtain an undue and paralysing influence. Where eternity is at stake, let us not be exclusively guided by the cold, calculating axioms of worldly policy. Selfishness may whisper, " Am I my brother's keeper?" and as the priest and the Levite, in the parable of the good Samaritan were probably willing to persuade themselves that their spiritual functions imposed upon them no obligation to afford *bodily* succour to the " wounded, half-dead man,"—so, my friend, may we be in danger of resting satisfied in withholding our spiritual aid from our dying patients, on the hollow and untenable ground that our responsibility extends only to the body and to time. Oh! let us be rather like the good Samaritan, and without hesitation or delay, endeavour to pour into the wounded spirit the wine and oil of heavenly consolation,—thus adopting our blessed Lord's special application of the parable—" Go, and do thou likewise!" Surely we may confidently hope that in rendering this obedience, we shall experience super-human aid; and though our path may be dark and rugged, and the obstacles many and powerful, yet may we cheerfully and implicitly rely on that Almighty God, who is " a Sun and a Shield" to those who put their trust in Him.

May I not add, as a collateral encouragement, that while thus aiming to promote the honour of the Divine Emanuel, we may humbly hope that he will be " *with us*," in granting efficiency to our strictly professional exertions ? When it is considered that the skilful or unskilful decision of a moment may save or lose a valuable life, and that even a well-selected remedy may prove salutary or detrimental as the Divine benediction is vouchsafed or withheld, how inconceivably important must we regard the guidance and the smile of Him, " in whom we live and move, and have our being," and in whom are all our springs of intelligence and of usefulness ! By " seeking the kingdom of God and his righteousness" in the way we have described, we may be rendered the happy instruments of giving occasion to our grateful patients, to unite with the sweet singer of Israel, in ascribing, from their inmost souls, blessing and praise to Jehovah, for having not only " forgiven all their iniquities," but also " healed all their diseases."

One especial ground of encouragement yet remains—that which rests upon *the actual success with which the God of all grace has been pleased to crown similar efforts*. He, who hath all power in heaven and on earth, *has* given efficiency to such exertions : and while, with " a single eye to His glory," they are " begun, continued, and ended in Him," we cannot doubt that the ardent desire and persevering endeavour to rescue immortal souls from endless perdition will be accompanied by those gracious influences which can at once direct, and animate, and bless. Thus, "our labours shall not be in vain in the Lord."

It has already been remarked, that, in aiming to subserve the spiritual as well as temporal interests of our patients, we shall usually retain, if not increase, their confidence and regard. Sometimes, however, it may prove otherwise; especially in reference to the relatives and friends of the sick. This was strikingly evinced in the experience of an aged and eminent, but now deceased physician, then practising in Westminster, as communicated by him to the writer of this letter. The veteran practitioner was called to the bedside of a young lady, whom he found passing to her long home, yet destitute of hope, unacquainted with the way to Christ, and peace, and heaven, and surrounded by relatives equally ignorant with herself. He placed in the hands of her attentive and (as it afterwards appeared) pious nurse, a volume of the "Village Sermons," requesting that a portion might be occasionally read to the youthful patient. On getting out of his carriage at the next visit, he was met by the mother, and thus abruptly accosted—" I will not trouble you, doctor, to go up stairs;" assigning no motive for so unceremonious a dismission, except such as might be read in a countenance of high displeasure. My sagacious friend at once penetrated her mind, and retired. After some time had elapsed, the nurse informed him that the young lady lived but a few days after his visit, yet long enough to afford a delightful evidence of having obtained pardon and peace through a crucified Redeemer. The very volume, it appeared, that excluded the physician from the family, was rendered instrumental in introducing the dying patient into spiritual life. And never can I forget the pious elevation and the grateful emphasis, with which my venerable friend closed his affecting narrative : " cheerfully," said he, " would I lose the best family in my professional connexion, if by my feeble instrumentality I could be the means of saving another soul from death."

Thus, my dear friend, I have endeavoured to set before you the principal encouragements for the endeavour. I have still to accomplish the most difficult part of my task— that of submitting to you a few suggestions on the *mode* of communicating serious counsel to the sick. This I must attempt in a future letter.

Believe me, with esteem,

Your very faithful friend,

T. H. B.

Tilford, Jan. 28th, 1836.

LETTER III.

ON THE MOST ELIGIBLE METHODS TO BE PURSUED.

My Dear Friend,

In accordance with your request, I now proceed to offer a few suggestions derived from personal observation, on the methods which appear to me best calculated to secure the important object of our present correspondence. You will remember that, even at a distance, I doubted my ability for properly executing this part of the undertaking; and I candidly own that my consciousness of inadequacy

has not diminished on a nearer view of the attending difficulties. Should, however, the plain remarks you are about
to receive, possess little value in themselves, they may, I am
willing to hope, prove indirectly useful, by engaging your
own attention more closely and continuously to the subject.

You are too well aware, how deeply the feeling of medical
responsibility has pressed upon myself, to suppose for a
single moment, that I would inconsiderately superadd to a
similar burthen upon you any unnecessary weight of obligation as connected with the spiritual condition of your patients.
I cannot, indeed, relinquish the opinion I have deliberately
formed, and which has been before avowed, namely, that
the peculiar facilities afforded to the medical practitioner
entail upon him a proportionate responsibility; yet am I
very solicitous not to endanger the peace of a conscientious
mind by incautious or exaggerated statements, or by urging
the adoption of any doubtful or impracticable measures.
On a subject of such manifest delicacy, as well as difficulty,
it is highly important that our views should be well defined,
and our opinions of the duties and obligations involved,
most carefully guarded and qualified, otherwise, we may
not only inflict a needless wound on a pious mind, but may
actually defeat the very object we desire to promote, by the
disheartening influence of plans of operation unfeasible in
themselves, or inconsistent with our proper, indispensable,
and untransferable duties. Allow me, therefore, to request
your attention to two preliminary observations.

First,—I would remark that the desire of promoting the
patient's religious welfare should never be allowed to interfere with the thorough performance of medical duties.
These cannot be superseded by any other claims. Under

this decided impression I would suggest, as a general rule, the propriety of giving your sole, undivided attention to the relief of the patient's malady, as well as to every circumstance and arrangement which his bodily condition may demand, before you permit yourself to advert to his spiritual exigences. You will kindly observe, that I recommend this as a *general* rule, which may possibly admit of some exceptions. For example, I can conceive that some highly-gifted individuals may have the power of interspersing, in an unobjectionable manner, a few religious hints among their medical inquiries and directions, and without materially distracting their attention, or endangering the temporal well-being of their charge. Yet, even with such facilities, there would sometimes, I apprehend, be a risk of dispersing those energies of mind which the physician ought assuredly, in the first place, to concentrate on his patient, in the earnest, persevering endeavour to remove his disease and preserve his life. Consequently, the talent referred to should be used with much judgment and caution. But I foresee that your habits of discrimination will lead you to doubt whether the example I have supposed really constitutes an exception to the rule. It certainly is not foreign to the *spirit* of the rule, which I think may be thus expressed :—that no attempt should be made by the physician to promote the religious welfare of the sick, which is incompatible with the full, efficient, satisfactory discharge of his medical duties and obligations.

The second preliminary relates to the distinction which it is important to mark between that *general* responsibility which, in my humble opinion, requires the physician to be always on the alert to profit by every incidental opportunity of employing his influence for the spiritual good of his patient; and that *special* obligation which may sometimes devolve upon him, (in consequence of the total absence of religious instruction,) to attempt, in a more particular manner, to rescue the sinking soul from perdition, and direct it to Him, who is able " to save to the uttermost." This distinction leads me to propose, as a second general rule, that, inasmuch as religious instruction forms a part of ministerial and relative duty, it would be highly inexpedient for the physician to add to his already onerous engagements, that of undertaking the spiritual supervision of his patient, except under circumstances of imperious necessity. Whenever, therefore, the aid of a Christian minister or a pious relation can be obtained, the medical practitioner may, I conceive, regard himself as free from any special obligation of that nature.

These limitations obviously imply that, in by far the greater number of instances, the religious influence of the physician should be exercised in an occasional, rather than in a stated and formal manner. If alive to the spiritual welfare of his patient, such opportunities of usefulness will not be wanting. Perhaps, nothing would so essentially contribute to the furtherance of the object, as the offering up of earnest supplications to the " Father of lights," for His especial guidance and help, before the physician enters upon his daily engagements, that he may be enabled both to discern and improve every suitable opportunity, which even in the ordinary exercise of his profession may be presented, of doing good to the souls of his patients.

In seeking, and humbly expecting, thus to employ your influence in this sacred cause, I feel the most encouraging persuasion that "your labours will not be in vain in the Lord."

It may be convenient to arrange the few thoughts which have occurred to me in reference to the *mode* of offering "a word in season" in a few leading particulars; premising that, next to the Divine blessing, the secret of usefulness will be found, I humbly anticipate, in the careful, discriminating adaptation of advice to the particular circumstances of the case. Age, sex, degree of intellect and cultivation, particular habits of body and of mind, the actual stage of the disease, the hopes and fears of the patient in relation to futurity, the religious knowledge already possessed, the presence or absence of spiritual instruction, and many other circumstances, will, I am persuaded, appear to you deserving of special consideration. I can, therefore, only hope to suggest a few general principles which may be indefinitely modified and applied, according to the varied and ever-varying circumstances of each individual case.

My first suggestion has already been anticipated. I refer to the importance of recommending and even urging the assistance of a Christian minister or a pious friend, in cases of serious and dangerous illness. I am aware that the very mention of the subject is sometimes productive of considerable alarm, and certainly requires much prudence and caution. With skilful management, however, the exciting of any injurious degree of apprehension and foreboding may generally, I would hope, be avoided. One may say, for example, in the course of conversation, to a patient apparently unconcerned or uninstructed in reference to Eternity, "You must find the change from active life to the confine-

ment of this room rather irksome. Yet some time for calm
reflection is really needful for us all. When withdrawn
from busy life, we can look upon the world at a distance, as
well as come into closer contact with ourselves. Indeed
serious consideration can never be unsuitable. Human life
itself is confessedly uncertain, and of course, under disease,
still more so. Should you not find a little conversation
with a pious minister interesting under your present circumstances?" In this familiar way, (pardon its homeli-
ness,) one may sometimes introduce the subject without
abruptness. From having had much personal illness, I
have been able to press the matter further, by assuring the
patient that such assistance has repeatedly proved very
consolatory to my own mind; thus, presenting a living instance of the incorrectness of the popular opinion that, to
propose the visit of a minister to the sick, is tantamount to
a death-warrant.

Should the recommendation prove entirely fruitless;
should the unhappy patient, notwithstanding our utmost
professional efforts, be so rapidly hastening into eternity as
to afford no opportunity of procuring more efficient spiritual
aid, the case will then present one of those *special* occasions before alluded to, which call for our more immediate
and devoted attention, in reference to the immortal spirit.
And who, that values his own soul, would not, under such
circumstances, endeavour, with all possible earnestness and
affection, to exhibit to the dying man the compassionate
and Almighty Redeemer, as able to save even at the
eleventh hour?

I may next suggest that the allusions of the physician to
the subject of religion should generally be *incidental* and

conversational; arising spontaneously from a solicitous regard to the particular situation of the sufferer. When such occasional advice appears naturally to flow from the heart, partaking of the disposition and character of the speaker, and having an evident bearing on the special circumstances of the patient, there will be little risk of its being regarded as superfluous or obtrusive. On the contrary, I believe, it will usually be welcomed as a gratifying proof of disinterested friendship. In this incidental way, one may sometimes refer to the experience of great and good men under similar sufferings, and to the signal support vouchsafed to them, and to the happy results of their afflictions. On some occasions, it may be useful to adduce the remarkable fact, that some of the brightest ornaments of the Church and of the world have ascribed much of their success in life to the discipline they were once called to endure in the chamber of sickness and seclusion.

May I add, that the occasional hints of the physician should also be *brief?* A single sentence well-timed, well-directed, appropriate, and expressive, will possess the great advantage of not wearying the attention of the sufferer, while it may, notwithstanding, supply ample materials for reflection during the succeeding hours of solitude and silence. "*A word* spoken in season, how good it is!"

Nor is it less important, I conceive, that such advice be expressed with *clearness and simplicity,* in a few plain words and short sentences, bearing a direct and obvious meaning, and free from ambiguity and circumlocution.

Allow me also to suggest that the advice should be *considerate and kind ;* the evident effect of genuine sympathy and tender concern. No word should be dropped that

R

might seem to imply an unmindfulness of the suffering, helpless, unresisting state of the patient, or oblige him to attempt a lengthened and laborious reply. One kind sentence delivered in a tone of kindness, and accompanied with a look of kindness, may, and often will, *juvante Deo*, penetrate the heart.

In certain states of disease, in which high excitement, or extreme debility prevails, it may sometimes be expedient to address a passing hint to a relative or friend who may be present rather than to the patient himself, thus leaving to the option of the latter, whether or not to reply to the observation.

Yet should the hints be *faithful*. Any approach to temporizing would be cruel in itself, and might prove fatally delusive in its consequences. It would be, in effect, to administer a moral opiate, from which the helpless victim might awake—only in Eternity.

Permit me also to remark that, whenever the circumstances of the case will permit, our allusions to spiritual subjects should be *attractive and encouraging*. Doubtless, the torpid insensibility of the sinner may require to be roused by an alarming representation of the direful consequences of transgression and unbelief; nor can we reasonably expect that mercy will be sought until it be felt to be needed. In general, however, I apprehend, that a cheering exhibition of the Almighty Saviour, as " full of grace and truth," as " ready to forgive," and " plenteous in mercy to all who call upon Him," will be found most effectual in softening the heart, and in exciting those earnest desires for pardon and acceptance, which are emphatically described, in our Lord's own test of sincerity, in the case of Saul,—" Behold, he prayeth." Let us, my friend, never forget that " he who *winneth* souls is wise." The promises of the gospel are, indeed, peculiarly adapted to meet the exigences of the afflicted and distressed. The blessed Redeemer was pleased to describe himself as having come purposely " to seek and to save that which was lost." Were we even restricted to the use of a single sentence, as a scriptural *vade-mecum* in the sick chamber, we should still have a volume of encouragement and consolation in our Lord's assurance,—" Him that cometh to me, I will in no wise cast out."

Upon the whole, my dear friend, the best preparation for speaking " a word in season," will be found in carefully studying the example, and seeking to imbibe the spirit, of the incarnate Saviour, that all-perfect Physician of the soul and of the body. What a lovely union of simplicity and sincerity, of faithfulness and tenderness, pervaded *His* addresses to the sick and afflicted! How much is comprised in that short sentence, " The gentleness of Christ!" He did " not break the bruised reed nor quench the smoking flax ;" but " came to bind up the broken-hearted," and heal their every wound. May we be enabled, by grace from on high, though necessarily in a very humble measure, to tread in His steps !

In truth, *the Christian-like deportment* of the physician comprises within itself a sphere of very important usefulness, affording ample scope for the development of those graces and affections which characterise the sincere follower of the meek and forbearing, the benevolent and sympathizing Saviour. And even should my friend find it sometimes difficult or impracticable to offer a word of spiritual

10

counsel as he could wish, he may yet, in his habitual demeanour, present to the patient and the surrounding relatives, a living "epistle" which they can read and understand, and which, by directing them to the source of every good gift, may issue in the attainment of true and saving wisdom.

In concluding this letter, I must not altogether omit to refer to *the season of convalescence*, as peculiarly favourable to religious impression. If ever the mind and the heart be open to the feelings of gratitude, love, and praise, it is under the circumstances of returning ease and health, and in the hope of being again permitted to enter on the duties and enjoyments of life. It is then that the physician, in my humble opinion, is more especially bound to avail himself of the grateful attachment of his patient, by referring any skill or care he may have evinced to the God of all grace, and thus endeavour to give a right direction to those kind and gladsome emotions, which are bursting from a full heart. It is then, I conceive, that the rescue from the grave should be held out as a signal warning, and as a powerful incentive. Then, also, by adroitly following out the convalescent's own suggestions, a powerful appeal may be made to his best feelings, and an affectionate plea presented for an immediate and entire surrender of himself, " body, soul, and spirit," unto an Almighty and most merciful Father, who " hath redeemed his life from destruction, and crowned him with loving-kindness and tender mercies."

At such a period, too, we may often recommend, with great advantage, some interesting volume adapted to our patient's state. Biography and easy letters, as being both interesting and not requiring much effort of attention, will often be found peculiarly acceptable. Indeed, the judicious recommendation of books and tracts may be regarded as an important mode of employing our influence during every period of illness, but particularly during the season of convalescence.

Such, my dear friend, are the few imperfect hints which have occurred to me. I might, indeed, have availed myself of the assistance of some valuable writers on the subject of affliction, particularly of the highly interesting work of my pious and intellectual friend, Mr. Sheppard, " *On Christian Encouragement and Consolation ;*" and the excellent " *Thoughts in Affliction,*" by another able friend, the Rev. A. S. Thelwall. I might also have enriched these humble letters by a reference to the " *Essays to do Good,*" of the eminent Dr. Cotton Mather, which contain some admirable suggestions on the same subject. From these several works I have formerly derived much instruction and pleasure, but was unwilling to have recourse to them on the present occasion, as well as from the wish of not unnecessarily extending these letters, as in compliance with your particular desire that I would send you the result of my own observation and experience.

With every kind wish,

Believe me, my dear Friend,

Ever faithfully your's,

T. H. B.

Tilford, March 1st, 1836.

LONDON :

G. J. PALMER, PRINTER, SAVOY STREET, STRAND.

MRS. HOPE,

ON

SELF-EDUCATION AND THE FORMATION OF CHARACTER;

ADDRESSED TO THE YOUNG.

1 vol. 18mo. price 2s. 6d. cloth.

PUBLISHED BY

J. HATCHARD AND SON, 187, PICCADILLY.

OPINIONS OF THE PRESS.

" Designed to impress on the mind of young persons that mere knowledge is not education—a doctrine often enough enforced in the Athenæum, and we welcome Mrs. Hope as an able ally."—*Athenæum.*

" Mrs. Hope having delighted the public with a Memoir of her highly gifted husband, has again appeared as an author. Her work shows that she has studied the best writers on education, and her views are decidedly in advance of the age. Parents and teachers will gain many useful hints from its perusal."—*Record.*

" The writer of this pleasing and useful compendium for youth is the widow of the late Dr. Hope, and she brings to her important task abilities of no common order, as well as that quality without which her task would be incomplete,—sincerity of purpose. It is a small but a valuable volume, and should form the manual of parents as well as of children, to whom it is more particularly addressed."—*Observer.*

" A little book, such as a child might read, and is occupied in developing a very sound principle, that no education is worth much which is not self-education; education of self in the fullest sense, of the memory, the intellect and the heart."—*British Magazine.*

UBLISHED BY J. HATCHARD AND SON,

187, PICCADILLY.

THIRD EDITION.

TOUR to the SEPULCHRES of ETRURIA,
in 1839. By Mrs. HAMILTON GRAY.

Contents.—Introduction—Veii—Monte Nerone—Tarquinia—Vulci—Tuscania—Cære or Agylla—Castel d'Asso—Clusium—Conclusion.

With Numerous Illustrations. Post 8vo. cloth, price 21s.

OPINIONS OF THE PRESS.

" Mrs. Gray's sepulchral picture gallery has no intervals of daub or vacancy. She has won an honourable place in the large assembly of modern female writers."—*Quarterly Review*.

" We warmly recommend Mrs. Gray's most useful, interesting, and instructive volume."—*Edinburgh Review*.

" A most interesting and valuable work, particularly as a guide-book, for any who may wish to visit that country."—*Athenæum*.

" A most agreeable volume, and a valuable guide-book to any traveller who may wish to arrive at the most remarkable points by the nearest cut. Mrs. Gray's volume has a vivid and life-like character throughout, and contains many descriptions of scenery, with the usual incidents of a tour, varied by sketches of manners and customs, English as well as native ; and as the author's objects led her out of the beaten track, she describes places never visited by common tourists."—*Spectator*.

By the same Author.

THE HISTORY OF ETRURIA. PART I.
TARCHUN AND HIS TIMES. From the Foundation of Tarquinia to the Foundation of Rome. 1 vol. post 8vo. price 12s. cloth.

" We shall content ourselves with giving such an outline of Mrs. Gray's theory of Ancient Erturian History as may excite those who delight in such researches to examine her work for themselves, and we can assure them that whether the perusal terminate in belief or scepticism, it is certain to afford pleasure. It was not without some misgiving we encountered Mrs. Gray in the field of conjectural history, but we rejoice to say our fears have proved groundless ; her theory is the most pleasurable that has yet been propounded on the subject of her researches—it is supported by analogies, few of which are forced ; one part of her learning bears the mark of being second hand, and the ingenuity of her deductions is equalled by the modesty with which they are propounded."—*Athenæum*.

CPSIA information can be obtained at www.ICGtesting.com
Printed in the USA
LVOW03s0922040114

368036LV00014B/809/P